THE PROTESTANT REVOLUTION

THE
PROTESTANT
REVOLUTION

FROM MARTIN LUTHER TO MARTIN LUTHER KING JR

WILLIAM G. NAPHY

FOREWORD BY

TRISTRAM HUNT

BASED ON AN ORIGINAL IDEA BY ALAN CLEMENTS

BBC
BOOKS

1 3 5 7 9 10 8 6 4 2

First published in hardback in 2007 to accompany the television series entitled *The Protestant Revolution*, first broadcast on BBC4 in 2007. Paperback edition published 2008

Published by BBC Books, an imprint of Ebury Publishing
A Random House Group Company

The Random House Group Limited Reg. No. 954009
Addresses for companies within the Random House Group can be found at www.randomhouse.co.uk
A CIP catalogue record for this book is available from the British Library.

ISBN 978 0 563 53920 9 (hardback) • ISBN 978 1 846 07523 0 (paperback)

The Random House Group Limited supports the Forest Stewardship Council (FSC), the leading
international forest certification organization. All our titles that are printed on Greenpeace approved
FSC certified paper carry the FSC logo. Our paper procurement policy can be found at
www.rbooks.co.uk/environment

Mixed Sources
Product group from well-managed
forests and other controlled sources
www.fsc.org Cert no. TT-COC-2139
© 1996 Forest Stewardship Council
FSC

Commissioning editor: Martin Redfern • Project editor: Christopher Tinker
Copy-editor: Patricia Burgess • Designer: Andrew Barron
Picture researcher: Cath Harries • Production: David Brimble

Colour separations by Dot Gradations, Wickford, Essex
Printed and bound in Great Britain by Clays Ltd, St Ives PLC

CONTENTS

FOREWORD

BY TRISTRAM HUNT

On a bright, blustery, spring day in April 2005 the body of Pope John Paul II was laid to rest with a requiem Mass in the crypt of St Peter's Basilica. Across the globe, billions watched the funeral on television, while official dignitaries crowded into St Peter's Square to pay their respects. Among them were the President of the United States, George W. Bush, and, representing Her Majesty the Queen, the Prince of Wales. To many, their presence seemed a proper reflection of the personal contribution of John Paul II to the twentieth century's turbulent history. But to religious commentators, the president's and prince's pilgrimage to Rome signalled something else: the final retreat of Protestantism from public life. That the representatives of two of the world's most iconic Protestant nations had dropped everything (including, in the case of the Prince of Wales, his wedding day) to attend the pope's Mass was graphic proof that the spirit of the Reformation had been abandoned.

On the eastern side of the Atlantic, that conclusion seems more and more the case. In an era of prosperous, Western secularism, British churches have been shedding congregations since the 1960s. While the 2001 census indicated that some 37 million people in England and Wales counted themselves as Christian, weekly attendance at Anglican services hovers around the 1.2 million mark.[1] Similar stories of declining numbers can be told for Methodist, Baptist and Church of Scotland services. Today, we might believe, but we don't belong. More than that, the cultural fabric of Protestantism – its essential moulding of Britain's intellectual, religious and creative life – seems to have been sidelined. The Reformation and the heroic split from Rome have been reduced to history.

Yet, despite the obituaries, its legacy lives on. Even in an age of nonchalant secularism, what this book and the accompanying television series show is the continuing impact of Protestantism in moulding our modern world. From literature to science, from gay marriage to the 'War on Terror', a vibrant struggle for Protestant principles remains alive in Britain, America and the developing world. Unbeknown to millions, the Protestant vision continues to shape their work life, home life, even their sex life. If we are to appreciate both the crafting of our own complex, national identities as well as some of the religious passions dictating modern geo-politics, we desperately need a continuing understanding of those epochal events of the Reformation.

Part of the problem is that, outside Northern Ireland, it is often difficult to detect the Protestant inheritance in modern Britain. Protestantism is something that goes on quietly, behind closed doors, in churches and chapels, at Sunday schools and prison ministries; the majority encounter the faith only at Christmas and Easter. When Protestantism does enter the public realm, it is rarely painted in the most favourable light: the Ulster cycle of Orange Order marches, Battle of the Boyne bonfires and anti-Catholic demonstrations, the low-level sectarianism in Scotland centred on Rangers versus Celtic football matches, the teaching of creationism in school biology lessons or demands for censorship from Christian evangelicals protesting against defamatory art, such as *Jerry Springer: The Opera*. Even in Lewes, East Sussex, where the annual Guy Fawkes bonfire night still attracts thousands of onlookers, the celebrations have become divorced from their Protestant pre-history.

Across Britain's suburbs and cities, the pulpit appears to wield ever less power. Sunday trading, gambling, pub opening hours – damaging reforms that Protestant churches passionately opposed – have all been sanctioned by successive governments. Perhaps more worrying for the heirs to the

Reformation, British society seems to be following a course of steady cultural re-Catholicization. The traditional Protestant reserve – the lonely, personal, unostentatious relationship with God – has been junked for the emotionalism of public mourning, icons and even shrines. The popular hysteria following the death of Princess Diana in 1997 was a long way from the quiet dignity that marked the passing of George VI and Winston Churchill. More prosaically, over the last ten years Britain's roadsides have become littered by personalized shrines to killed loved ones, many of them thereby recognizing an ongoing relationship with the dead. So even while Protestantism remains the official British religion, its theological impact on public life seems increasingly marginal.

Nonetheless, our mental and physical landscapes continue to be shaped by its legacy, not least in architecture. From the austere beauty of Ely Cathedral's whitewashed Lady Chapel to the geometric elegance of St Paul's Cathedral, from the Methodist chapels of the Black Country to the Baptist churches of south London, the Protestant inheritance has carved out our cityscapes and rural villages. Many such chapels have been deconsecrated – turned into carpet warehouses, bijou apartments, even wine bars – but their vernacular aesthetic (that ready embrace of the world as it was) has become a part of our familiar, if often squalid, everyday environment.

The Protestant aesthetic has extended from architecture to art. All too often, we are given to think that when it comes to culture, Catholicism held the trump card. From the poetry of Chaucer and Dante to the frescos of Giotto and Michelangelo, the power and glory of Rome effortlessly over-shadowed the dowdy, mechanical philistinism of Protestantism. And certainly the early Protestant reformers did themselves no favours. While Luther himself had few theological difficulties with Church art (and adored choral music), many of his more radical followers regarded icons and images as affronts to God and obstacles to salvation. The outbursts of icon-oclasm that scarred northern Europe during the mid-sixteenth century were an attack on the religious sorcery of imagery, not the aesthetics of art.

In their place the Reformation moulded a new, definably modern

10

approach to art. Under Protestant influence, art moved from the Church to the home, its subject matter from the saintly canon to the secular world and its purpose from divine assistance to aesthetic contemplation. Indeed, art historian Professor Joseph Koerner has made the case that in the world of modern art one can trace clear Reformation tendencies: the iconoclastic impulse (now directed against the authority of 'art' rather than the Church) along with an often puritanical minimalism.[2] This is apparent in the mid-twentieth-century avant-garde work of Jackson Pollock, Barnett Newman and Lucio Fontana. And maybe also in the work of such young British artists as Rachel Whiteread, whose 2005 work 'Embankment' consisted of 14,000 translucent white boxes piled high. In its confrontational iconoclasm, its celebration of whitewashed simplicity, there seemed something proteanly Protestant in Whiteread's installation.

But Protestantism was always a religion of the word rather than image. Luther had reworked his faith through the exacting text of St Paul's Epistle to the Romans, and opening up the mysteries of the Bible to the people has always been at the intellectual core of the Protestant project. Unsurprisingly, Protestant communities – especially Puritan ones – were among the most literate and educated. Readings from Scripture were common parts of Protestant services, while sixteenth-century godly house-holds might typically contain devotional tracts, a copy of the Bible, and one of the many editions of John Foxe's *Acts and Monuments* (1563). Reading and learning were central components of the Puritan existence.

Ian Watt's 1957 study, *The Rise of the Novel*, made clear the connection between this Protestant culture of the word and the development of the modern novel.[3] Crucial to this was the Protestant spiritual temperament – that ever present, internalized sense of self-doubt and struggle – and its literary manifestation in the form of the diary and autobiography. In many Puritan, particularly Calvinist, denominations there was also a strong conception of God's direct action in the world: how His hand was everywhere apparent. This gave rise to a detailed examination of each earthly event – however insignificant – in the hope of seeing God's purpose behind it.

These uniquely Protestant concerns were readily apparent in the diaries and autobiographies of the early seventeenth century, and then in the fictional work of John Bunyan and Daniel Defoe. With its caricatures, laboured symbolism and rambling narrative, it is difficult now to appreciate the enormous literary significance of *The Pilgrim's Progress* (1678 and 1684), but it has proved one of the defining texts of English literature. From Bunyan to Defoe to Samuel Richardson, then on to the great nineteenth-century novels of Charles Dickens and George Eliot, Watt clearly traced the lineages of a Protestant legacy. Indeed, with its Puritan heroine Dorothea and Dissenting villain Bulstrode, there is a strong case to be made for *Middlemarch* (1871–2) as one of the high peaks of Anglo-Protestant culture.[4]

Does such a tradition have any influence on our culture today? The practice of great English diary-keeping continues. And if *Bridget Jones's Diary* (1996) is not quite worthy of Samuel Pepys, is it too fanciful to see in her self-lacerating catalogue of calories and cigarettes a modern, secular equivalent of the type of spiritual diary that godly men kept in seventeenth-century Essex? More obviously, the novel remains a vibrant literary form in English culture. Ironically, some of the greatest twentieth-century English novelists – Evelyn Waugh and Graham Greene among them – have been self-consciously Catholic. But the Archbishop of Canterbury, Rowan Williams, has made the case that the novelist A. S. Byatt, in her tortured characterization, delight in wordiness and often morally focused plot lines, is an obvious inheritor of the Protestant literary tradition.

In America this Puritan culture is far more obvious. Over the last two decades, the evangelical community has rediscovered its literary ethic. And while Tim LaHaye and Jerry B. Jenkins are no George Eliots, their Left Behind series of evangelical novels – accounts of the lives of people stranded on Earth after the Second Coming – have proved staggeringly popular, with 60 million copies shifted since 1995. So too the format of the spiritual diary. One of the most influential books in American Protestant communities today is Pastor Rick Warren's *A Purpose-Driven Life* (2002). According to the promotional material, 'The most basic question everyone faces in life is

"Why am I here? What is my purpose?" Self-help books suggest that people should look within, at their own desires and dreams, but Rick Warren says the starting place must be with God and his eternal purposes for each life. Real meaning and significance come from understanding and fulfilling God's purposes for putting us on Earth.'[5] They are sentiments that could have come straight from *The Pilgrim's Progress*. And in its accessible, diary-like format Warren's work resembles a modern version of Puritan devotional literature. But one vital change between now and then is that in the seventeenth century Protestantism was influencing contemporary culture, while in contemporary America evangelical communities are often engaged in a conscious cultural retreat from mainstream, secular society.

The stark differences between the evangelical Protestantism of modern America (essentially Calvinist in inspiration) and the more lethargic Anglicanism of England (predominantly Arminian in outlook) highlights one of the historic drivers of Protestantism: national identity. Protestantism's focus on 'a priesthood of all believers' inspired by the word of Scripture led to the translation and printing of Bibles in the common tongue. In order that the people could be brought to the Protestant faith, they had to read the word of God in their own language.

From the outset, Protestantism often developed as a national faith, nowhere more so than in England, where the nationalization of faith (the transition from the Church in England to the Church of England) was driven home by the Tudor State's conscious elevation of Protestantism as a patriotic calling. Thomas Cranmer's Book of Common Prayer (1549), *Foxe's Book of Martyrs* (1563), the *Protestant Wind* of 1588 (whereby God saved England from the Spanish Armada), the King James Bible, and another *Protestant Wind* in 1688 (whereby God saved England from Catholic King James II) cumulatively conjoined Protestantism to England's role in the world. First with England and then, following the 1707 Act of Union, with Britain, Protestantism underpinned an emergent national identity. And while many congregations sympathized with fellow believers struggling in the Low Countries, central Europe or the Americas, Protestantism helped to cement that unique sense of election: of England as Israel, a country called forth to serve God's purpose. Indeed, it was the very same language of manifest destiny and divine providence that the Pilgrim Fathers would use to describe their new-found land across the Atlantic.

Yet while Protestantism did much to forge national cultures – art, literature, music – in many cases the legacy continues today independent of the religion. One of the abiding ironies of Protestantism is that its ready embrace of the world, its belief that God could be found in our everyday existence, led to an embrace of society that progressively segued into secularism. For the Protestant ethic's focus on the wonders of the world as it was – its refusal to flee the sins of man into nunneries and monasteries – gave rise to a mindset that saw the world function just as well in the absence of God.

So today we have inherited a Protestant mindset often devoid of its divinity; it is a secular legacy separated from the theology. One can witness elements of this cultural bequest in our obsessive approach to timekeeping, our national preoccupation with gardening and home-making (an updating of the evangelical focus on the 'sacred hearth', now reworked with 'domestic goddesses') and our approach to work and welfare. Both in Margaret Thatcher's war on the work-shy and Chancellor Gordon Brown's determination to reform welfare and 'make work pay', there lies the residual Protestantism of their Methodist and Calvinist upbringings. In many areas of our life where we seem so modern and rational – public policy, business efficiency, even the psychiatry of self-examination – we are repeatedly engaging with the secular seedlings of the Protestant Revolution.

This removal of God from the Protestant carcass is especially evident in British politics. The Tory party has long since dropped its battle cry of 'Church and King', and, it is fair to say, the Church of England could rarely be regarded today as 'the Tory party at prayer'. Led by Charles Kennedy, a Roman Catholic and recovering alcoholic, for much of the last six years, the Liberal-Democrat party is similarly detached from its Puritan origins in the Nonconformist movement. The journey from William Gladstone to Kennedy (via Lloyd George) is a telling story of Protestant descent. While

Christian Socialism remains nominally alive in the Labour party, for the majority of Labour members, neither Methodism nor Marx seems to have much of an impact on their political philosophy. As Tony Blair's spin-doctor famously put it, 'We don't do God'. Only in Northern Ireland and parts of Scotland (notably, the west-central communities of Ayrshire and Lanarkshire) does Protestantism still dictate the political agenda.

This is not to suggest that Protestant churches have no influence in political debate. From the Campaign for Nuclear Disarmament to the anti-apartheid struggle, Jubilee 2000 and 'Make Poverty History' campaigns against Third World debt, Protestant and Catholic congregations have helped marshal public opinion. Indeed, many of them have been inspired by the historic role Protestant congregations (typically Nonconformist) played in the campaign to abolish the slave trade in 1807, and the later anti-colonial movement. That sense of an international Protestant conscience, its global gaze, has been rediscovered in recent years. Few of its members might realize it today, but, for example, the origins of the Greenpeace environmental group can be found in the ancient Quaker tradition of 'bearing witness'.

But the days of political parties being partly formed around Protestant denominations is long gone. As such, this is part of that broader unravelling of Protestantism within Britain's public realm. The endless anxiety we feel today over the nature of Englishness or Britishness is itself partly a reflection of the vacuum left by the retreat of Protestantism. It was, in the idiom of the British historian Linda Colley, part of the ideological, commercial and military maelstrom that helped to forge British identity in the eighteenth century.[6] In its absence, one of the pillars of what historically constituted Great Britain has been removed. Officially, the Church of England remains a national Church, but we live in a multicultural, multi-faith society that poses new challenges for our modern sense of national identity. The next supreme governor of the Church of England, the Prince of Wales, has appreciated that reality with his wish to be known as 'Defender of Faith' rather than the old (misapplied title) of 'Defender of the Faith' (hence his presence at the funeral of Pope John Paul II).

But what was the President of the United States doing in Rome? For the roots of modern America are intimately entwined with radical Protestantism and the flight from popery. The Pilgrim Fathers and early pioneer settlers from England and the Netherlands fled to the New World to build a pristine commonwealth free from the kind of tyranny and irreligion (as much Anglican as Catholic) they had witnessed in seventeenth-century Europe. And while the founders of the republic (men such as George Washington and Thomas Jefferson) might have been, for the most part, Deists and free-thinkers, a strong strand of radical Protestantism remained within the American psyche. Indeed, for much of modern American history this translated into popular, anti-Catholic prejudice. The Ku-Klux-Klan was, in origin if not in practice, as much an anti-Catholic as anti-Semitic and racist organization. But the President's visit to the Vatican shows just how far this nativist mindset has shifted – particularly among the southern states of America – in the last thirty years.

For one of the great differences between modern America and 'old Europe' is the strength of faith on the western side of the Atlantic. From being a consciously Enlightenment, rationalist republic in the years after the American Revolution (1775–83), with relatively few taking part in organized religion, America had become a land of popular religiosity.[7] President George W. Bush, himself a born-again, evangelical Methodist, has spoken of religion in America as undergoing a 'Third Awakening'. And the fastest-growing churches are those outside the traditional groupings. While the Episcopalians and Presbyterians continue to lose followers, churches such as the Pentecostalists and other non-denominational faiths have expanded massively. Some of these faith groups are identifiably Protestant in their obsessive focus on the words and meaning of the Bible, in their belief in a personal relationship with God, and a 'priesthood of all believers'. However, many also seem to be more in the line of radical Reformation sects, rather than traditional Protestant churches. Led by charismatic, occasionally televangelist preachers, such as Rick Warren and Joel Osteen, or the old guard of Jerry Falwell and Pat Robertson, theirs is an emotional, revivalist faith based on the direct power of prayer and the personal role of Jesus Christ in your life. There is little room for the nuances of doctrine or theology in much modern American evangelicalism.

What does unite many of these aggressively autonomous churches is an increasingly conservative politics. For many of the years following the Second World War, the Protestant intervention in American political life was decidedly progressive. It was the Baptist churches that stood at the forefront of the civil-rights struggle in the 1960s, and it was from the southern Baptist movement that Democrat Jimmy Carter began his journey to the White House. Yet in response to the counter-culture of the 1960s – the strong sense that liberalism, feminism and secularism were undermining the religious foundations of the American way – evangelical conservatives began to enter public life. Inspired by such figures as Billy Graham, conservative congregations began to make their voices heard. And starting in the 1980s, they made the Republican party their political vehicle of choice – so much so that by the late 1990s, conservative evangelicals, organized by such consummate strategists as James Dobson and Richard Land, were able to dictate congressional, even presidential choices. The election of George W. Bush in 2000 and 2004 could not have happened without the assistance of the religious right.

Owing to their political power, the influence of evangelical Protestants on public policy has been significant. Putting aside age-old enmities, conservative pastors have joined with the Catholic Church to campaign against the right to abortion, same-sex marriage, even stem-cell research and gene therapy. Indeed, one of the most deleterious effects of evangelicalism on American public life has been the assault on scientific inquiry. Rather than regarding Protestantism and rationalism as historical bedfellows (a tradition stretching back to the founding of the Royal Society in the seventeenth century), US evangelicals have sought to undermine the principles of scientific method in numerous fields, from evolution by natural selection to climate change and even astronomy. In many schools creationism and 'intelligent design' have started to replace the Darwinian orthodoxy.

On foreign policy they have also made their mark. Conservative evangelicals have helped to shape America's unquestioning alliance with Israel, and even hardened opinion towards the US invasion of Iraq in 2003. At the time, one influential southern Baptist pastor declared, 'We should offer to serve the war effort in any way possible … God battles with people who oppose him, who fight against him and his followers.'[8] Many leading evangelicals regard the War on Terror as part of a greater eschatological, end-of-day struggle between black and white, good and evil, Islam and Christianity. What is perhaps more worrying is that President Bush often seems to be one of them.

Yet the great strength of Protestantism is its culture of self-government. From its earliest days, one of the hallmarks of Protestantism has been the practice of breakaway congregations seeking their own religious truth – even more so now; within the broad, Protestant communion there flourishes a market of competing, contradictory churches. So in contrast to the family-values conservatism of the Southern Baptist Convention there flourishes the organization of Metropolitan Community Churches, with a specific focus on ministering to the gay, lesbian, bisexual and transgender communities. In political discourse there exists the determinedly liberal evangelicalism of pastors such as Jim Wallis, who want to take back Protestantism for progressives.[9] And in contrast to the creationism of the evangelicals, there are numerous scientist believers, such as Francis Collins, who combines his work on the Human Genome Project with a deeply held, Protestant faith. Indeed, it is central to his sense of scientific inquiry.[10]

However, while America might be the fulcrum of Protestantism today, it won't be tomorrow. The centre of Christian gravity is moving from the northern hemisphere to the southern one: in 1900s' Africa there were 10 million Christians; in 2000 that number had swollen to a staggering 360 million.[11] As with every form of Protestantism in every different nation, African Protestantism has its own particular, cultural locus. The spiritual and oral traditions of African society have been transmuted into Protestant practice, with the Pentecostal church proving to be one of the fastest-growing communities.[12] Where missionaries once roamed, the Anglican Church remains powerful, but is now subject to the same political and cultural battles it faces in England and America. On the one hand, its progressive tradition drawn from the anti-colonial struggle remains vibrant, most obviously embodied in the saintly figure of the South African archbishop, Desmond Tutu; on the other hand, the evangelical, conservative wing is powerfully represented by Nigerian archbishop Peter Akinola and his fervent campaign against homosexuality within the Church.

As such, the conservative temperament of African Protestantism – much of it supported by close financial links to the US evangelical movement – is coming up hard against the predominant liberalism of the Anglican communion. The appointment of a gay bishop, Gene Robinson, by the Episcopalian Church in New Hampshire, USA (following in the wake of the appointment and enforced resignation of gay priest Canon Jeffrey John as Bishop of Reading), is currently threatening to divide the worldwide Anglican faith. Archbishop of Canterbury, Rowan Williams, is in the unfortunate position of trying to hold the fort against that quintessential Protestant urge for schism, division and debate. But while the disparate energies and cultures of Protestantism often threaten to cripple any binding institutional authority, these offshoots have the much needed capacity to reinvigorate the Church.

In our globalized world, the transnational transmission of faith and doctrine is becoming ever easier. A clear example of this is the revival of Protestantism in Britain's inner cities on the back of black British communities of African descent. Adventist, Pentecostal and evangelical churches are flourishing, even as the traditional Church of England struggles to retain its congregations. As ever with Protestantism, new forms and new contexts continue to determine its doctrinal and social progress. As William Naphy puts it, Protestantism's continual capacity for reformation has frequently proved an exceptional strength: 'It has, for five centuries, allowed Protestantism to respond relatively quickly and effectively to changing cultural circumstances by reinventing itself for each new age.'

So despite the presence of the prince and the president at John Paul II's funeral, despite the talk of obituaries and eulogies, the energy and ambition of global Protestantism still thrives. It not only remains the faith of millions of Christians, but is also an essential part of our cultural inheritance and contemporary social landscape. And it is evolving with the problems of the day: from the politics of debt relief to inter-faith relations, the battle over contemporary sexuality and the limits of scientific inquiry, the place of Protestantism in our nominally secular society continues to be enormously influential. It behoves us to understand its complexities – its theology, its controversies, its sense of purpose. To know our own culture, to appreciate the geo-politics of America or the trajectory of the developing world, we need to get to grips with the faith that drives hundreds of millions of people. Almost five hundred years after Martin Luther sparked the Reformation, its legacy continues to shape much of our modern world. Its almost unique ability to change with the age makes it ever more challenging to decipher.

Tristram Hunt
NOVEMBER 2006

1   www.statistics.gov.uk and www.cofe.anglican.org

2   See Joseph Koerner, *The Reformation of the Image* (Chicago, 2003).

3   Ian Watt, *The Rise of the Novel* (London, 1987).

4   See Raphael Samuel, 'The Discovery of Puritanism, 1820–1914: A Preliminary Sketch', in *Island Stories* (London, 1999).

5   www.purposedrivenlife.com

6   See Linda Colley, *Britons: Forging the Nation, 1707–1837* (Yale, 1992).

7   See R. Finke and R. Stark, *The Churching of America, 1776–1990* (New Brunswick, 1992).

8   See Charles Marsh, 'Wayward Christian Soldiers', *New York Times*, 20 January 2006.

9   Jim Wallis, *God's Politics: Why the Right Gets It Wrong and the Left Doesn't Get It* (San Francisco, 2005).

10 Francis S. Collins, *The Language of God: A Scientist Presents Evidence for Belief* (Free Press, 2006).

11 See Philip Jenkins, *The Next Christendom: The Coming of Global Christianity* (Oxford, 2002).

12 See Stephen Hunt and Nicola Lightly, 'The British Black Pentecostal "Revival": Identity and Belief in the "New" Nigerian Churches', *Ethnic and Racial Studies*, 24, 1 (2001).

1

SOWING THE WIND WITH REFORM

WHAT CAN BE MORE RUINOUS THAN TO LET
SUCH WORDS AS THE FOLLOWING COME TO THE
PEOPLE'S EARS? – 'THE POPE IS ANTICHRIST;
BISHOPS AND PRIESTS ARE MERE GRUBS; MAN-
MADE LAWS ARE HERETICAL; CONFESSION IS
PERNICIOUS; WORKS, MERITS AND ENDEAVOURS
ARE HERETICAL WORDS; THERE IS NO FREE
WILL; EVERYTHING HAPPENS BY NECESSITY' …
I SEE, UNDER THE PRETEXT OF THE GOSPEL,
A NEW, BOLD, SHAMELESS AND UNGOVERNABLE
RACE GROWING UP – IN A WORD, SUCH A ONE
AS WILL BE UNENDURABLE TO LUTHER HIMSELF.

DESIDERIUS ERASMUS
(C.1469–1536)

IF LEGEND CAN BE BELIEVED, THE PRIEST AND theologian Martin Luther nailed a set of 'questions for debate' (in Latin) to the doors of Wittenberg church on 31 October 1517. His intention was to advertise a university dispute about a series of debating points, ninety-five in total, and consequently referred to as Luther's Ninety-five Theses. He was concerned about practices that he considered inappropriate: the way in which the Church was raising funds (in part to finance the rebuilding of the Vatican basilica, the present-day St Peter's). Beyond provoking a lively theological and ecclesiastical debate at the university, it is not immediately clear what Luther hoped to accomplish. What *is* clear is that he had no intention of sparking a revolution and of breaking apart Western Christianity. But that is what he did.

Less than a century and a half later, by 1650, much of Europe had been convulsed by wars about religion as a result of Luther's 'accidental revolution'. Hundreds of thousands of people had died, towns had been laid waste, disease and famine had stalked the land. Armies had marched from Spain and Italy in the south, from Sweden in the north, across Ireland and Poland and the Czech Republic and Hungary. Monarchs had lost thrones and, in one spectacular case (Charles I of Great Britain), their heads. European foreign policy was thrown into disarray – Catholic France funded Protestant armies and Calvinist Hungarians looked to the Turkish sultan to protect their freedom of worship. Indeed, the conflicts left Christian

Europe's southeastern flank open to Turkish Muslim advances, with the result that thousands of Christians (Orthodox, Roman Catholic, Lutheran and Calvinistic to name but a few) fell under Muslim power and, ironically, were forced to coexist. Moreover, this religious rivalry and denominational competition was exported around the world and became a factor in European global competition in the opening phase of Europe's first 'push for empire'. Spaniards and Portuguese spread Catholicism in the east; Dutch Calvinists undermined Jesuit missions in Japan; British Protestants and French Catholics fought for dominance in North America.

Whether or not Luther's hammer ever struck a blow in Wittenberg is unimportant. Within a century blows were being exchanged across Europe, and Christianity began to crusade against itself. More than at any time in the past, states and churches, ministers and magistrates, priests and politicians became almost obsessed with the beliefs of individuals. What people believed — not what they did — could get them killed. And yet, more than at any time in the past, people's ability to think, question and decide religion for themselves became easier and more common. By the mid-seventeenth century it seemed as though almost everyone in Europe had picked up a hammer and was nailing theses on to every door, wall or tree they could find. How this accidental revolution happened, and its impact on the way the West thought and acted is fundamental to understanding how the modern world came into existence. One thing, though, is certain from the outset. If Luther had seen where his theses would lead, he would almost certainly have hammered his head rather than the nail.

However, any discussion of the Reformation, Luther, and what followed must begin over a century before Wittenberg. From the late fourteenth century throughout the fifteenth century the late medieval, Western Church was the scene of calls for reform. Some were dramatic, others less so. Most were unsuccessful, but left an indelible stamp on the mindset of the Church and its parishioners. At some level and to some extent most Christians in Western Europe were, by 1500, very well aware that things needed to change, and that change was being demanded from above and below. As we shall see, though, the 'changes' that were being mooted were very different from what Luther actually set in motion and what eventually emerged.

Real problems arose – and with them calls for reform – in the late fourteenth century, when different nations in Europe recognized, in 1378, two different popes. One was based in Avignon (accepted primarily by France, as well as by Spain and Scotland) and the other at Rome (backed by the Holy Roman Empire, England and most Italian states). Urban VI and Clement VII posed a difficult problem for Western Christianity. With a strong theological commitment to papal supremacy (the idea that the pope, as successor to St Peter, was head of the Church), Christianity now had two heads – in this case, definitely not better than one. This was clearly a situation that required immediate resolution, but there was no mechanism for doing so. Very quickly, though, leading churchmen and scholars began to call for a general council (a gathering of leading clergymen and theologians). This council would constitute a 'supreme legislative body' capable of sorting out the number of popes and any other matters that might arise. In effect, it was the first step towards producing a system of checks and balances, and giving the Church a government. This was the conciliarist movement.

The first serious attempt to use a council to settle the issue of multiple popes was the Council of Pisa, which, in 1409, simply elected a third pope. Fortunately for the Western Church, the next council, meeting at Constance in Switzerland, was more successful. It deposed two of the popes, accepted the abdication of a third, and elected Martin V as the single new pope. This ended the Great Schism in the West, as well as the so-called 'Babylonian Captivity' (papal residency in Avignon). It also ended conciliarism. Martin V and subsequent popes showed no interest in erecting a system of 'constitutional' government for the Church, much less bringing in checks and balances on papal power, and accepting the supremacy of anyone or anything (such as a council) over them. However, this did set an interesting precedent, and during the Reformation meant that councils were often seen as a means of resolving the debates sweeping the Church.

Conciliarism was not the only reform movement. Its focus was on the structure and government of the Church, and it was largely motivated by a desire to resolve a specific problem (multiple popes). Two other movements, though, with entirely different motivations and goals, arose at the same time. The first appeared in England in the 1380s, when the philosopher and theologian John Wyclif began to call for a Church that was humble and poor. He was particularly incensed by ecclesiastical wealth in both land and finery (the gold, silver, jewels and ornamentation seen in churches), though he was not so offended as to give up his well-paid posts in the Church. He also believed that the Bible should be placed in the hands of ordinary Christians, and that it was the standard against which doctrine and practice should be checked. Opponents called him and his followers Lollards (probably from the Dutch *lollaerd*, 'a mumbler') since they 'spoke nonsense'. In the end, Lollardy was suppressed and, interestingly, English Church officials banned all English-language versions of the Bible. Although a sensation at the time, especially in England, the movement met with little success, and rather quickly faded into the background. It did, however, throw into stark relief the question not only of the Bible, but also of its language.

The second major movement to arise during the Great Schism was considerably more successful and had a lasting impact in central Europe. Wyclif's ideas spread, rather bizarrely as a result of foreign-policy ties, from England to Bohemia (in the modern Czech Republic) and had an impact on the preacher Jan Hus at Prague University. Hus and his followers, Hussites, were much more successful than Wyclif in that their ideas became linked with ethnicity (an important issue in explaining the success of some reformations, to which we shall return). As a Czech-speaking movement, Hussism provided an epicentre for resistance to German-speakers. Hus also attacked the wealth of the Church and highlighted many other areas of perceived abuses, especially among the clergy. Hus became so successful that he was summoned to the Council of Constance (which would elect Martin V and end the Great Schism) to explain his ideas. He was provided with a safe conduct by the Holy Roman Emperor. Sadly, this availed him not at all, and the council finally sealed the end of the schism with Hus's blood – he was burnt at the stake as a heretic.

Unlike Lollardy, though, Hussism did not fade away. News of Hus's execution was met with fury and violence in Bohemia. His followers split, and civil war ensued. Despite fratricidal infighting and efforts by forces loyal to Rome, Hussism survived in two predominant forms. The Utraquists, of whom there were two types, were the less radical version, largely resembling the Roman Church except in two key areas. First, they worshipped in the vernacular, the language of the people; second, the common people received both the bread and the wine at Communion (hence their name – from *utraque*, 'each of two'). The norm elsewhere was for the bread to be given to all, but the wine to be taken only by the celebrating priest. The more radical variety of Hussism, the Union of Bohemian Brethren (*Unitas Fratrum*) shared these views, but went well beyond them. The Brethren rejected the notion of transubstantiation – that the bread and wine became the body and blood of Christ. They also denied any concept of a priesthood separate from the rest of the believing community (in effect, they held to a priesthood of all believers). They also believed that the Christianity of the early Church and the New Testament called for a radical separation from general society and, especially, the State. They also stressed Christ's instruction to 'turn the other cheek'. They therefore opposed all forms of violence, capital punishment, military service and taking oaths (including in courtrooms).

Many of these issues will be highlighted in the story of the Reformation that follows. The most important point to grasp at this point, though, is that by 1500 there was a part of Europe that was already beyond the control of Rome. Not only was there an established, functioning form of Christianity that rejected the papacy before Luther, but, in Bohemia, there were actually two varieties. These two, as we shall see, were foretastes of the features of Protestantism set to emerge in the course of the 1500s. The Utraquists were a structured church (denomination in the modern sense) very similar in hierarchy, worship and theology with Rome, but rejecting papal control. The Brethren were less interested in theology and considerably more concerned with constructing an entirely different type of society, community and way of life that were distinct and separate from the wider community.

A NEW PIETY

It would be a mistake, though, to imagine that calls for, or awareness of the need for, reform came solely from the top levels of society or a few learned theologians and their followers. Indeed, in some senses reform was well under way by the time of Luther, and was almost a mass movement. Two specific examples will suffice for the general trend. The first was the *devotio moderna* (new devotion or new piety) and the second was humanism. In their own way these two movements were changing not only the way people thought about religion and their church, but also the way in which they practised their faith and worshipped their God. The changes were slow, often minimal and usually seemingly inconsequential. Cumulatively, however, these two movements laid much of the groundwork for what would follow in the Reformation.

The *devotio moderna* began in Holland during the late 1300s (in many ways in the aftermath of, and in response to, the Black Death and the subsequent bouts of epidemic plague) and spread across the Low Countries, Germany, France and parts of Italy. The movement, with its emphasis on the supposed original simplicity of the early Church and its faith, appealed to lay people and clerics alike. Clergy responded to the movement's call for a more holy, devout life by keeping the vows they had taken. Lay people were especially attracted by an emphasis upon an inner devotional life, apart from (though often complementing) the Church's institutional means of salvation (for example, the sacraments of the Mass or extreme unction – the last rites). With between a third and half of all clergy dying during the plagues of the last half of the fourteenth century, these institutional means were considerably less available, and in some parishes lay people were largely left to their own resources.

Adherents (perhaps better described as exponents) of the *devotio moderna* also took to heart many of the more theologically orientated ideas of the period. Thus, purely external and superficial acts of formulaic piety and devotion were criticized. Likewise, many asserted, as forcefully as Luther would do early in the Reformation, that God could be understood not only by scholarly theologians, but also by the humblest peasant. The catastrophic psychological impact of the Black Death also brought to the fore an appreciation of the mortality and sinfulness of all mankind (surely God was striking his people with plague for their sins) and the urgent need for salvation.

However, this movement did not lead to a call for a change to the structures of the Church: rather, it was a plea for all individuals to take a more active part in the devotional life of the Church and its worship. In particular, and in stark contrast with later reformers, exponents of the *devotio moderna* often stressed the intimate and mediating nature of the sacrament of the Mass when adored or taken by a Christian. Great stress was also laid on the physical sufferings of Christ (and, at times, his mother the Virgin Mary) and his victory over them – all the more critical and poignant for a society piling its dead into plague pits (like 'lasagne', as the Italians noted) in their thousands.

The movement arose in the Low Countries, with Geert de Groote as a key figure. He was not a priest, but was licensed to preach (in and around Utrecht), although his licence was eventually revoked because of his sermonic attacks on clerical abuses. The movement attracted much lay support, and this became more or less organized into the Brethren of the Common Life. The Brethren were associations (sometimes sharing accommodation) of lay people, including women, and 'secular' priests (those who were not monks). The communities were often semi-monastic in style, but never wholly cut off from the world. A monastic version did develop among the Windesheim Canons (founded 1387) under Florentius Radewijns.

However, the movement was most successful in its impact on the way in which lay people actually worshipped, and the types of piety they displayed. It was both intensely personal and explicitly secular in its determination that the new devotion would be imbedded in 'this world'. The best-surviving window into this new, personal type of religiosity and piety is the *Imitation of Christ* by Thomas à Kempis from Cologne. During this period, though, other works were also important, for example, the *Spiritual Ascensions* by Gerhard Zerbolt, a priest and librarian at Radewijn's foundation in Deventer. Indeed, his work was certainly read by Luther, though it is impossible to say with certainty that he or any other reformer was heavily or directly influenced by the *devotio moderna*. However, what can be said is that many lay people, especially in northern Europe, were influenced by the movement and, as a result, favourably inclined to types of religion that placed an emphasis upon personal and individual piety, and a more direct relationship with the divine.

HUMANISM

While the *devotio moderna* had an important impact on the practice of religion in much of Europe, humanism had a much greater influence, especially in the understanding of religion. Beginning in Italy during the Renaissance, humanism placed its emphasis on rediscovering the culture of the ancient world. In particular, this meant reviving classical Latin, encouraging a familiarity with Greek and, in the context of religion, placing a similar importance on a knowledge of Hebrew. This new learning, 'humane letters' as it was called, was in contrast to medieval scholasticism (sacred letters), which stressed philosophical and theological exactitude. This contrast and critique is best exemplified by the humanists' jibe (entirely unfounded) that scholasticism had become so obtuse that adherents might spend hours arguing about how many angels could dance on the head of a pin. Humanism was, therefore, a new way of thinking about the past, a new way of reading documents, a new way of expressing oneself (normally in 'correct' Ciceronian Latin).

In some cases, this new emphasis upon Latin, classical learning and ancient culture became almost slavish, if not actually pagan. The poet Dante Alighieri, fortunately for Italian, decided (only just) not to compose his *Inferno* in Latin. His fellow poet Francesco Petrarca (Petrarch) saw some of his own works as an attempt to rival the elegant Latin of Virgil's *Aeneid*. Many authors opened their literary works not only with invocations of Christ, but also pagan deities or the muses. For Italians especially, humanism was 'getting in touch' with their ancestors. They were simply eliding over the Middle Ages or the Dark Ages (humanist terms that give an idea of what they thought of the centuries immediately behind them), and plugging back into their greater cultural past. Consequently, Italian humanists would speak of Caesar as 'one of us' and Hannibal as a 'foreigner'.

In art, humanism and the Renaissance allied to return to the forms and aesthetics of the ancient world. The sensuality and, indeed, semi-pornography of some Renaissance art evokes this spirit. It is perhaps interesting to speculate how a society so enthusiastically throwing off its medieval (and Christian) heritage was so immune to the call of Luther and other reformers. Equally, one cannot help but note that the almost hedonistic revelry in classical culture was considerably less a feature of the Renaissance in northern Europe, where the Reformation would eventually take root. Indeed, it is perhaps more accurate to suggest that the form of humanism most important to this discussion was the one that placed an emphasis upon linguistic analysis of documents and the rediscovery of the 'exact' or 'correct' meaning of ancient texts, particularly the Bible.

While humanism was important it should not be overestimated. The heartland of humanism and the Renaissance was Italy, and Italy was largely deaf to the Reformation. Italian humanists did despise clerical abuses and what they considered to be the stupidity of traditional theological debate, but at the core of their ambivalence to the institutions of the Church seems to have been a general revulsion at hypocrisy, not hedonism. Italian humanists were not appalled at lavish living or pure pleasure. What seems to have annoyed them was the pomposity and hypocrisy of clerics engaging in such behaviour, while pretending not to. Italian humanists were not so much calling for reform of the Church's morals, as for life to be embraced in this world instead of the next. Had this sort of call been heeded, there would have been change, but it would not have been reformation.

An excellent example of this disdain for institutional reform is the humanist Gian Francesco Poggio. As a secretary, he accompanied (the anti-) Pope John XXIII to the Council of Constance (the one that burnt Hus). Instead of concentrating on the council's deliberations, he spent much of his time browsing the libraries of the monasteries in the area – and borrowing (permanently) their most valuable works. To the extent that he noticed Hus and his companions, he was largely positive and deplored their persecution. The bulk of this papal secretary's life epitomized Italian humanism. He wrote in Latin and spent much of his life deciphering, copying and editing newly discovered Latin and Greek manuscripts. He was also an archaeologist, especially of Rome's ruins. He may have deplored much of what he saw in the Church as old-fashioned and hypocritical, but he seems to have given little thought or concern to more substantive problems, such as what was believed or how faith was to be lived.

Italian humanists were simply not interested in reforming the Church. To the extent that one can discover any clear religious beliefs, some were pagan or semi-pagan, and many were Deists. They stressed the attainment of perfection in this life, by which they meant not moral perfection, but rather literary and 'social' perfection. Living right meant living well, not living out some moral or spiritual code. Indeed, many were amoral, if not immoral by the standards of their day (and perhaps, at times, of the present day too). They disdained the Church, but were quite happy to take its office, benefices and pensions. They preferred the sensual pleasures of Ovid to the austere, introspective other-worldliness of the New Testament. Since they greatly exceeded the amorality and immorality of many clergy, they could not take any practical interest in spiritual or theological reformation. The great historian Jacob Burckhardt has suggested that humanists were '(de-)moralized' by spending so much time steeped in the literature of a hedonistic, pagan past.

Humanism in northern Europe was a considerably more austere, serious and spiritual movement. It would be frivolous to suggest that the cold of the north made hedonistic cavorting a little less attractive (or practical) than it was in Italy. Nevertheless, there was a distinctly different climate to northern European humanism. There was less a feeling that the classical world was 'their' world and less a desire to rediscover 'their' ancestors. The aesthetics of northern humanism focused on the beauty of a fully understood text and a pleasing translation, not the perfect form of Michelangelo's *David* or an Ovidian crudity amusingly expressed in Ciceronian Latin.

Desiderius Erasmus of Rotterdam is the best example of this northern style of humanism. He loved classical literature; indeed, his first published work (*Adagia*, 1500) was a collection of Latin and Greek proverbs. He used his excellent command of Latin (for example, in 1502 in his *Enchiridion Militis Christiani — Manual of a Christian Knight/Warrior*) repeatedly to lampoon clerical abuses and to call for greater piety and an adherence to true religion. Indeed, in his 1509 work *Encomium Moriae (In Praise of Folly)*, he blasted abuses throughout society, especially in the Church. That he thought this work would cure rather than kill is apparent in its dedication to his friend Pope Leo X (Giovanni de' Medici). Throughout his life he walked a precarious line between embracing society and lambasting it. Erasmus attacked abuses wherever he saw them, and through his satires provided much of the vitriolic polemic that would be used so effectively against the Church by the reformers. Importantly, his more serious writings provided the intellectual weaponry to assault many of the traditional truths of the Church. These included *The Whole New Testament* (1516) with notes (which were often satirical and biting) and a new Latin translation meant to replace the Vulgate, and his *Paraphrases of the New Testament* (1517 and later). Just as important was his critical reading of the books of the New Testament. He questioned the authorship of James the apostle, and the epistles to the Ephesians and the Hebrews. He approached the biblical texts with a cold rationalism, and treated them no differently than he (or any other humanist) would treat any other ancient document.

The role that Erasmus played (while remaining loyal to the Church) in the later Reformation and the establishment of a 'modern' view of religion is best expressed in a hardly supportive evaluation. In the *Catholic*

Encyclopaedia (1909) the famous 'liberal', Catholic theologian Joseph Sauer (1872–1949) wrote:

> The literary works issued by Erasmus ... made him the intellectual father of the Reformation. What the Reformation destroyed in the organic life of the Church Erasmus had already openly or covertly subverted in a moral sense ... [H]e regarded Scholasticism as the greatest perversion of the religious spirit; according to him this degeneration dated from the primitive Christological controversies, which caused the Church to lose its evangelical simplicity and become the victim of hair-splitting philosophy ... [Thereafter] there appeared in the Church that Pharisaism which based righteousness on good works and monastic sanctity, and on a ceremonialism beneath whose weight the Christian spirit was stifled. Instead of devoting itself to the eternal salvation of souls, Scholasticism repelled the religiously inclined by its hair-splitting metaphysical speculations and its over-curious discussion of unsolvable mysteries ... Even his concept of the Blessed Eucharist was quite rationalistic and resembled the later teaching of Ulrich Zwingli. Similarly he rejected ... Confession, the indissolubility of marriage, and other fundamental principles of Christian life and the ecclesiastical constitution. He would replace these ... [with] the simple words of the Scriptures, the interpretation of which should be left to the individual judgement. The disciplinary ordinances of the Church met with even less consideration; fasts, pilgrimages, veneration of saints and their relics, the prayers of the Breviary, celibacy, and religious orders in general he classed among the perversities of a formalistic Scholasticism. Over against this 'holiness of good works' he set the 'philosophy of Christ', a purely natural ethical ideal, guided by human [wisdom]. Of course this natural standard of morals obliterated almost entirely all differences between heathen and Christian morality, so that Erasmus could speak with perfect

seriousness of a 'Saint' Virgil or a 'Saint' Horace. In his edition of
the Greek New Testament and in his 'Paraphrases' ... he
[foreshadowed] the Protestant view of the Scriptures.

Erasmus, rather to his horror, provided the reformers with the ammunition
both cerebral and vicious to attack, wound and tear asunder the body of
Christ, the Church.

And yet Erasmus was no Protestant. He not only wrote that 'Luther's
movement was not connected with learning', but also that he could 'find a
hundred passages where St Paul seems to teach the doctrines which [are
condemned] in Luther'. Most importantly, he rejected and abhorred the
chaos that seemed to follow in Luther's wake: 'I would rather see things left
as they are than to see a revolution that may lead to one knows not what' —
the pithiest description and warning of the results of Luther's accidental
revolution. Much of his life's work was taken and shaped, in the hands of
reformers, into a bat with which to beat the Church. Erasmus desperately
desired reformation in the Church, the key word for him being 'in'. The
status quo was bad, but schism was worse. Schism, however, is what he got.

2

REAPING THE FIRST HARVEST
OF REFORM

THIS MOST MISERABLE ANARCHY CAUSES
ME SUCH ANGUISH THAT I WOULD GLADLY
LEAVE THIS LIFE ... ANARCHY STRENGTHENS
THE PRESUMPTION OF THE WICKED, AND
THE NEGLECT OF LEARNING THREATENS
TO BRING ON ANOTHER AGE OF DARKNESS
AND OF BARBARISM ... CONTEMPT OF
RELIGION PARADES QUITE OPENLY.

PHILIPP MELANCHTHON, THEOLOGIAN AND EDUCATOR
(1497–1560)

MARTIN LUTHER WAS BORN IN 1483 INTO A WORLD that was ripe for change. That change was needed and probably coming was accepted by almost everyone. Luther's parents certainly wanted his life to be different from their own. They were determined that their newborn son would rise in the world. To this end, his father decided that he should receive a university education and eventually become a lawyer. Much of the past may seem, as the novelist L. P. Hartley put it, like a 'foreign country', but the desire of Luther's father, who worked in copper mining, to see his son earn a better and more secure living is decidedly, recognizably modern. Luther was sent to various schools, eventually studying in an academy operated by the Brethren of the Common Life in Magdeburg. He then moved to Eisenach, and later entered the University of Erfurt in 1501 at the age of seventeen. Graduating as a Master of Arts in 1505, he then began his legal studies.

That same year his entire life – and probably the course of world history as well – changed like a thunderbolt. Indeed, because of a thunderbolt! According to Luther, in the midst of a storm he was nearly struck by lightning. He cried out to St Anne for protection, vowing to become a monk if he were spared. He immediately left law school, sold his library and became an Augustinian monk at the monastery in Erfurt. Luther was a dedicated and devoted monk. More accurately, he was an obsessive and compulsive monk, so much so that he later said, 'If anyone could have gained heaven as a monk, then I would indeed have been among them.' But despite all his pious devotion to fasts, prayer, pilgrimage and Confession, he could not lose the feeling that his sin would eventually doom him. Wallowing in his own despair, Luther was almost certainly close to a breakdown when his superior, Johann von Staupitz, sent him back to university to study theology. He began his studies and teaching in Wittenberg in 1508; by 1512 he had a doctorate, and was hired as a lecturer at the university – the post he held for the rest of his life.

If too much time contemplating his soul had led Luther nearly to despair, then a career focused on theology led him to reform. During the course of 1513–16 Luther lectured on the Pauline letter to the Romans. He became convinced that salvation was entirely a gift from God received through faith – a concept that came to be known as 'justification by faith'. In other words, a simple belief in the saving ability and power of God (through Christ's death) was able to save without any need for specific action. This did not, however, mean that a person had only to have some faith, or that the faith came from the person. Rather, faith was given by God as a gift that allowed the person to accept, indeed embrace, God's gracious gift of salvation. Luther no longer saw the biblical commands to righteousness as a call to something impossible, but rather as something that God gave sinners freely. Once he came to this conclusion, Luther began to examine both the teachings and practices of his Church in the light of this free gift of grace. This led him to question, in particular, the Church's stress on merit – not only of the individual, but also of the saints. The idea that damnation or salvation were based on some system of spiritual book-keeping with debit and entry columns was repugnant to him. This entire debate for Luther crystallized around one practice that, to him, became the epitome of this emphasis on earning salvation through human activity or merit. That practice was the granting of indulgences.

CHALLENGING THE CHURCH

Indulgences remitted or cancelled punishment for sins that had been absolved and forgiven in the confessional, but that still had to be removed or purged in purgatory. Indulgences could be earned (by making a pilgrimage, for example), or bought outright either for a person or, more creatively for the purposes of fund-raising, for a dead relative. During the late 1510s the pope required enormous sums of money to fund the rebuilding of the Vatican basilica (the present St Peter's is the result, having replaced the earlier structure built under the emperor Constantine the Great in the early fourth century). In addition, some of the money was meant to repay the loans owed to bankers by Albrecht, Archbishop of Mainz and elector of the Holy Roman Empire, which he had incurred when he bought the archbishopric/electorate. The leading 'salesman' employed was a Dominican monk named Johann Tetzel. Not only was there an historical animosity between Augustinians (such as Luther) and the Dominicans, but Luther was horrified by Tetzel's techniques. It is probably apocryphal, but the sales jingle attributed to Tetzel gives a reasonably fair idea of how easy it was to abuse the system:

> *Sobald der Gülden im Becken klingt*
> *Im huy die Seel im Himmel springt.*
> (Soon as the coin in the box rings
> The soul into heaven springs.)

To Luther this overt sale of indulgences was an abuse that would delude people into thinking that they could ignore true repentance and rely instead on a piece of paper. Luther preached against the practice and, according to tradition, on 31 October 1517 (celebrated throughout the Lutheran world as 'Reformation Day') he nailed a notice about a university debate on the traditional noticeboard for such events – the door of the castle church in Wittenberg. This notice contained ninety-five separate points (or theses) for debate and discussion, hence they are known as Luther's 'Ninety-five Theses'. In general, these focus almost wholly on the sale of indulgences and the greed that motivated it. Luther sent a copy to his superior, Archbishop Albrecht of Magdeburg (also of Mainz), who forwarded the list to Rome. The subject of indulgences was suitable for debate as it was an open question as far as Church doctrine was concerned. However, Albrecht and others suspected that an attack on papal power underlay the theses.

In the normal course of events that would have been the end of the tale. Luther might have received a slap on the wrist or faced censure from his superiors. Alternatively, and much more likely, he would have held his debate to general indifference and universal forgetfulness. However, one significant factor intruded – the printing press. Some enterprising printer spotted the explosive and populist nature of what Luther had said, and this led to a general printing and reprinting of the theses by presses across Germany. Within weeks they were appearing as pamphlets (more like wall posters) throughout Germany, and within two months they were available in various countries. Clearly, it was not Luther's intention that his theses, written in Latin, would circulate widely. The enterprising printers, on the other hand, had seen their potential wider interest, especially once they had had them translated into German.

Taking advice from his theological advisers, Pope Leo X had Luther's views refuted, especially as the theses called into question the theological reasons given for using indulgences that had received papal support as early as 1343 in Clement VI's bull *Unigenitus*. It is worth pausing a moment to note that a 'bull' is a papal decree, so called because it has a large, embossed seal – a *bulla* in Latin. Bulls are always known by the opening word(s) of the Latin text. Luther, in emphasizing that merit was conferred by God, was suggesting that the Church's claim of access to a 'treasury of merit' (that is, the 'extra' merit accumulated over the ages by the saints) was not only false, but also misleading and ultimately worthless.

At this point, Luther became embroiled, accidentally and probably unwittingly, in the politics of the Holy Roman Empire and the papacy. Luther's secular ruler, the Elector Frederick, wanted to protect 'his' theologian, and since there was the chance that he would be the next emperor, the pope did not desire a confrontation. A series of meetings and discussions soon followed, involving Luther and a string of papal representatives:

Cardinal Cajetan, the papal chamberlain Karl von Miltitz, and the theologian Johann Eck. During the course of these meetings, held in Leipzig (June–July 1519), Luther's views, especially his denial of papal sovereignty, became clearer and harsher. Most damagingly of all, Eck got Luther to say positive things about Jan Hus.

This, more than anything, sealed the issue in the minds of many traditionalists and papal supporters. Worse, by this point Luther's works, which continued to pour from his pen, were circulating throughout Europe. And the more Luther wrote, the more topics he discussed, and the more his ideas began to deviate from the accepted norms of the Church. It is worth noting, though, that many of the issues Luther debated were not settled by the Church (this would come later in the century during the various sessions of the Council of Trent). What was new, though, was that these debates began to be aired and discussed more widely and more thoroughly by lay people, not just theologians in universities. Luther's resulting revolution may have been accidental, but his use of popular appeal through vernacular printing was entirely intentional.

Three of these works (all published in 1520) stand out not only for their expressions of Luther's ideas, but also (being addressed to large audiences) for their impact (often unintended, as we shall see). The first, *To the Christian Nobility of the German Nation*, introduced the idea of a priesthood of all believers, suggesting that reformation, rather than being the work of councils or clerics or theologians, was a task given by God to all Christians. This idea was explosive. The work also contained multiple attacks on traditional doctrine, and for the first time labelled the pope as the Antichrist – the arch-enemy of Christ, a perverted mirror image of the Saviour – Satan himself. Luther also denounced clerical celibacy. Much of what he said recalled complaints made by reformers, from Hus to Erasmus, in previous decades. But the really dangerous idea, as we shall see, was the priesthood of all believers.

Luther's second work, *On the Babylonian Captivity of the Church*, was more explicitly focused on doctrine taking its name from the chaos surrounding the pope's residence in Avignon and the multiple popes of the Great Schism. Luther questioned both the number and understanding of the sacraments. He called for the cup to be given to lay people in communion (another move linking him with Hus). He accepted only the Eucharist (communion), Baptism and Confession as true sacraments (later he would drop Penance); Confirmation, Marriage, Holy Orders (that is, being a monk, nun, or priest) and Extreme Unction (last rites) were all rejected. Luther used his title, which referred to the embarrassing recent history of the papacy, to suggest that the Church and all Christians were held captive by a threefold set of chains: the cup being denied to lay people, the doctrine of transubstantiation (that the bread and wine changed into Christ's body and blood) and the 'sacrifice of the Mass' (that the priest replays Christ's sacrifice on the cross during every Mass). In a theological and institutional sense, this work was much more daring and dangerous. It called into question fundamental beliefs about salvation and how it was brought to humans from God. It also suggested enormous changes to the way in which Christians would, or could, worship God. Nevertheless, the treatise is much less polemical and confrontational, being focused on belief and practical piety.

The final work, *On the Freedom of a Christian*, deals with the freedom that God's grace gave to a Christian to live a life of love and service. Luther addressed it to Leo X himself in an attempt at conciliation following the pope's threat (a few months previously) in another bull, *Exsurge Domine*, to excommunicate Luther as a heretic. He stressed that he was not attacking the pope personally – only the abuses and corruption that surrounded him. The situation escalated rapidly. On 12 December 1520 Luther burnt the bull and other papal writings, saying: 'As for me, the die is cast; I despise alike the favour and fury of Rome; I do not wish to be reconciled with her; or even to hold any communication with her. Let her condemn and burn my books; I, in turn, unless I can find no fire, will condemn and publicly burn the whole pontifical law, that swamp of heresies.' On 3 January 1521 he was formally excommunicated by the bull *Decet Romanum Pontificem*. In effect, the revolution that was the Reformation had begun.

Fortunately for Luther, though, imperial politics intervened, or this would almost certainly have been the end of the Reformation. Although the elector had not become emperor, the man who did – Charles V – was unwilling to throw his new, fractured realm into greater chaos. Instead, Charles prevaricated and procrastinated. He summoned Luther under a safe conduct (the same type that had failed to save Hus over a century before) to the Diet (imperial council) at Worms on 22 January 1521. Here Luther faced his old opponent Johann Eck. Confronted by a table groaning under a pile of his published works, he was asked to acknowledge them and to accept or reject the ideas in them. After a day to contemplate his answer, Luther stood before the emperor and his council and said: 'Unless I am convicted by Scripture and plain reason, I do not accept the authority of popes and councils, for they have contradicted each other. My conscience is captive to the Word of God. I cannot and will not recant anything, for to go against conscience is neither right nor safe.'

According to tradition, he ended his answer with: 'Here I stand. I can do no other. God help me. Amen.' Even if he did not utter these words, the overall tenor of what he said was clear – and, in the long run, extremely important. Although he was no advocate of individualism, Luther neverthe-less declared both his own personal ability to decide theological issues, and also his own responsibility for his beliefs. By asserting the primacy of his own conscience and its relationship with the Word of God, he opened the floodgates to the sort of splintering and schism that would produce the old Dutch proverb: 'One Dutchman [one might just as easily say, Protestant], a theologian; two Dutchmen, a church; three Dutchmen, a schism.'

This threw the Diet into an uproar. While discussion raged about what to do with Luther, he wisely slipped away from Worms. On his way back to Wittenberg he was taken into 'protective custody' by the elector and secreted away in Wartburg Castle at Eisenach, where he was safely hidden for nearly a year. In the meantime, the emperor acted, and on 26 May 1521 Luther was formally declared a heretic and an outlaw in the empire; in addition, his writings were banned. Protected from the heretic's stake,

Luther busied himself in his castle exile translating the New Testament into German (published in 1522).

Bereft of Luther, the situation in Saxony began to move forward quickly and chaotically. Luther's writings continued to pour forth. He attacked aspects of Confession, and condemned Archbishop Albrecht's ongoing sale of indulgences. He continued to strengthen his view that saving grace was entirely a gift, and that salvation did not in any way depend on a quality or action in a person. Philipp Melanchthon and others received written advice from Luther, as they turned to him for guidance when others exceeded his reforming zeal at Wittenberg. Clerics began to renounce not only their vows of celibacy, but also the whole concept of clerical vows. Luther rejected vows that were taken to acquire salvation, but was open to the idea of vows more generally. He agreed that private Masses (that is, Masses said by priests in private) should be abolished. As monks and priests began to move against elements of the traditional worship service or repudiate the Mass entirely, Luther called for calm and order. However, having turned human conscience loose, he could only look on with concern as his followers, such as Andreas Karlstadt (1486–1541), demanded the abolition of the private Mass, Communion with both bread and wine, the removal of pictures from churches, and the destruction of what they considered to be idolatrous images in the form of statuary and other works of art.

Luther's efforts came close to collapse with the arrival in Wittenberg of the so-called Zwickau Prophets around Christmas 1521. Thomas Dreschel, Nicolas Storch and Mark Thomas Stübner came from Zwickau to Wittenberg, asserting that Luther had not gone far enough. In particular, they rejected the traditional practice of infant baptism, insisting that baptism should be reserved for adults. Although opposed by Melanchthon, the prophets got a sympathetic hearing from Karlstadt. At first Luther advised conciliation and caution, but when he returned to Wittenberg on 6 March and subsequently had a meeting with the prophets, he rejected them and their ideas completely. Luther now took firm control of the situation. A new style of worship, not radically different from many parts of the

Mass, was introduced, as was a hymnal. Luther's use of music and singing to spread his ideas was inspired, and proved to be extremely successful. He also issued a treatise, *Temporal Authority: To What Extent It Should Be Obeyed*, which argued that secular authorities had no control over the soul.

The rise of the prophets (the first stirrings of what would later be called Anabaptism – from the idea that they were re-baptizers, 're-' being a translation of the Greek 'ana-', since everyone had already been baptized in infancy) was but a sign of worse to come. It was clear that Luther's ideas concerning a priesthood of all believers, freedom of conscience, and rejection of secular control over the soul were being read much more radically than he intended. Never one to speak softly or circumspectly, his fulminations in conflict with his Catholic opponents provided other more radical reformers with ready ammunition to use against his more cautious approach. Luther was clearly determined that the unintended and accidental consequences of his actions would never be revolutionary.

The immediate problem though was that Luther had opened Pandora's box and unleashed more than he had bargained for. It became clear at once how disastrous and unintended the consequences of this would be. In 1524 one of the empire's periodic peasant revolts began. Normally, these would involve a considerable amount of posturing that would eventually end in a settlement in which some of the peasants' demands would be met. This revolt, though, was to be decidedly different, with horrific results. The peasants took Luther's rhetoric to heart and enlarged on his attacks against clerical corruption and the ecclesiastical hierarchy into an attack on social structures more generally. They *intended* revolution.

Revolts broke out in Swabia, Franconia and Thuringia, and attracted support from both peasants and disaffected nobles (knights and minor gentry). The latter groups traditionally provided leadership in these sorts of revolts. However, this revolt also found a leader in the radical Anabaptist theologian Thomas Müntzer. The revolts coalesced and became widespread, threatening to overthrow the existing social order and, as was apparent to most observers, spread a type of reformation much more in tune with the prophets than Luther. Nevertheless, Luther seemed initially to support the peasants, as he condemned the rapacious greed of the nobility, which had driven the peasants to revolt. However, as the revolt intensified and the peasants became ever more successful and destructive, Luther grew horrified, and he condemned the rebels in his *Against the Murderous, Thieving Hordes of Peasants* (1525), which called upon the secular authorities to slaughter the rebellious peasants.

It is perhaps too cynical to suggest that since Luther relied on support and protection from the princes, he was afraid of alienating them. This may have played a part, but it is much more likely that Luther's innate conservatism and his acceptance of social hierarchy meant he was truly appalled and frightened as much by the peasants' successes as their demands. His call upon the nobility to visit swift and bloody punishment upon the peasants was seen by many of the putative victims as a betrayal, but it also had the effect of encouraging many others (who saw how the wind was blowing) to melt away from the rebel forces. The revolt was finally crushed at Frankenhausen (15 May 1525) by nobles who supported Luther *and* those who supported the pope. Neither liked the other, but both shared a fear and hatred of the peasants and their radical religious ideas.

TWO TYPES OF REFORM

Although he was captured and executed, Müntzer's ideas were not crushed, and they deserve some careful consideration. From the very first years of the Reformation two different types of Protestantism developed. Traditionally, these have been known to scholars as the magisterial and radical reformations. The former describes a type of movement that closely allied itself with secular rulers or magistrates, hence, 'magisterial'. The radical movement rejected much of the existing social and economic structures and called for a radical reorganization of society and culture. The two names are apt, but focus on the institutional and societal characteristics of these varieties of the Reformation. In particular, this traditional nomenclature has obscured the truly revolutionary nature of the radical movement and would suggest that the two types are quite distinct. In fact, they were not.

Both movements spring from the same root – Luther's rejection of a type of institution and type of salvation focused on mediation. That is, a religion where the vast bulk of the people were dependent on a handful of 'professional' religious figures (priests, monks, nuns, cardinals, bishops and popes) to deliver salvation. Luther declared that individuals had to read and interpret the Bible for themselves, and that ultimately they and they alone were responsible (through their conscience) for what they believed. Salvation was individually granted to a person by God's grace through the medium of faith. Both types of reformation shared these beliefs. The difference lay in what sprang, in practice, from these beliefs. Luther supported a dramatic and thorough reform of the stucture of the Church, but did not envisage his ideas leading to an equally complete change in society. He – and most other humanists and magisterial reformers – thought that the Bible was 'clear' and its message 'plain': that Scripture would interpret itself, that all men of good will (no matter how humble) who studiously read the Bible would and could see the truth. The *same* truth!

There was also a parting of ways about exactly what society and community meant. For the magisterial reformers (especially with their insistence on infant baptism), society and the Christian community (or body of believers) were the same group. Indeed, society could in some way be Christian. The radicals, by and large, did not see the two groups as the same. Rather, the Christian community was a group of individuals within the wider society (the world), but called by God to be separate from it. They tended to think that societal institutions were as likely to be godly as the magisterial reformers thought the ecclesiastical institutions of the Roman Church were likely to be. The magisterial reform was, in that sense, a 'communal' reformation, which saw society as something that could and should be Christianized. As such, the use of coercion in regulating not only behaviour but also belief made sense. Radicals, believing that the bulk of society was unchristian, saw no need for coercion; rather, they wanted purity and separation. Any coercion within their own group extended simply to threatening an errant individual with expulsion and 'shunning'. This was almost certainly effective, and considerably less drastic than execution.

These two approaches to reform and Protestantism will resurface time and again. They appeal to those asking a range of different and, at times, mutually exclusive questions. What is right belief? How is belief policed and controlled, and should it be? How do (or can) Christians and Christianity make a difference in society? Is the faith a communal activity (for example, including infants in some way), or individual (involving mainly professing believers), or both? Which is more important: right behaviour or right belief? Can they be separated? The magisterial reformers might therefore be called 'communal' reformers, and the radicals 'individualists', but this would overlook the enormous stress laid on the communities in which the radicals 'gathered' (as they would term it) from the wider society. Perhaps 'corporate' and 'separatist' would be more accurate descriptions because the magisterial reformers did see Christianity as something that could (indeed, had to) encompass the whole of society, its institutions as well as its people, while the radicals wanted to separate from the world. Finally, in one area they disagreed greatly and that was on the use of force. The magisterial reformers accepted and used force, while most (though not all) radicals were pacifists. It would be perjorative in the modern world to talk of coercive and voluntary reformations, but these too highlight the distinctions. What is most obvious is that 'magisterial' and 'radical' may be convenient terms, but they are hardly obvious in their meaning, or necessarily informative.

In order to understand the radical (or Anabaptist) movement and why magisterial Protestants as well as Catholics feared and hated it so much, it is important to look at Müntzer and his immediate successors in some detail. Müntzer had left Zwickau and travelled widely, preaching in Bohemia (now in the Czech Republic), Thuringia (Germany) and Switzerland. Unlike later Anabaptism, Müntzer was willing to utilize force to create his utopian Christian society, in which all distinctions of social status were eradicated, and possessions were held in common for the common good (as the early Church had in Jerusalem – Acts 2:44, 4:32). Anabaptists frequently noted that the enthusiasm of the magisterial reformers for returning to the early Church of the apostles, having purged the contemporary one of later traditions and practices, did not extend to 'holding all things in common', nor to the elimination of the tradition of infant baptism.

Müntzer believed that the end of the world was imminent (as did some of the magisterial reformers). He also preached that God continued to speak (reveal truth) directly to mankind through prophets, such as himself. He is often accused of anti-intellectualism, and, in truth, he had little time or use for theological debates, having taken to heart Luther's ideas about the clarity and simplicity of the Bible, and the importance of even the simple ploughman interpreting the Word of God. He did, however, also produce the first completely new (that is, non-Catholic) order of worship in German, *The Order of German Church Service*. He also preached in both Latin and German at Prague University during his brief stay in Bohemia. He may have disregarded theology, but he was not himself uneducated.

Apart from rejecting infant baptism (though there is no direct evidence that he ever received believer's baptism), he also preached that the bread and wine in Communion were only symbols. In this he prefigured the reformer of Zurich, Ulrich (or Huldrych) Zwingli, and part of Luther's seemingly illogical and stubborn response to Zwingli and his ideas may stem from an earlier experience with Müntzer. Zwingli, as we shall see, was no Müntzer, but Luther may have heard echoes of Müntzer's (dangerous) theology when Zwingli spoke. Finally, and most frighteningly to the magisterial reformers and their magistrate supporters, was Müntzer's teaching that God still spoke and revealed truth, and that the Spirit did more than simply interpret the Word of God (the Bible). Catholics could and did rightly charge that Luther's views on the priesthood of all believers turned every person loose to come to his or her own understanding and interpretation of any and every verse of the Bible – with cataclysmic consequences. Müntzer and other Anabaptists went even further in claiming that God might reveal even more than was in the Bible, thereby exponentially multiplying the possibilities for personal and, thus conflicting and separate, interpretations.

REFORMATION IN SWITZERLAND

However, any further discussion of Anabaptism must await an examination of the reformation in Zurich and the life and work of Ulrich Zwingli. A contemporary of Luther, Zwingli began to move away from the Roman Church at about the same time. Indeed, it is not clear that there was any direct 'Lutheran' influence on Zwingli; rather, it is probably better to see Zwingli as a humanist who arrived at many of the same conclusions as Luther. If nothing else, this stresses the extent to which both were part of a much wider intellectual movement that was questioning many of the accepted truths of their day.

Although Zwingli and Luther disagreed on many aspects of religion, the heart of the debate between them was the understanding of the sacraments, especially Communion. It is perhaps worth mentioning just one minor disagreement, though, to hint at the extent to which even magisterial reformers could have views that would have significantly differing impacts on the reformations they headed. Luther loved music in church and wrote many hymns; Zwingli, although himself an accomplished musician, thought music distracted from worship and hearing the Word preached, and banned it altogether. Not a significant difference perhaps, but to the worshipper in the pew this would have made a Lutheran church service radically different from one in Zwinglian Zurich.

But the sacraments of Baptism and Communion were the areas of greatest debate, and, in the long run, proved the obstacles not only to agreement, but even to a united stance against a resurgent Roman Church (that is, parishes submitting to the supremacy of the Bishop of Rome, the pope) — which can now rightly begin to be called Roman Catholic. For Luther, the sacraments *did* something; for Zwingli, they were merely symbolic. As E. Brooks Holifield succinctly put it (*The Covenant Sealed*, 1974):

When Luther called the sacrament a covenantal seal, he meant that baptism visibly ratified and guaranteed God's promises, as a royal seal authenticated a government document on which it was inscribed. Only secondarily was baptism a pledge of obedience by men. For Zwingli, however, the sacrament was primarily 'a covenant sign' which indicated that all those who received it were willing to amend their lives to follow Christ.

For Luther, then, baptism marked someone as having received God's free gift of grace through faith. Zwingli, however, saw it as a contractual pledge in which both parties had obligations, and that could lapse if either party failed to fulfil his side of the 'bargain'. Zwingli's upbringing in Switzerland, where oaths and bonds were crucial to the culture, almost certainly led to this understanding and emphasis. It smacked of the same sort of 'works' salvation' that Luther had seen and rejected in Catholicism. Having said that, it was fairly clear that a form of words could have been devised that would have allowed Luther and Zwingli to agree.

The greater debate, though, was over the Eucharist, and here it proved impossible to reach an agreement. In 1529 at the Marburg Colloquy (conference) Luther and Melanchthon met Zwingli and Johann Oecolampadius (1482–1531), the reformer of Basle. After much debate and discussion, it became clear that understanding of the Eucharist was the main barrier to unity. Luther believed, and famously wrote on the conference table, that the bread really was Christ's body – *Hoc corpus meus est* ('This is my body'). Although he rejected the Catholic doctrine that the substance of the bread and wine was completely transformed (hence transubstantiation) into Christ's body and blood, he believed that the substance of Christ's body and blood was present with (hence consubstantiation) the bread and wine. Zwingli did not reject an Aristotelian view of reality (which is absolutely necessary for a belief in either transubstantiation or consubstantiation, and which is completely at odds with the modern view of reality based on the atom). Rather, he simply insisted that the words Christ used meant that the bread is his body in the same way that he said 'I *am* the gate' or 'I *am* the light'. For Zwingli, Jesus was speaking symbolically, not literally.

In effect, Zwingli was suggesting that one had to use common sense to distinguish when Jesus was speaking *literally* or symbolically. He saw no specific reason to think that Jesus meant that the bread was literally his body, and as many opponents then and now of Luther's view said, Christ's *body* was in Heaven seated at God's right hand. Luther proposed that Christ's body could share in the divine aspect of omnipresence (everywhere at the same time in the same way). Zwingli and others believed that the idea of Christ's physical body being ubiquitous undermined the fundamental doctrines about how Christ was fully human and fully divine (two substances in one person), which was inextricably linked with the Trinitarian doctrine that God is three persons in one substance. Or, as that powerful early sixth-century statement of the theology of the Trinity, the so-called Athanasian Creed, puts it:

> We worship one God in Trinity and Trinity in Unity. Neither
> confounding the Persons, nor dividing the Substance. For there is
> one Person of the Father, another of the Son, and another of the
> Holy Ghost ... So the Father is God, the Son is God, and the Holy
> Ghost is God. And yet they are not Three Gods, but One God ... For
> the right Faith is, that we believe and confess, that ... Jesus Christ ...
> is God and Man. God, of the substance of the Father, begotten before
> the worlds; and Man, of the substance of His mother, born into the
> world. Perfect God and Perfect Man ... [N]ot by conversion of the
> Godhead into Flesh, but by taking of the Manhood into God. One
> altogether, not by confusion of substance, but by Unity of Person.

Ubiquity threatened to 'confuse' the two persons united in the one substance of Jesus. It may well seem an obtuse point, but, as we shall see, the Reformation freed people to question every doctrine and practice of the Christian faith, including the nature of Christ and the nature of God.

For our perspective, though, the most important aspect of the Marburg Colloquy and the failure of Luther and Zwingli to unite were twofold. First, it meant that Protestantism was weakened in the face of the coming forces of the Counter/Catholic Reformation, with Protestants often willing to work with Catholics to the detriment of other Protestants. Second, it allows us to focus on two of the key issues of the Reformation – the priesthood of all believers and the simplicity/clarity of Scripture.

Both Catholics and Protestants believed that the Scripture reveals truth under the direction of the Holy Spirit. Any given verse might have a number of different interpretations (that is, might speak about more than one thing), but ultimately any truths that arose from any given verse would not be contradictory. In that sense, the meaning of the Bible is 'clear' and 'plain'. The question, though, is how a decision is made about which overarching interpretation (that is, truth) is really 'true'. How this question is answered explains why Catholicism works the way it does and why Protestantism works (or more accurately does *not* work) the way it does.

Catholicism teaches that the interpretation of any given verse is ultimately understood through the *magisterium*, the guiding teaching role, of the Church. In other words, a Catholic turns to the Church (its theologians, priests, bishops and, ultimately, the pope) for the 'true' meaning. The Church, in the exercise of this *magisterium*, is guided by the Holy Spirit, as well as the accumulated wisdom of thousands of years of thought on a given subject. The result is a settled interpretation that can, however, adapt and evolve over time as the Holy Spirit makes a verse or passage 'clearer'. This additional clarity will not produce contradiction, only greater depth of understanding. It can allow for a slow change that may seem to produce contradiction: for example, a Church that once prosecuted Galileo for denying the truth of the Bible now accepts that the Earth rotates on its axis and revolves around the sun. It is worth recalling that Catholics and Protestants would have agreed with the comments of Cardinal Robert Bellarmine on Galileo's ideas:

But to want to affirm that the sun really is fixed in the centre of the heavens and only [turns upon its axis] without travelling from east to west, and that the earth is situated in the third sphere and revolves with great speed around the sun, is a very dangerous thing, not only by irritating all the philosophers and scholastic theologians, but also by injuring our holy faith and rendering the Holy Scriptures false. (See, for example, these passages: Joshua 10:12–14; II Kings 20: 8–11; Psalms 93:1, 96:10; Habbakuk 3:11; ed.)

In some cases though, this *magisterium* can be a straitjacket stopping change (for example, the view that priests must be male).

Protestantism has no such mechanism for group and collective inter-pretation. Indeed, Luther's assertions about the priesthood of all believers work entirely against such an approach. So why did Luther say it if it would simply produce as many interpretations as there are people? Well, he did not think that is what would happen. Luther, Zwingli and almost every other reformer or humanist was working with a simple yet profoundly naive presupposition. They could almost all read the New Testament in the orig-inal Greek, also in Latin and in their own native languages. These were educated men. They simply believed that men of good will, led by the Holy Spirit, would come to the same interpretation, since there was only one, true interpretation. With no mechanism for settling differences of interpre-tation Luther and Zwingli were left with a stalemate and schism. Both taught that Scripture was clear and that there was only one truth. And yet both failed to agree on what the word 'is' meant in one of the central doctrines of their faith – in what happens when Communion takes place.

Why did (and does) Protestantism constantly and frequently splinter into very small groups (denominations), sometimes coming together at a later date in unions and reunification? The answer is simply this: it has no mechanism for settling debates. When a Protestant states that a verse says and definitely means something, it is (no matter how important the issue at stake may be) almost always possible to find another Protestant (or indeed an entire other Protestant denomination) that will disagree and propose an entirely different meaning. Catholicism, on the other hand, will agree that the Bible reveals truth and that that truth is plain and clear, but it understands that there is a difference between that as a theory and the reality of the diverse interpretations that sinful humans might find in the Bible. Catholicism relies on hierarchy and tradition to ensure a unity of interpretation and to settle differences; those who disagree place themselves outside the Church. Protestantism has no such mechanism, but instead relies on a conviction that the Holy Spirit will (or at least should) ensure a unity of interpretation. When this fails, schism results and a new denomination is born. It is messy, but also immensely inventive and exciting.

However, while this digression may have provided some illumination, it also left Zwingli in Marburg arguing fruitlessly with Luther. There is more to tell of Zwingli's story. Beginning just a couple of years after Luther's Ninety-five Theses, Zwingli introduced radical change into the faith in Zurich. But his story begins well before the 1520s. Like any good humanist, Zwingli was educated in a number of institutions. He studied in Vienna, Berne and Basle, finally receiving a theological degree in 1506. At the same time, he became a priest (unlike Luther, Zwingli was a parish priest not a monk and university lecturer) in Glarus in his native Switzerland. There he continued his studies in Greek, learnt Hebrew and read many of the works by Erasmus. His work among the people also led him to follow many of his parishioners to Rome, serving as their chaplain when they became mercenaries in papal service, to protect the pope's territorial possessions in Italy against, variously, the French, the Spanish, and other Italian states. His growing renown as a preacher saw him move first to the abbey church at Einsiedeln near Zurich, and then, in 1518, to the city's Grossmünster church.

It would seem that Zwingli began to move away from his traditional faith during his first years in Zurich. In 1519 he opposed the preaching of indulgences. The following year he renounced the salary (pension) he had been receiving from the pope as a result of his chaplaincy work in Rome. By 1522 he had convinced the Zurich government to ban anyone from entering mercenary service or receiving a mercenary-related salary. It was this same year that Zwingli's break with Rome became obvious. During the Lenten fast (when Christians were not supposed to eat meat) a number of men openly ate sausages. Zwingli was present, though, interestingly, he did not eat the sausages. The resulting controversy saw him condemn such fasts as mere 'human commands' and publish his first explicitly reformed work, *Vom Erkiesen und Fryheit der Spysen (On Choice and the Liberty of Meals)*.

The situation developed rapidly thereafter in Zurich once the city's politicians approved and held a disputation (debate) between Zwingli and advocates of the 'old faith'. The government sided with Zwingli, and in quick succession images and pictures were removed from the churches, vernacular worship was introduced, and the Mass was 'cleansed of superstitious' practices. By the end of 1524 convents and monasteries had been closed, and music ceased to be a part of the church service. This was also the year that Zwingli began to produce (alongside Luther's Bible) his own Swiss-German translation of the Bible, the *Froschauer Bibel* (published in stages between 1524 and 1531).

The city finally embraced the Reformation officially on 13 April 1525, which was Maundy Thursday in Easter Week; the Mass ceased and was replaced by the Lord's Supper according to a rite written by Zwingli. Men and women sat on opposite sides of a table that extended down the middle of the church, and were served bread and wine from wooden utensils. Although supporters of the old faith seem to have been non-existent (or already to have left), there were problems. Turned loose on their Bibles, the simple peasants owing allegiance (and taxes, rents and, especially, ecclesiastical tithes) saw nothing in the Scripture that required them to pay. Only after negotiation and some concessions was a potential peasants' revolt prevented.

The biggest problem Zwingli faced, though, came from the Anabaptists. Again, believers turned to their Bibles and found that not all of Zwingli's vision was apparent in its pages. In particular, many found that infant baptism made little sense when compared with the practice of baptism as it appeared in the Bible, which seemed to suggest that baptism should follow, not precede, an experience of faith. Also, as with many other radical reformers, Zurich's (proto-) Anabaptists were unhappy with Zwingli's close collaboration with the government. They likened this (indeed, this became a recurring theme for Anabaptists) to the early Church's connection with, and (as all reformers stressed) corruption by, the emperor Constantine and Rome's imperial state. Zwingli appeared to be making the same mistake that had led Christianity into the religious dead end of Roman Catholicism.

Zwingli and the state responded with speed and ferocity. In a bout of horrific irony, it was decided that since the Anabaptists were such lovers of water, drowning them would be the appropriate punishment. One of the Anabaptists, Felix Mann, was drowned in January 1527; a year earlier the more famous Conrad Grebel had avoided this fate by managing to escape, but died of plague.

Grebel, the so-called 'Father of Anabaptism', had spent eighteen months in the movement and performed the first adult believers' baptism. Even Zwingli admitted that he had few disagreements with Grebel, saying that they only parted company over 'unimportant outward things, such as these, whether infants or adults should be baptized and whether a Christian may be a magistrate'. But, as we have seen, these made all the difference. Infant baptism and cooperation with magistrates suggested a view that society and its institutions as a whole could be (and, indeed, were) Christian; Grebel's view saw only space for a 'remnant' of believers in a wider, unbelieving world. Rejecting the magistrates and their powers of coercion, Grebel inadvertently found himself not only being an early exponent of freedom of conscience and separation of Church and (or, more accurately, from) State, but he also had a lasting impact on Anabaptist groups, such as the Amish and Mennonites, as well as Baptist, Brethren, pietistic and free church movements thereafter. Finally, along with the Bohemian politician and author Petr Chelčický, Grebel is considered one of the earliest advocates of Christian pacifism in the Reformation.

As a legacy, though, Grebel's greatest impact may have been his indirect contact with the great Moravian Anabaptist Balthasar Hübmaier. Like most of the other reformers, both magisterial and radical, he had received a humanist education. He attended Latin school in Augsburg (near his birth-place, Friedberg) and then went to the University of Freiburg before grad-uating with a doctorate in 1512 from the University of Ingolstadt, where he became vice-rector in 1515. Although a successful preacher, he was not a great university administrator, so he left to become a parish priest in Regensburg in 1516, and then, in 1521, in Waldshut.

The following year, Hübmaier met Heinrich Glarean (who taught Grebel) and Erasmus in Basle, and in 1523 he met Zwingli and partici-pated in one of the key disputations in Zurich, which ushered in the city's reformation. To what extent Grebel had a direct personal impact on Hübmaier is not clear, but it is certain that during his time in Zurich he came to reject infant baptism. In 1525 he welcomed another of the Zurich Anabaptists, Wilhelm Reublin, to refuge in Waldshut. That same year, in April, Reublin baptized Hübmaier and sixty others. By December Hübmaier was forced to flee the approaching Austrian (Catholic) army and seek refuge in Zurich with his former debating partner Zwingli, who promptly had him arrested. A direct debate with Zwingli and others was held, and Hübmaier used Zwingli's words against him, but Zwingli said he was being misquoted. Hübmaier offered to recant, but then withdrew the offer; he eventually did recant after being tortured on the rack – a 'moment of weakness' he regretted the rest of his life. He was then released and fled to Nikolsburg in Bohemia. Two years later Hübmaier and his wife were arrested by the Austrians. In Vienna he was tortured again, refused to recant, was tried as a heretic and, on 10 March 1528, burnt for his beliefs. Three days later his wife had a stone tied around her neck and was thrown into the Danube to drown.

The Anabaptists of Zurich, as well as the Zwickau Prophets, showed many of the reformers the dangers of Anabaptism and uncontrolled bibli-cal interpretation. For the most part, though, these radicals were few in number and, apart from Müntzer and his peasant followers, non-violent. As we shall see, this view was to change, and the fears first occasioned by Müntzer would return a thousand times worse in the early 1530s. But before turning to a more militant form of radicalism, it is important to revisit Zurich and Zwingli to complete the development of the Reformation in Switzerland. By and large, Protestantism was most successful in those Swiss cantons that were heavily urbanized, while Catholicism was retained in the rural cantons, such as Uri, Schwyz, Unterwalden, Lucerne, Zug and Freiburg. Each urban centre had its Zwingli: St Gallen had Vadian (Joachim von Watt); Schaffhausen had Dr Sebastian Hofmeister; Basle had Johann Oecolampadius (present at the Marburg Colloquy). Berne was treated to a personal visit by Zwingli and the Reformation was adopted there. Eventually, by 1529, the list expanded to include Constance, Biel and Mulhausen.

Much to the dismay and shock of many Swiss, this divided situation quickly degenerated into open warfare. Zwingli, an opponent of mercenary service, was not, however, averse to war, and cajoled Zurich into moving against the Catholic cantons. The war was rather lacklustre, and Berne, Zurich's chief ally, was lukewarm, while the Catholics failed to get their hoped-for support from Austria. A truce was agreed that forced the Catholics to allow each village to vote to stay Catholic or become Protestant. This outbreak of democracy was not extended to villagers in Zurich's territory, though. Zwingli opposed any conciliation with the Catholic cantons, and eventually they felt compelled to resort to arms and march against Zurich. The surprise attack was successful in that Zwingli went out to war with his parishioners and was killed, in full armour and with sword in hand, at Kappel. A month later (June 1529) another peace treaty was signed that more or less solidified the division of Switzerland into Catholic and Protestant cantons, but pulled the Swiss back from the brink of full-scale civil war and the possible dismemberment of the Confederation.

Thus ended the first phase of the Reformation. True, Geneva was becoming Protestant at the same time (the early 1530s), but its story, under John Calvin, lies in the next chapter. One other significant event belongs to this earlier period, namely, the one attempt at a 'magisterial' Anabaptist reformation – or rather, the establishment of an Anabaptist city-state. If most Europeans, Catholic and Protestant, found the Peasants' War and Müntzer frightening, what would happen in Münster in Westphalia was terrifying.

REFORMATION IN GERMANY

Anabaptists, preaching the imminent end of the world (the apocalypse) under the leadership of the (theoretically) Lutheran pastor Bernhard Rothmann, along with Jan Matthys, a Dutch baker from Haarlem, and Jan Bockelson, a tailor from Leiden (hence his more common name, John of Leiden), were able to stage a coup against the magistrates and take control of Münster. Matthys had been a follower of Melchior Hoffman (see page 86) and had gathered a considerable following in the Low Countries. He declared that Münster was the New Jerusalem of the Book of Revelation, and after the coup Anabaptist refugees flooded into the city to await the return of Jesus and the end of the world.

On 5 January 1534 adult-believers' baptism was introduced into the city, and well over a thousand adults were baptized. Bursting with refugees, the city began to prepare for the end of the world and Christ's conquest of it. Unfortunately, the city's exiled Catholic bishop wanted his see (bishop's seat) back, and he laid siege to the town. On Easter Sunday 1534, believing in his own invincibility as God's prophet (a second Gideon, after the Old Testament judge, Gideon, who led a divinely selected army against overwhelming odds and won), Matthys sallied forth from the town with thirty followers and was cut to pieces – in his case, quite literally. His head was severed and placed on a pole for all in the city to see, and his genitals were nailed to the city gate. John of Leiden now took control and was crowned king of the New Jerusalem as the successor to King David.

Münster now began a truly peculiar experiment in radicalism. John of Leiden justified his actions by the authority of visions he claimed to have had directly from God. He 'returned' to the Old Testament and legalized polygamy (as the patriarchs had practised it), taking sixteen wives himself;

one of these he personally beheaded (which was *not* polygamy as the patri-archs practised it). Not only did he claim scriptural support for his polygamy (an important time to recall the preceding discussion about how the truth of the Bible was to be decided among Protestants), but he also ensured that the many single and widowed refugee women had the 'protec-tion' of a husband. Finally, a community of goods was declared, though some exceptions were made to keep the few remaining merchants in the city peaceful. The city fell to its besiegers (by now comprising both Catholic and Protestant troops) on 24 June 1535, and John of Leiden and his lead-ing supporters were tortured and executed. Their bodies, and later their bones, were exhibited in cages hung from the steeple of St Lambert's Church in the city. The cages – and the pincers that were heated red-hot to tear their bodies – remain on view to this day, though the bones have been removed.

At this point it is worth briefly discussing emerging Protestant ideas about the family and sex. Protestants rejected celibacy – integral to the institutional life of medieval Catholicism – on two levels. In theory, they accepted that celibacy was the ideal state, continuing to hold to the older and wider Christian view that sex distracted from the spiritual and was, at its lowest level, a 'base', even 'bestial', activity of the flesh. This did not change. However, Protestants did reject the idea that celibacy was possible for almost anyone through vows and the active aid of the Holy Spirit – the notion underpinning the Catholic approach to monks, nuns and celibate parish priests. Luther and the other reformers held that very few were 'gifted' with celibacy, and that the vast majority of people should marry.

This resulted, accidentally, in the family acquiring an enormous eleva-tion in status. In particular, the family of the pastor became the model for the rest of society, rather than, like a priest, being set off as different. For Lutherans, this also meant the reinterpretation of Mary as the dutiful, ideal housewife and mother, rather than as the Virgin Queen of Heaven. It also meant that the normal state for men and women was married. The single person was no longer someone upholding a religious ideal, but a figure of suspicion. Family life increasingly became the ideal through which Christianity was lived. Men and women were no longer encouraged to free themselves from the flesh, but rather to experience and control their flesh within the marital, familial unit. Everyone was supposed to marry.

The epitome of this idea – very much unintended by Luther – was the emergence of Mormonism in the second quarter of the nineteenth century. Mormonism so elevated the family and procreative sex that even God has a heavenly wife. The soul that occupies each human is, in fact, the offspring of God and His wife breathed into each individual, just as God breathed life into Adam. Mormon couples procreate on Earth, and in due course become a divine, heavenly couple in their own universe, where they are united in marriage and procreation for all eternity. Indeed, the heavenly couple 'populating' this universe were a fleshly, marital couple in a pre-existent, alternative universe. Of all the unintended consequences of the reformers' accidental revolution, this is probably the most unimaginable. Luther and other reformers upheld and valued marriage, but, in keeping with Christ's teaching, they never believed that the marital unit existed beyond death. When death parted a couple, it did so eternally. The surviving spouse was therefore free to remarry. Mormonism, however, took this Protestant emphasis on the family, added a stress on procreation, and elevated it to an eternal state of existence. Münster saw some peculiar ideas about marriage being put into practice, but there was never any suggestion that monogamy or polygamy were anything other than as described in the Bible.

Returning to Münster, one can readily see that the rebellion there was a turning point for Anabaptism. It never again had the opportunity to gain political power. Unsurprisingly, the magistrates adopted the most stringent measures to suppress a movement that they believed was committed not only to the overthrow of normal social structures, but of the State itself. For those who opposed the use of force, differentiating themselves from the Münster rebels became a key goal and a significant part of their rhetoric. Many non-resistant Anabaptists found leaders in Menno Simons and the brothers, Obbe and Dirk Philips. These Dutch Anabaptists had strenuously and unwaveringly repudiated the distinctive doctrines of the Münster Anabaptists. This group eventually became known as Mennonites, after Simons. They rejected all violence, preached compassion and the love of one's enemy, and never aimed at any political revolution.

The image of Anabaptism, though, was not helped by the followers of Jan van Batenburg, who was eventually burnt at the stake. Batenburgers believed that every person and every thing was literally owned by God, and that they were God's chosen children. Thus they could do as they pleased. (This is an extreme form of antinomianism, which regarded predestination and election as a licence to sin without any threat of eternal repercussions, highlighting the fact that it is possible to hold this view without believing in predestination.) Therefore there was nothing wrong in making a living by robbing those who did not belong to their sect. In fact, killing an unbeliever could be pleasing to their God (rather as killing a heretic could please the God of an inquisitor or a Protestant magistrate). The Batenburgers also shared the views of the radical Münsterites on polygamy and property: all women (note, not men) and all goods were held in common. A few Batenburger marriages did occur, and van Batenburg retained the right to present a deserving member of his sect with a wife from the sect's 'stock' of women. Although never numbering more than a few hundred, this band provided endless material for anti-Anabaptist polemics in subsequent centuries.

In August 1536 the leaders of the various Anabaptist groups influenced by Melchior Hoffman met in Bocholt in an attempt to maintain unity. The meeting included some Batenburgers, survivors of Münster, David Joris and his sympathizers, and the non-violent Anabaptists. The main points of contention were polygamy and the use of force against unbelievers. Joris proposed a compromise that said it was not yet the right time (presumably a time closer to Christ's return would be right) to fight against the civil authorities, and that it was unwise to kill any non-Anabaptists, since this let their enemies label them as common thieves and murderers. The gathered Anabaptists, in a rare show of unity, agreed to this compromise, but it did nothing to slow the tendency towards schism that infected all varieties of Protestantism.

LUTHER'S LEGACY

It would be rather unfair to the Reformation to leave this first phase on a Batenburger note. Rather, let us return to Luther and close, as we began, with his reformation in Wittenberg. What exactly did Reformation mean in practice for the lay people in Wittenberg? How radical was it? Luther's *German Mass* (1526) had weekday services and catechetical instruction. He strongly rejected, however, all but the lightest of changes to the actual worship service, adopting only those he considered necessary to eliminate erroneous doctrine and superstition. Indeed, Luther advocated liberty in liturgy, but suggested liturgical uniformity among churches in any given area (an ideal suggestion, since Lutheranism was fairly dependent on the whims of both city councils or landed princes). He considered liturgical uniformity to be an outward expression of unity in faith, while liturgical variation indicated possible doctrinal variation. He was very opposed to changes being introduced by individuals or individual congregations. Luther was content to reform through preservation, and preserve in reformation what the Church had inherited from the past. Consequently, while Luther condemned aspects of the Mass that suggested the Eucharist was a sacrifice, or that taught the doctrine of transubstantiation, he was willing to retain an east-facing altar table and various pieces of clerical garb: the stole, chasuble and alb. It would seem, though, that he did think more changes would be introduced later, but that little should be done at this early stage in the Reformation lest the lay people be too greatly offended at having their normal worship life radically altered. The more Luther began to appreciate the possible scale of the revolution he had set in motion, the more he tried to moderate it.

Baptism was also altered through Luther's *Baptismal Booklet*, and ordination was replaced (in 1525) by a simple ceremony in which hands were laid on the new minister and a simple prayer said. This may have provided for a Lutheran parish church, but it did not solve the need for a structure above the parish level. As few bishops rushed to Luther's reformation, much of the administration of the Church in areas that converted fell directly to the civil authorities. Luther would have preferred to have had evangelical (Protestant) bishops, but reality meant that the princes and town councils had to become 'bishops of necessity'.

At this point, Luther and his supporters had time to turn their attention to the lay people themselves. The result of their first 'visitation' (effectively an interview of parishioners by ministers) was shocking in revealing that many people were not only not Protestant, but they could not really even be termed Christian. Luther had himself been a visitor–inspector, and, as a result, wrote two catechisms – instructional booklets with questions and 'correct' answers – in 1529. He realized that more was needed than catechism, and stressed the need for education. Luther declared that it was the duty of the civil authorities to provide schools and to see that parents sent their children to them. He even advocated the establishment of elementary schools for girls.

None of this would have been possible without the support of secular rulers, especially some of the empire's great princes. When it became clear, in the late 1520s, that the new emperor, Charles V, was willing to unite with his traditional political foes, the papacy and France, to crush Protestantism, Luther's defenders took action. Philip of Hesse sought to assemble a league of all Lutheran and Zwinglian states. Luther resisted any alliance that might aid heresy, but was led by Philip as far as Marburg (see pages 52–4), where any hopes of a united front were dashed. However, the threat from the Ottoman Empire put Charles's plans on hold, and he called the Diet at Augsburg in 1530 to unite the empire against the Turkish foe. Melanchthon attended (Luther was still formally an outlaw and heretic) and presented the Augsburg Confession as a statement of what it meant to be 'Lutheran' – and it is from this point that one can really begin to use that word.

For good or ill, by 1530 Europe was divided. The Augsburg Confession made explicit and formal what had already been apparent. Western

Christendom was now divided into two formal creeds or forms of belief: Catholic and Lutheran. In the next chapter we shall see how these two creeds were joined by a third (Calvinism/Reformed), then a fourth (Anglican), and a plethora of others (various radical groups). But even in 1530 it was obvious that the inherent dangers in Luther's teaching of the priesthood of all believers, and the humanists' understanding that biblical truth was clear and plain, had been realized. Catholic and Lutheran creeds were already accompanied, and opposed by, Zwinglians and Anabaptists. One schism had sprouted three, but unlike the ancient hydra, one did not have to cut off a head to get another head to grow. Protestantism was already showing a unique ability, indeed enthusiasm, for splintering and schism.

3

REAPING THE SECOND HARVEST
OF REFORM

HERESIES AND SCHISMS, THEREFORE, ARISE
WHEN A RETURN IS NOT MADE TO THE
ORIGIN OF TRUTH, WHEN NEITHER THE
HEAD IS REGARDED, NOR THE DOCTRINE
OF THE HEAVENLY MASTER PRESERVED.

JOHN CALVIN
(1509–64)

FROM THE AUGSBURG CONFESSION IN 1530 AND the reformatory work of Luther and Zwingli, the only logical place to begin this chapter is Geneva in Switzerland. In the early 1530s Geneva's citizenry began and, with the military help of Protestant Berne and Catholic Freiburg, completed a revolution against the Duke of Savoy and the Catholic bishop of the city. In the process, the city committed itself to Protestantism, thereby losing the support of Freiburg. It was clear that the city magistrates who hired John Calvin (in 1536) to assist their main evangelical preacher, Guillaume Farel, not only wanted to join the Swiss Confederation (a goal not achieved until 1815), but also intended the Genevan Reformation to follow the model of state-controlled reform seen in Zurich and elsewhere in Protestant, urban Switzerland.

Hiring Calvin was to prove a stroke of genius: he had been educated as a humanist lawyer at Paris and Orléans. Indeed, as an exemplary humanist, his first published work was a critical edition with commentary of Seneca's *De Clementia*. His first stay in Geneva ended abruptly in 1538, when he and the leading reformer of Geneva, Farel, clashed with the city's politicians over changes to the city's religion designed to bring Genevan practice into line with that of Berne, the city's main military protector and chief ally. Calvin was fired and expelled. Eventually, he settled in Strasburg, where he came into close contact with the great Strasburg theologian and reformer Martin Bucer. However, his stay there was also short, for in 1541 Geneva recalled Calvin and he returned to be the city's chief minister, the post he held until his death.

While the first wave of reformers discussed in the previous chapter were often highly original, if not radical and dangerous, in their thought, Calvin's forte was in systematizing the ideas of the Reformation. In particular, he did much to connect these ideas not only with the theology of the Church fathers (those writing in the first four or five centuries of the Church), but also with some of the best theological thinking of the Middle Ages. He took as his starting point the greatness and holiness of God. Most now associate him with predestination, but it is important to remember that most of the early reformers were as predestinarian as Calvin – indeed, Luther was probably more explicitly so as a result of his dispute with Erasmus over freedom of will.

Calvin is also justifiably famous for the system of Church governance he helped create in Geneva, which became the model for many denominations in subsequent decades. These are variously known as Reformed, Presbyterian or Calvinistic. The system relied on a semi-democratic relationship between elders and ministers in a given church. In areas that followed this model, layers of administration above the church level were later adopted, and these might be known as presbyteries, sessions or classes. These bodies were largely made up of ministers. In some reformed denominations there were also bishops or superintendents. The system in Geneva was never intended for use elsewhere, and Calvin's flexibility in advising other churches allowed the basic model to be very adaptable indeed. In theory, though, the basic structure had four offices:

DOCTORS were largely theologians who taught both lay people and pastors. To the extent this developed in Geneva, the doctors taught at the academy (later university) founded at Geneva in 1559.

PASTORS preached, administered the sacraments and exercised discipline by teaching and admonishing the people.

DEACONS oversaw institutional charity, including hospitals and anti-poverty programmes. In Geneva, though, this was a political office entirely in the control of the magistracy.

ELDERS were laymen (usually twelve to a church/panel) who assisted the pastors in the administration of discipline through their joint body, the Consistory. In Geneva the elders were also serving magistrates drawn from the city's three ruling councils.

In most other Reformed/Calvinistic denominations both the elders and deacons were drawn from the laymen of a given church and were normally nominated by the other elders and the minister – though the consent of the (male) congregation was essential.

The Consistory (and the discipline it administered) is perhaps the most radical feature of Calvin's reform, but it was not novel. Indeed, the more Anabaptists talked about holiness and the need for a disciplined community, the more enthusiastic magisterial reformers became about establishing their own disciplinary credentials. The Consistory dealt with all aspects of behaviour and belief, but after the initial few years, during which it focused on latent Catholic practices, the Consistory largely concentrated on preventing interpersonal, especially domestic, conflict. It was an intrusive body, but the enthusiasm with which people voluntarily submitted them-selves to disciplining bodies in other countries confirms what appears in Geneva: discipline was not pleasant, but it kept the peace and was, as a result, tolerated.

Nevertheless, Geneva's leading politicians, while enthusiastic that disci-pline and order were maintained, were less than enthusiastic when it was applied to them personally. Many came to resent that all but one of the ministers was French (that is, foreign) and that Calvin showed little interest in promoting any locals into the ministry. For a city just freed from an eccle-siastical ruler (the bishop) and his foreign, secular lord (the Duke of Savoy), the possibility of being controlled – or, more accurately, humiliated – by French ministers was intolerable. As a warning note placed in one of the city's churches put it:

Gross hypocrite, you and your companions will gain little by your pains. If you do not save yourselves by flight, nobody will prevent your overthrow and you will curse the hour when you left your monkery. Warning has been already given that the devil and his renegade priests were come hither to ruin every thing. But after people have suffered long they avenge themselves … We will not have so many masters. Mark well what I say.

(Attributed to Jacques Gruet (executed 1547), a local Genevan who opposed Calvin)

The debate and anti-French feelings continued until 1555, when a political crisis saw the expulsion of the leading magistrates and their supporters, who were opposed to the style of Reformation Calvin wanted – they felt it was too unlike the Zwinglian model they preferred.

In the course of these long-running disputes, Calvin proved himself to be an astute politician, just as his work in the Consistory and pulpit showed him to be a conscientious and effective pastor. However, he also demonstrated his credentials as a staunch magisterial reformer and opponent of truly radical change. In this context, the name that stands out is that of Michael Servetus, a Spanish doctor of medicine, who, interestingly, had hypothesized the pulmonary circulation of the blood long before William Harvey received credit for the discovery. He had fled Spain and eventually settled in Vienne in Catholic France, where he was arrested for denying the doctrine of the Trinity. He escaped and fled to Geneva in the apparent hope of converting Calvin, despite having had some less than friendly correspondence with him.

His ideas, however, were never likely to do more than infuriate Calvin. In 1531 Servetus had published a treatise *De Trinitatis Erroribus* (*On Errors about the Trinity*), in which he rejected the Trinitarianism of the Nicene Creed and said that God the Son (Christ) was the union of the divine *Logos* (Word) with the man Jesus – the result miraculously born from the Virgin Mary through the intervention of God's spirit. This was generally (and correctly) interpreted as a denial of the Trinity (indeed, Servetus said the doctrine of the Trinity was a 'three-headed Cerberus', a monster, that only led believers into confusion and error). Shortly before his execution he expanded these ideas on God and Christ in *Christianismi Restitutio* (*The Reinstitution of Christianity*), which was almost certainly meant to be a play on the title of Calvin's great work *Institutio Christianae Religionis* (*Institution of the Christian Religion*, or more commonly *The Institutes*). He had sent a copy to Calvin, who had made it clear in his reply, and in his comments to others, that he considered Servetus a heretic meriting death.

The arrival of Servetus in Geneva was a public-relations nightmare for Calvin and the city's magistrates. As a small independent city-state on the border of Catholic France, Geneva had consistently argued against punishing people for their religious beliefs. By which, of course, they meant Protestant beliefs. Calvin hoped for the conversion of France, and Geneva's merchant magistrates wanted to be able to trade unhindered in the kingdom. Since Servetus was already under sentence of death in Catholic Vienne (Calvin had supplied much of the material needed to prove Servetus's guilt), the city tried at first to send him back. When this failed, Protestant opinion was canvassed throughout Switzerland, and the response was unanimous: Servetus had to die. He was quickly burnt at the stake. While many of Calvin's ideas were radical and, as we shall see, his followers in France and the Netherlands were anything but 'conformist' and conservative, he was not a radical reformer, and was more than willing to coerce a conscience. But it is equally fair to concur with the assessment made by the poet Samuel Taylor Coleridge that 'If ever a poor fanatic thrust himself into the fire, it was Michael Servetus'.

While the death of Servetus earned Calvin a place among those who persecute for the sake of conscience, there was more to his work in Geneva than just upholding Christian orthodoxy or reordering the city's Church structure. In one area Calvin also began — or, rather, participated in — his own accidental revolution. In union with Geneva's city government, he altered attitudes towards usury or lending money at interest. Based on various biblical ideas (for example, Deuteronomy 23:19–20), Christianity had traditionally forbidden the practice among its own brethren. Likewise, Jews would not lend at interest to other Jews, and, even today, Muslims will not lend at interest to other Muslims.

It would be wrong to think that Calvin opened the floodgates of capitalism. Lending at interest was strictly limited and controlled in Geneva. The maximum rate was 5 per cent (not compoundable). However, further restrictions applied. The money could be loaned only as part of a shared venture. For example, an individual could loan, say, 100 florins to a merchant to buy a shipment of cloth, and expect an eventual repayment of 105 florins. However, if the cloth were lost, perhaps through a fire, before the transaction was complete, the money was not repayable. This was, therefore, less like interest than buying a type of stock in a venture with an eventual return (dividend) spelt out as interest in the contract. But as with Luther's accidental revolution, this set in train an acceptance of the concept of interest, which would expand in later years.

In particular, the Dutch took the idea and developed it into the limited stock company during the seventeenth century. This worked as follows. A successful shipment of spice from the Indies normally generated a profit of well over 100 per cent. So if ten merchants each bought and outfitted a ship apiece at 1000 guilders, they could expect to get 10,000 guilders each upon the fleet's return and the sale of the spice. However, if four ships sank (a reasonable attrition rate), six merchants would make 10,000 guilders each but four would make nothing. The Dutch pioneered the idea of shares. The same ten merchants banded together, outfitted the entire fleet for 10,000 guilders, and looked for a shared return with shared liability for any losses. If four ships sank, the ten merchants would still share 60,000 guilders in return, thereby spreading the liability (risk) involved in global trade. Eventually, the merchants sold even more shares of the risk/profit to nonmerchants, often guaranteeing a small return (in effect, interest), with the possibility of an even greater return (a dividend). Thus, what began as a minor, very restricted innovation in Calvin's Geneva had the very unintended consequence of allowing the likes of the Dutch East India Company to develop, and later paved the way for the gathering of capital necessary to finance the Industrial Revolution. Through no fault of Calvin and his Calvinistic Dutch successors, modern capitalism was born.

DEVELOPMENTS IN SPAIN AND ITALY

Returning to the still smouldering ashes of Servetus, it may come as a surprise to learn that Catholic Spain could produce someone with his extreme, radical views. In fact, though never influential, radical religious thinkers were not unknown in Spain. The best example is the Alumbrados (The Enlightened Ones) sect who sought secret, separately revealed truth from God through personal mystical experiences. One famous case involved a labourer's daughter, La Beata de Piedrahita. In 1511 she was examined by the Inquisition (the Catholic ecclesiastical body that examined individuals for heresy and breaches of canon (Church) law) for claiming to have had conversations with Jesus and the Virgin Mary. Such mystical experiences were not then (or subsequently) unknown in Catholicism, but the content of her talks was suspect. In the end she was spared from execution as a result of intervention by some powerful patrons. There is no direct evidence that Servetus was influenced by the Alumbrados, but together they suggest that religious foment was not unknown in Spain. Indeed, in 1527 Ignatius Loyola, founder and first leader of the Jesuits, had been examined for his supposed connections with the Alumbrados, a charge never forgotten by Catholic opponents of the Jesuits.

The Alumbrados movement may have been connected with the Illuminés (also The Enlightened Ones) sect in France, who first began to appear in 1623, just when the country seemed to have settled its religious turmoil and Protestantism and Catholicism fell into an uneasy period of coexistence. The Illuminés attained some following in Picardy, but were largely suppressed by 1635. Another group of Illuminés, almost certainly unconnected, would appear in 1722, and seem to have managed to survive until the mid-1790s. These groups, along with other more peculiar groups (such as the

Rosicrucians, who also appeared in the early seventeenth century and claimed to be able to combine the esoteric principles of religion with the mysteries of alchemy), remind us that even France, seemingly over its reformation phase and, for the most part, happily Catholic, was still able to produce some very interesting religious movements. Innovation and schism were not the sole preserve of Protestants, even after the various sessions of the Council of Trent tried to lock Catholicism into tight uniformity.

It is perhaps also worth noting that a similar nascent movement of mystics, which might have coalesced into reform, also existed in Italy. The so-called Spirituali (Spiritualists) were members of a Catholic reform movement from about 1510 to the 1560s. Among them were a number of cardinals: Gasparo Contarini, Giovanni Pietro Carafa (later Pope Paul IV), Jacopo Sadoleto, and Reginald Pole (later Archbishop of Canterbury under Mary I). These Italian 'evangelicals' proposed to reform the Catholic Church from within through a spiritual renewal and internalization of faith by each individual – very much a combination of humanism and the *devotio moderna*. They believed in the importance of studying the Bible, and seemed to have accepted justification by faith (Luther's key doctrine). The Spirituali took many of their ideas from older Catholic and humanist texts, but they were also inspired by the Protestantism, especially the Reformed variety, easily within reach over the Alps in Switzerland. Although Spirituali occupied positions of power within the Church hierarchy, they failed to achieve much change, and more traditionally minded and 'loyal' groups, such as the Jesuits, determined to reform Catholicism through their own hierarchy and doctrines. In fact, they set the Church on a course of confrontation with the Protestants, dooming any hope of a moderate, reconciling course. In large part, the Spirituali's lack of success stemmed from their hope for Church reform without a challenge to Catholic authority; that is to say, for a peaceful, humanistic renewal from within. This made them suspect to Protestants, who thought they were lukewarm and cowardly, and to conservative Catholics, who simply suspected them of heresy.

But the action of the Reformation never took place in Spain or Italy, and we must return to the small city-state Republic of Geneva. In the course of the 1550s Calvin oversaw the eventual triumph of his version of the Reformation. Alone, this would have made Geneva similar to Zurich. However, Geneva was also a place of exile for reformers from various European countries, and, most importantly, had become a centre for Protestant printing presses, which churned out literature of a Calvinistic nature. It is for these two reasons, as well as the character and abilities of Calvin himself, that Geneva became as important as Wittenberg. Calvin's theology and approach to Church government (ecclesiology) spread first to France, then to the Netherlands, eventually to Scotland, and, to a lesser extent, even had an influence in England. From the British Isles, Calvinism would move across the Atlantic to leave an indelible mark on the nascent character of the colonists and later citizens of the thirteen American colonies.

REFORMATION IN FRANCE

For Calvin, though, the great goal was always the conversion of his native France. Unfortunately for him, as well as for most of France, this mission-ary effort resulted in nearly four decades of civil war. Francis I, coming to the throne in 1515, saw himself as a Renaissance humanist monarch, and was initially quite sympathetic to the calls for reform. He made the great humanist Guillaume Budé his chief librarian, and hired agents across Italy to find and buy rare books and manuscripts. Not only did the royal collec-tion expand dramatically, but the king read many of the books he bought. In addition, he made his collection available to scholars in order to increase their knowledge – a truly humanist gesture. He was joined in his humanist and Renaissance endeavours by his older sister, Marguerite, Queen of Navarre, who was herself a great supporter of reform, and an accomplished author (her great work, the *Heptameron*, is a classic). It is no surprise, there-fore, that Calvin and other French reformers placed great hope in the king inaugurating a princely reform, as had happened in so many German states.

This explains Calvin's dedication of his French version of *The Institutes* (1541) to Francis.

The best example of this support for reform was the so-called Circle of Meaux. The Bishop of Meaux, Guillaume Briçonnet, implemented reform in his own diocese. He strove to improve the education of his clerics, as well as monastic morality and discipline, though his efforts were opposed by some, especially the Franciscans. He attracted a number of leading humanists to assist him, and these formed the 'circle'. Among them were Guillaume Farel, who initially convinced Calvin to stay and labour in Geneva. However, the bishop was not an 'evangelical', and his support for humanist-style reform never led him to Protestantism. That some of his advisers were more positive towards Luther and the growing reformation movement allowed the bishop's opponents, in his diocese and elsewhere (in particular the Parisian theological faculty at the Sorbonne), to move against him and he was questioned before the *parlement* (sovereign court) of Paris on suspicion of heresy. Although spared, the bishop was forced to abandon his reforming agenda, and his circle was disbanded — with many making the final move to Protestantism soon after.

The conservative theologians at the Sorbonne were not content with this single victory, and continued a campaign against leading humanist reformers, despite the king's protection of them. However, the king was captured by the Spanish at the Battle of Pavia in 1525, and this gave those at the Sorbonne freedom to act. Their most spectacular prize was the execution of the leading humanist Louis de Berquin for heresy. The king had returned in 1526 and had initially managed to save Berquin, who had been arrested and condemned at the instigation of the Sorbonne's theologians, but as the situation became more extreme, Berquin was executed. Although the king clearly wished to save him, the situation had deteriorated to the point where even he had to accept Berquin's condemnation. In effect, his death set an example of the regime's seriousness about combating heresy. The final break for Francis came in the 1530s, and two events stand out. In 1533 Nicolas Cop, the newly appointed rector of the

University of Paris, used his inaugural address (possibly co-written by Calvin) to oppose religious persecution and advocate the preaching of the Gospel (usually code for Protestant ideas). The result was pandemonium and many of Cop's supporters fled. The next year, before the controversy was able to die away, another outrage occurred. Placards attacking 'the horrible, great and insufferable papal Mass' appeared in many provincial cities, and, so it was reported, were even stuck to the door of the king's bedroom at Amboise. Francis was incensed and deeply shocked. Printing was taken under royal censorship, and a brutal repression followed in which two dozen 'Protestants' were executed and scores, including Calvin, were forced to flee – in Calvin's case, never to return. Calm was quickly restored, and two amnesties (in 1535 and 1536) were extended to those heretics who would recant their views.

From this point onwards into the reign of Henry II, the situation in France remained outwardly peaceful. Most of the leading advocates of reform fled and, like Calvin, used bases abroad (mostly notably Geneva and Strasburg), from which they sent literature pouring into France. The movement continued to gain adherents, but quietly and clandestinely.

The first Protestant 'church' was secretly established in 1555, and growth continued apace during the final years of Henry II's reign. The entire situation was thrown into turmoil, first by the death of Henry as the result of a freak jousting accident (a lance pierced his eye), and the subsequent death a year later of his son Francis II, whom the Protestant nobles had tried to kidnap just months before he died (the so-called Conspiracy of Amboise). This left France with a ten-year-old king, Charles IX, under the regency of his Italian mother, Queen Catherine de' Medici. Determined to secure her son's inheritance and keep the kingdom stable, she steered a conciliatory course between the arch-Catholic house of Guise and the Huguenot (French Protestant) house of Bourbon. Her chancellor, Michel de l'Hôpital, urged toleration.

This toleration extended to a truly bizarre attempt at conciliation reminiscent of the Marburg Colloquy. In September 1561 the regent organized the Colloquy of Poissy, to which she invited the Guise Cardinal of Lorraine, plus leading Protestants, such as Theodore Beza and Peter Martyr Vermigli, from Switzerland. Some progress was made, but the endeavour eventually foundered on the question of the Eucharist/Mass. The court, frightened by the drift to violence and extremism (the Conspiracy of Amboise, for example), and having failed at unification, issued the Edict of Saint-Germain (1562), which allowed the Huguenots to worship publicly outside towns and privately within them. The Guises were incensed, and when the duke and his retinue came upon a group of Protestants worshipping in the Guise town of Vassy in Champagne (thereby violating the edict), they massacred them.

With the edict quickly revoked, the Protestants, under the leadership of their nobles, immediately took up arms 'in self-defence'. Protestants seized control of, and garrisoned, a number of key French towns, and open warfare erupted. Leaders of both sides were taken captive in battle, and the Duke of Guise was assassinated. Catherine managed to negotiate a truce and issued the Edict of Amboise in 1563. This new edict largely repeated the terms of the first edict, as did almost every truce that followed. Both sides became concerned that the situation in France would become internationalized. The Guises and Catholics looked on in horror as revolt swept across the Low Countries, and the Bourbons and Huguenots feared Habsburg (that is, Spanish and imperial Catholic) intervention. Warfare resumed, but was quickly quelled by yet another edict, the Peace of Longjumeau, in 1568.

The continued threat to the stability of France as a unified nation finally convinced the regent, always a committed Catholic, to throw in her lot with the Guises. The edict and all toleration were revoked, and war resumed. The Protestants proved equal to the fight, and the military stalemate that followed was quickly recognized by the Peace of Saint-Germain (5 August 1570) and the return of the basic toleration of 1562. Catherine now decided to take a more devious route. She organized an assassination attempt against one of the leading Protestant nobles, which failed (although Admiral Coligny, the intended victim, was injured). With Coligny and many leading Protestants in Paris for the marriage of the king's sister Marguerite de Valois (a Catholic) to the Protestant Henry of Navarre, later Henry IV, the time was judged right to strike. The Crown moved to arrest or assassinate most of the nobles, and the Parisian Catholic crowd – staunchly anti-Protestant – took its cue from the State, and a general massacre of Huguenots in Paris occurred. It became known as the St Bartholomew's Day Massacre (24 August 1572). Violence spread to other parts of France, and thousands of Huguenots (men, women and children) were brutally murdered, much to the delight not only of the Guises and their supporters, but even Philip II of Spain and Pope Gregory XIII (who struck a commemorative coin to celebrate this 'victory' over heresy). The result, though, was simply to harden Huguenot resolve and to convince many that the Crown could not be trusted.

With the death of Charles IX in 1574, his brother, Henry III, came to the throne: he was young but not a minor. However, he was as trapped by the situation as his mother and brother had been. On one hand were the Guises, now leading the well-organized Catholic League; on the other was a Huguenot army that largely controlled the southwest of France. There also remained the continued threat of outside intervention, which would have further endangered the viability of the nation. The entire situation became explosive when Henry's younger brother and heir, Francis, Duke of Anjou and Alençon, died in 1584. As Henry had no children and was not, so it was said, of a sexual preference likely to produce a child, the heir apparent to the French throne was none other than Henry of Navarre, a Bourbon and a Huguenot (having renounced his conversion to Catholicism, which had saved his life during the 1572 massacre, when he had been captured in Paris).

Henry initially tried to lead the Catholic League, while advocating a policy of conciliation and moderation. This failed to appease the leaguers, and when, in 1588, Paris rose against the king in favour of the new leader of the league, Henry of Guise, the king fled and threw in his lot with Henry of Navarre. The Guises proposed to make Henry's aged uncle, Cardinal

Charles de Bourbon, his heir. The king agreed to attend a meeting of the Estates General at Blois that same year to discuss the succession. He now followed the path of his mother and brother in trying to solve the problem by cutting off the head of the opposition. Henry of Guise was lured to a private meeting with the king and assassinated. This was as successful as the massacre in 1572 – it simply enraged the leaguers and convinced them that the king was a heretic. Even the theological faculty at the Sorbonne declared it would be a 'pious act' to kill the king. In his own turn, the king was duly assassinated the next year by a monk. With Charles Bourbon in Huguenot custody, Henry of Navarre became Henry IV, titular (and Protestant) king of France. Calvin's dream of a princely reformation seemed at hand.

However, it quickly became clear that Paris and the Catholic north and east of France would not accept a Protestant king. The League now allied openly with Habsburg Spain (a horrible situation to any French patriot), and the nation was on the verge of collapse and dismemberment. Henry turned to England for support (anathema to all Frenchmen as well). A growing segment of French opinion supported some moderate (indeed, any) solution. These *politiques* put the State and its survival above denominational allegiance. For the many leaguers, the key event came in 1590 when Henry renounced, for a second time, his Protestantism and was, for a second time, received into the Catholic Church, saying, or so tradition has it, that 'Paris is worth a Mass'. Many moderate Catholics now began to drift towards the king. Desultory warfare continued, but with the withdrawal of Spanish forces in May 1598, the League was doomed. A month earlier (13 April 1598) the king had issued the Edict of Nantes, which largely restored the provisions of the 1562 edict of toleration. This edict stood until it was revoked by Louis XIV in October 1685. Although it ended the wars of religion as such, a final Huguenot revolt in the 1620s saw them stripped of their arms, but the edict left intact. Henry IV fell victim himself to assassination in 1610. It was, and remains, a matter of debate whether or not Henry's edict was actually meant to be a permanent peace treaty or was simply a truce (as Louis XIV would later argue).

In effect, the Reformation in France had failed, and the Huguenots remained a small minority largely cut off from the wider society and culture. More importantly, on both sides the wars led to the development of key ideas about the State, the people and the monarchy. At various points both Protestant and Catholic thinkers began to stress that there existed a contract between those who governed and the people they ruled. Should rulers breach this implicit contract, the people had a right to change them. Indeed, the people even had a right to kill their ruler. It was always stressed that this popular power was best exercised under the leadership of the 'natural' leaders of a society, namely, lesser nobles or magistrates, but the ideas are the very same that underpinned the opening lines of the American Declaration of Independence in 1776:

> Governments are instituted among Men, deriving their just powers
> from the consent of the governed, – That whenever any Form of
> Government becomes destructive of these ends, it is the Right of
> the People to alter or to abolish it, and to institute new Government,
> laying its foundation on such principles and organizing its powers in
> such form, as to them shall seem most likely to effect their Safety
> and Happiness ... when a long train of abuses and usurpations,
> pursuing invariably the same Object evinces a design to reduce
> them under absolute Despotism, it is their right, it is their duty, to
> throw off such Government, and to provide new Guards for their
> future security.

REFORMATION IN THE NETHERLANDS

The Dutch Reformation, already alluded to earlier, followed a similarly violent path, but produced a different outcome – the one most feared by the French *politiques*: the dismemberment of the pre-existing political unit, the Low Countries. Initially, reform broke out in Antwerp in present-day Belgium, then the chief city of the Habsburg possessions in the Low Countries. It was the involvement of the Habsburgs that allowed the revolt to continue so long and so bitterly. Charles (later Charles V, Holy Roman Emperor) was born in Ghent, and at the age of six he inherited title to his possessions in the Low Countries. In 1516 he succeeded his grandfather Ferdinand I as king of both Castile and Aragon (which Ferdinand had inherited from his wife, Isabella). This meant relocation to Spain and, more importantly, possession of the great wealth and power of the Spanish Empire, which was just on the cusp of rapid and massive expansion in the New World. After the death of his other grandfather, Maximilian (Holy Roman Emperor), he inherited extensive possessions in Austria and stood as the most likely person to be elected as the new emperor. He faced opposition from Francis I of France and Luther's protector, the elector Frederick, but in 1519 he was successfully elected the new emperor (though he was not crowned by the pope until 1530). He thus united under his personal rule, through various forms of allegiance, an extensive 'empire': Spain, the Low Countries, parts of Italy, the Holy Roman Empire (basically, modern-day Germany and Austria), as well as territories in what is now the Czech Republic, Poland and Hungary. However, these holdings were not organized or centralized, a situation Charles hoped to rectify. One part of this campaign to rationalize his empire came in 1549, when he united his Low Countries holdings, by the Pragmatic Sanction, into a single, heritable unit.

In this situation, Protestantism (originally of a Lutheran variety) grew apace, protected by the *laissez-faire* attitude of the wealthy merchants of the southern Netherlands (Belgium). As early as 1521 Charles had issued edicts against Luther and his writings; his works were publicly burnt and, because he was an Augustinian, the Augustinian monastery in Antwerp was closed as a hotbed of Lutheran ideas. The friars there recanted, but two who refused were burnt in 1523, earning the dubious honour of being Protestantism's first martyrs. This persecution seems to have cut the legs from under Lutheranism in the Netherlands. However, support for reform continued, and private meetings (conventicles) at which reformation ideas were discussed were held for the next two decades. Largely, though, people at these meetings continued to participate in the life and worship of the Catholic Church.

The reformation movement, to the extent that it existed, was diverse and often radical. Indeed, Anabaptism was prominent from the start thanks to the efforts of Melchior Hoffman, who prophesied the end of the world, leading to an exodus of Dutch Anabaptists to Münster. These conventicles and the burgeoning support for reform, especially radical reform, was dealt a horrific blow by the events at Münster just over the Dutch–German border. Swift and brutal repression followed, and once again it seemed as though reform was at an end in the Low Countries.

There was an abortive attempt to organize Protestantism (on the model of Strasburg) in the mid-1540s. The authorities were able to nip this in the bud, and the main protagonists were killed or forced into exile. Having crushed Lutheranism in the 1520s and Anabaptism in the 1530s, it appeared that the 1540s had seen off the Reformed churches as well. However, aided by refugees and the enthusiastic work of Protestants in the French-speaking southern Netherlands, a Reformed church was finally established in Antwerp in 1554, with a Dutch-speaking church also organized there in 1555. In an effort to prevent another successful round of persecution, these churches organized into cells of eight to twelve members. They kept a low profile, but also, unlike their disorganized predecessors, separated themselves from Catholic worship.

There was a decided lack of enthusiasm on the part of the city officials to engage in yet more persecution and execution. It was disruptive and bad for business, especially with neighbouring Protestant states. In addition, those within the Reformed churches increasingly found themselves on the 'patriotic' side of a growing debate with Charles and his successor, Philip II of Spain. In addition to unifying the Netherlands in 1549, the imperial government wanted to centralize and rationalize the chaotic administration of the Low Countries. This, of course, meant substantial and substantive changes to traditional patterns of governance – almost always in favour of the imperial bureaucracy and to the detriment of local bases of power. A harbinger of this radical revision of government had already occurred in 1528, when Charles had replaced the Utrecht guild council with a royal regent, and had built a heavily armed castle in the city to ensure his regent stayed in power.

Charles, however, was a 'local boy', and was unlikely to push change too far or too fast: although his repressive Perpetual Edict of 1550 did appear dangerous, it still relied largely on local political support for implementation. Many officials decided to take a tolerant view, even deciding that non-violent Anabaptists were more misguided than dangerous, and refusing to move against them or the even more politically and socially acceptable Reformed. His son, Philip, however, was far away in Spain and knew nothing of the Low Countries he inherited in 1556 (just as the Reformed were beginning to organize in earnest).

By 1565, nobles and other political leaders called for a more moderate policy, and had petitioned that the Inquisition (which had proved especially unpopular in the Netherlands) be removed. This suggested to the Reformed that a reformation under the leadership of lesser magistrates was imminent, and many refugees poured back into the Netherlands. In June 1566 a nationwide meeting (synod) was held, and the Reformed churches came out of the closet (or conventicles). Large outdoor meetings (resembling the camp meetings of the American Second Great Awakening, see page 162) were held, on one occasion outside Antwerp attracting 25,000 listeners. It was clear that charismatic preachers of the Reformation were able to attract large crowds of interested, or maybe just curious, spectators. But that did not mean that the churches within the cities were changing hands.

The Reformed openly and dramatically moved inside the cities in August 1566. Emboldened and militant, they swept into churches across the Netherlands and began the systematic destruction of religious images that they labelled 'idols'. The regent in the provinces of the Netherlands, Margaret of Parma, took fright at this iconoclasm, and legalized Lutheran and Reformed (Calvinist) worship, though there were few Lutherans beyond the German-speaking merchant enclave in Antwerp, and the Anabaptists were noticeably not included in the edict. This initial response was modified in later months, as Margaret found many leading nobles drifting to her (Catholic) side, having been appalled and frightened by the violence of the iconoclasm. Toleration was rescinded, the churches closed, a Spanish army of 10,000, led by the Duke of Alva, arrived; thousands were executed and tens of thousands sentenced *in absentia*. Nevertheless, the Reformed had seen their own strength, and were as amazed as French Protestants had been at the same time. Indeed, although short-lived, this period of Protestant success is still known by Dutch Calvinists as the Wonder Year.

Alva's heavy-handed policies proved disastrous in the long run. His Council of Troubles, which had passed sentences of death and exile over so many refugees, did score some notable own goals, though. In particular, the execution of the Counts of Egmont and Horne (both loyal Catholics) for being overly tolerant, horrified and infuriated many, especially those moderate Catholics who had turned to Margaret after the inconoclasm of 1566. Alva coupled this brutality with offers of amnesty to all who would return to Catholicism – in 1570 nearly 35,000 renounced Protestantism in the dioceses of Antwerp, Mechelen and 's-Hertogenbosch alone. This approach did work in the short term. Most Protestants were executed, forced into exile or returned to Catholicism. But Alva's repression of local political-power structures to facilitate his policy made him enemies, and many leading nobles had also fled. Most notably, William I of Orange (*stadtholder* – governor-general or viceroy – of the provinces of Holland, Zeeland and Utrecht, as well as Margrave of Antwerp) had gone into exile to avoid the same fate as Egmont and Horne. He took up residence with his father-in-law, the (Lutheran) elector of Saxony. Philip declared his lands and titles in the Netherlands forfeit to the king, and William was declared an outlaw.

It was William who returned in 1568 at the head of an army determined to drive the 'evil councillor' from the land and restore the 'correct' relationship between the king (Philip) and the people. This was a recurring way for leaders of rebellions to present their actions, not as treason, but as loyal and necessary revolts designed to restore peace. This rather unwanted intervention on behalf of Philip against his appointed general began the Dutch Revolt (also known as the Eighty Years' War) at the Battle of Heiligerlee on 23 May 1568. Initially, William met with success, and numerous cities fell to his forces. Crucially, though, William's rebellion was motivated more by disgust with Alva and his policies than any great enthusiasm for Protestantism. Once Spanish forces could be released from fighting the Turks in the Mediterranean after the Battle of Lepanto (1571), Alva was reinforced and he was able to defeat the rebels, though he failed to capture William.

Once again Spain seemed on the brink of securing the Low Countries for Catholicism. However, Alva again blundered. In an effort to pay for the war and the consequent occupation and garrisoning of the provinces, he introduced a new tax. Not surprisingly, this prompted both Catholics and Protestants to move towards the rebels. William's rebel forces had been continuing a guerrilla campaign throughout the conflict (largely by sea from English ports). In 1572 these so-called Sea Beggars took the ports of Brielle and Flushing. Not only did this give them bases of operation, but it was a signal for Protestants – and disaffected Catholics – to rise again in rebellion. Much of the important northern province of Holland rose up (though Amsterdam did not, remaining in Catholic hands until 1578). The revolt spread, and was proving even more successful than the first rebellion.

At this point, Philip decided, rather as Margaret of Parma had, to try conciliation in order to split moderates away from William. For this purpose, Alva was replaced in 1573 by Luis de Requesens. However, two events served to undermine this new policy. In 1575 Spain was forced to declare bankruptcy: its wars had placed more demands on the treasury than even the massive influx of New World wealth could meet. Then, early in 1576, Requesens died. This left both a political and, more importantly, an economic vacuum among the Spanish forces. In November 1576 the unpaid Spanish soldiers garrisoned in and around Antwerp mutinied and sacked the city to recoup their back pay through pillage. This 'Spanish Fury' put steel into the spines of the rebels, and forced many moderates and Catholics either into outright opposition to Spain, or neutrality.

In an effort to unite the provinces' Catholics and Protestants in a broad, anti-Spanish front, the Pacification of Ghent was negotiated, which allowed for the toleration of both denominations. Calvinists, sensing victory, were unwilling to abide by the agreement, and this gave Spain time to send in another army under the Duke of Parma (Alexander Farnese). He was able, through a more intelligent policy, to peel the mostly Catholic southern provinces away from the rebellion. On 6 January 1579 these provinces signed the Union of Arras, which affirmed their loyalty to Spain and ended any hopes of a united, independent front against Spain by all seventeen provinces in the Low Countries. A few weeks later, on 23 January, William oversaw the union of the provinces of Holland, Zeeland, Utrecht, Guelders and Groningen in the Union of Utrecht, which was subsequently joined by some southern cities (Bruges, Ghent, Brussels and Antwerp). Technically, the northern union remained loyal to Philip as well, but in 1581 it declared that Philip had broken his 'contract' with the people, so he was deposed by the Oath of Abjuration.

Unable to envisage a state without a monarch, the union's parliament, the States General, tried to recruit a replacement for Philip. William (of the House of Orange) may now seem to have been an obvious choice, but he was only a local noble and did not have sufficient standing among (and above) his fellows to be chosen – indeed, the House of Orange did not become a royal house until the early nineteenth century. He and his heirs continued as *stadtholder* only. Initially, the States General turned to the Protestant queen of England, Elizabeth I, but she had no desire to provoke a war with Philip of Spain, and declined to step in. A more likely candidate was Francis, the Catholic Duke of Anjou and younger brother of Henry III of France. He had insisted on the abjuration, but in the end his Catholicism, and the determination of the States General to limit his power, made the arrangement collapse. Anjou left in 1583, and died the following year. Ultimately, the States General had to accept reality and simply ruled the union as a republic.

War raged on, with the Spanish slowly recovering much of Flanders and Brabant. The city of Antwerp was finally captured, but the vagaries of war had devastated the former political and economic capital of the Low Countries — its estimated population of 100,000 in 1570 had fallen to 40,000 in 1590. Most of the north remained in rebel, now largely Calvinist, hands and was thoroughly Protestantized in the 1570s and 1580s. In 1584 William was assassinated by a Spanish supporter, and his place taken by his son Maurice of Nassau (Prince of Orange — after the family's enclave around Orange in France).

The revolt began to turn against the northern provinces in the mid-1580s, and the United Provinces (as they were now called) turned outwards for allies. In 1585 England actively intervened, sending the Earl of Leicester to the Netherlands with an army of about 7000 foot soldiers and cavalry. He failed to make any headway, particularly in his attempts to disrupt the ongoing trade between the two halves of the Netherlands, which he rightly argued was in fact helping the Spanish. It was also allowing northern merchants to get very rich. He left within a year, and the States General now turned to Maurice and made him commander-in-chief at the age of twenty.

He proved to be a tactical genius, and now began the 'Ten Glory Years' in which the present boundaries of the Netherlands were defined. Just as importantly, his campaigns ensured that most of the fighting took place along the frontier, which left much of the United Provinces (especially Holland) free to recover and prosper economically, thereby providing the funds for the ongoing revolt. Fortress after fortification fell to Maurice: Bergen op Zoom (1588), Breda (1590), Zutphen, Deventer, Delfzijl and Nijmegen (1591), Steenwijk and Coevorden (1592), Geertruidenberg (1593), Grol, Enschede, Ootmarsum and Oldenzaal (1597). Not only did Spain suffer these reverses, but it also lost its Armada sent against England in 1588, and in 1595 Henry IV of France declared war on it as well. Philip was once again forced to declare bankruptcy and get out of the rebellion-crushing business.

Accepting the inevitable, or at least the inevitability of being unable to solve the problem from Spain, Philip ceded the Netherlands, including his claim to the United Provinces, to his daughter Isabella and her husband (Philip's nephew), Archduke Albert of Austria. Spanish power in the south was secure, but the Protestant control of the Scheldt estuary meant that Antwerp was being economically strangled and that Amsterdam was beginning to replace it as the financial heart of the Low Countries. Not surprisingly, the business-minded merchants of the north began to lose interest in the south. Nevertheless, against the advice of Maurice, a final campaign was begun to 'liberate' the south in 1600. Although tactical victory was achieved, the United Provinces eventually withdrew their forces. In effect, this was the end of the war. Desultory fighting continued until a truce was negotiated in 1609. The United Provinces had *de facto* independence, but it was not officially recognized until 1648 (see page 123).

On the west and north of the Continent, this brought the second phase of Reformation largely to an end. Germany and Scandinavia were Lutheran; France remained Catholic, but with a legally tolerated and protected Protestant minority; the United Provinces were officially Reformed, but in practice Catholicism and Anabaptism were tolerated. Two large areas remain to be considered: the British Isles, which adopted two differing approaches to Protestantism only uneasily united by the early 1600s, and central Europe, where almost every conceivable religious group existed (from Islam and Judaism to Catholicism, Protestantism and anti-Trinitarianism) and, for a time, flourished in anarchic pluralism.

REFORMATION IN THE BRITISH ISLES

Church reform in the British Isles was a very different affair from what went on in continental Europe, but only in some ways, important though they were. In England, which effectively meant Wales and Ireland too, the reform was very much a conservative movement driven by the king. In Scotland the Reformation would outwardly resemble the Calvinistic reformations in France and the United Provinces, being led largely by ministers and nobles (lesser magistrates) against the wishes of the monarch. However, these superficial similarities belie some rather startling differences.

It is probably safe to say that had Henry VIII been able to gain some measure of direct national control of the Catholic Church within his realm(s), as had the kings of France and Spain, and the rulers of many Italian states, there would not have been a Reformation. The English Church was centralized, efficient, well staffed, and apparently enjoyed popular support. Despite this, in 1534 Henry's parliament passed the Act of Supremacy, making him Supreme Head of the Church of England and repudiating papal supremacy. And this was despite the fact that Henry had already written a book attacking Luther and all his works, for which the pope had awarded him the title *defensor fidei* (Defender of the Faith) – a title still used by his successors, and one that features on British coins to this day. Between 1535 and 1540, under Henry's chief minister, Thomas Cromwell, the monasteries were dissolved and the veneration of saints was attacked, as were pilgrimages and pilgrim shrines. Extensive ecclesiastical holdings and income passed into the hands of the Crown, to be sold on to the nobility and gentry. Not only did this generate enormous income for the State, but it also guaranteed strong vested interests against any restitution of Catholicism (or, at least, Catholic monasticism).

It is perhaps tempting to see all this as the ultimate triumph of Wyclif and the Lollards. This would be entirely mistaken. In fact, as just about every schoolchild knows, the actual explanation was much more mundane and seedy. Henry VIII was King of England and Lord of Ireland (later King of Ireland) from 1509 until his death. As the second Tudor monarch after the War of Roses, it was essential that he secure his family's dynastic hold on the throne by producing a male heir. Although his wife, Catherine of Aragon, had been pregnant at least seven times (the last time in 1518), only one child, Mary, had survived beyond infancy. Henry had produced a male, Henry Fitzroy, by Elizabeth Blount, one of his many mistresses. By 1526 it was clear that Catherine was unlikely to produce another child, and the king was anyway enamoured of Anne Boleyn. The two issues combined to convince

Henry that his only option was to end his marriage with Catherine – by divorce or annulment – either of which would require papal dispensation.

Henry also claimed that his conscience had been plagued by the fear that he had committed incest in marrying Catherine, the widow of his brother Arthur. Catherine swore that her marriage to Arthur had not been consummated, so the matter was dropped. This was the first salvo in Henry's efforts to find a valid reason for ending his marriage. He then applied directly to the pope for an annulment on the grounds that the dispensation to marry his brother's widow, granted by Pope Julius II, was void. He also wanted permission to marry anyone, a request that would allow him to marry Anne, which would clearly have been incestuous since he had had sex with her sister, who was still living, and at the time sex with a 'sister-in-law' (which she was, in effect) was seen as such. As Pope Clement was effectively the prisoner of Charles V, he was never likely to support the annulment as Charles would not allow his aunt, Catherine, to be humiliated.

Stymied at this second attempt to end his marriage, the king enlisted Cardinal Thomas Wolsey. The result was a papal commission that was to consider the matter and decide if the original bull of Julius II was valid. Little headway was made, and when the Spanish presented a letter that Julius had sent to Spain outlining the dispensation, the commissioners were unable to consider it, since they were allowed only to examine facts relating to the bull itself. Although the commission was now a lame duck, the inquiry continued, and on 18 June 1529:

> The Queen was summoned to the great hall of the Black Friar's
> convent in London. The King, on a raised platform, sat at the upper
> end. Some distance away Catherine was given her place. The Cardinals,
> sitting lower than the King, flanked the royal presence, and near
> them the Archbishop of Canterbury and the bishops were given
> position. Dr. Richard Sampson (afterwards bishop of Chichester)
> and Dr. John Bell (afterwards bishop of Worcester) led those who

pleaded for the King. Representing the Queen was John Fisher (bishop of Rochester) and Dr. Standish ... Bishop of St. Asaph.

(Documents presented by Henry's legal team to the papal legate)

The meeting produced high drama, but little else. It certainly did not get the king the freedom he sought.

Henry's wrath turned on Wolsey and other leading churchmen. Wolsey was stripped of his titles and wealth, and only escaped punishment by dying on his way to trial. Henry now appointed laymen to posts previously reserved for clerics: Sir Thomas More became the new Lord Chancellor, and Thomas Cromwell, 1st Earl of Essex became the Secretary of State. Henry also gained the support of Thomas Cranmer, the Archbishop of Canterbury, who, on 25 January 1533, participated in the marriage of the king and Anne Boleyn. Four months later, in May, he declared the marriage to Catherine null and void. The timing was perhaps the wrong way around, but it suited the king. Princess Mary (Tudor) was declared to be a bastard, Henry's marriage to Catherine having never been 'real', and Catherine was stripped of her title as queen and made dowager Princess of Wales, her first husband having been Prince of Wales. Catherine would remain in England under this title until her death in 1536.

Henry had what he wanted – Anne Boleyn – but Anne failed to deliver her part of the bargain. She gave birth to a daughter, Elizabeth. Sir Thomas More accepted Anne as the new queen, but refused to accept that Parliament had any power in religious matters. He asserted that the pope remained head of the Church and therefore refused to accept the Act of Supremacy; he was tried and beheaded as a traitor. For his loyalty to papal supremacy, he was later declared a saint of the Catholic Church.

Angered at the treatment of Catherine, the pope excommunicated Henry in July 1533. Parliament, guided by Thomas Cromwell, now moved to secure Henry's position, and, through a series of Acts in 1534, formalized the break with Rome and the pope. The Statute in Restraint of Appeals prohibited appeals from English ecclesiastical courts to Rome, and prevented the English Church from making any regulations without the king's consent; the Ecclesiastical Appointments Act allowed the king to nominate bishops (a power held by the kings of France and Spain as well, though they at least accepted that, technically, the pope had the final say); the Act of Supremacy made Henry Supreme Head of the Church of England and repudiated papal supremacy; the Treason Act made it high treason to deny the king's supremacy in the English Church. It also became illegal to send ecclesiastical revenues, such as Peter's Pence, to Rome. The Act of Succession (also 1534) removed Mary from the succession, declared Anne's offspring the legal successors, and threatened treason and death to anyone who even dared to produce any literature suggesting that Henry's marriage to Anne was illegitimate.

At this point all Henry had done was, in effect, to create an English Catholic Church (albeit one with a decidedly greedy eye on Church lands and incomes). All apparent opposition to Henry's religious policies was quickly suppressed. Several dissenting monks were tortured and executed. Cromwell, the new Vicegerent in Spirituals (who acted as supreme judge in religious matters on behalf of the king), was sent to visit monasteries, theoretically to ensure that they followed the new laws, but in reality to assess their wealth. In 1536 Parliament allowed the State to seize the possessions of the 'lesser' monasteries, which had annual incomes of £200 or less.

This, and Henry's other religious policies, sparked a general revolt in the north of England. In 1536 the so-called Pilgrimage of Grace rebellion broke out. As was often the case with rebellions in this period across Europe, the ruler initially granted both concessions and amnesties. Henry did just this, but broke his side of the bargain almost immediately, and a second revolt occurred in 1537. The leaders of the rebellion were eventually captured, convicted of treason and executed. In 1538 Henry sanctioned the destruction of shrines to the saints. The following year the rest of the monasteries were dissolved, and their lands and incomes seized by the Crown. With the dissolution of the monasteries, the numbers of Lords Spiritual (clerics) in the House of Lords was greatly reduced (there no

ABOVE

1 *The Mocking of Noah* (c. 1515) by Giovanni Bellini. The story of Noah's humiliation by Ham was used to support the idea of three races and that one (black Africans) was eternally subservient. (See pages 170 and 220.)

LEFT

2 *The Holy Family* (1509/10) by Lucas Cranach the Elder. For Lutherans, the Reformation and its rejection of the Cult of Saints also meant the reinterpretation of Mary as the dutiful, ideal *Hausfrau* (housewife and mother) rather than as the Virgin Queen of Heaven. (See page 62.)

3 *Martin Luther in front of Charles V at the Diet of Worms* (1521). According to tradition, Luther, faced with the demand that he repudiate his beliefs, refused, saying: 'Here I stand. I can do no other. God help me. Amen.' (See page 44.)

4 *Katharina von Bora, future wife of Martin Luther* (1526) by Lucas Cranach the Elder. The Reformation's rejection of celibacy meant that the single person was no longer someone upholding a religious ideal but a figure of suspicion. Family life increasingly became the ideal through which Christianity was lived. Luther and other leading reformers led by example, taking wives – in Luther's case, a former nun. (See page 62.)

ABOVE
5 *Peasants' Revolt Massacre* (1525). Luther's call upon the nobility to visit swift and bloody punishment upon the peasants was seen as a betrayal by many peasants, who had supported his demands for reform. (See page 47.)

LEFT
6 John Calvin. In the course of disputes with Geneva's government, Calvin proved himself to be an astute politician – as his work in the Consistory and pulpit showed him to be a conscientious and effective pastor. His followers founded denominations variously known as Calvinist, Reformed, and Presbyterian. (See page 71.)

Scotorum primum Te Ecclesia CNOXE, docentem
Audijt, auspicijs estq reducta tuis.

a a 4

LEFT
7 John Knox became the leading reformer in Scotland, and Protestantism was secured by ensuring that the young king, James, was raised a Protestant after the abdication and exile of his mother, Mary Queen of Scots. (See page 105.)

BELOW
8 *Galileo Galilei before members of the Holy Office in the Vatican in 1633* (1847) by Joseph-Nicolas Robert-Fleury. The Catholic Church condemned Galileo and upheld a literal reading of the Bible, which asserts that the earth did not – and could not – move (Ps. 93:1; 96:10). Straightforward historical accounts (Joshua 10:12–13; 2 Kgs 20:9–11) taught that the sun moved around the earth. (See page 54.)

RIGHT

9 *Thomas Cranmer* (1545) by Gerlach Flicke. Cranmer was the principal author of the first Book of Common Prayer, which replaced the Latin and Catholic worship service when the Mass was abolished under Edward I. (See page 98.)

BELOW

10 *Riot in St Giles' Cathedral, Edinburgh, 23 July 1637.* Opposition to attempts by Charles I to enforce Anglican practices in Scotland reached a flashpoint when he introduced an Anglican Book of Common Prayer, resulting in riots during church services, as depicted in this contemporary engraving. (See page 132.)

The Arch-Prelate of St Andrewes in Scotland reading the new Service-booke in his pontificali: assaulted by men & Women, with Cricketts stooles Stickes and Stones.

ABOVE
11 *Charles I* (1628) by Gerrit van Honthorst. Charles's attempts to bring religious uniformity to his kingdoms and to curtail parliamentary restrictions on his 'divine right' to rule led to the Wars of the Three Kingdoms and, eventually, his own execution. (See page 130.)

LEFT
12 *Archbishop William Laud* (*c.*1636) by Anthony van Dyck. Laud was a fervent supporter of Charles I, whom he encouraged to believe in divine right. His support for rituals, vestments, kneeling and candles led to him being accused of popery (i.e. Catholicism) by his Puritan opponents. (See page 144.)

RIGHT

13 Title page from published version of the National Covenant (1638). Not only did many Scots sign their names to the National Covenant but they also published both the covenant and their names, much as those supporting American independence did in subscribing to the Declaration of Independence over a century later. (See page 132.)

BELOW

14 'A Crowd Queues to Sign the National Covenant in front of Greyfriar's Churchyard, Edinburgh, in 1638', from *Scottish Pictures*. In the National Covenant, Scots asserted that episcopacy was contrary to God's Word and that kings ruled by consent and contract not divine right. (See page 132.)

THE
PROTESTATION
OF THE GENERALL
ASSEMBLIE OF THE
CHURCH OF SCOTLAND, AND OF
THE NOBLEMEN, BARONS,
GENTLEMEN, BORROWES, MI-
NISTERS AND COMMONS;

Subfcribers of the Covenant, lately
renewed, made in the high Kirk, and at the
Mercate Croffe of Glafgow, *the* 28, *and* 29.
of November 1638.

Printed at *Glafgow* by *George Anderfon,*
in the Yeare of Grace, 1638.

LEFT
15 *Oliver Cromwell* (1656) by Sir Peter Lely. By the end of the wars, Cromwell had united the Three Kingdoms (England, Scotland, and Ireland) into a single state called the English Commonwealth, in theory a republic, but, in practice, more of a military dictatorship. (See page 134.)

BELOW
16 *Quaker Meeting* (1699). Much of Quaker thought was based on trying quietly to hear what God was saying. Traditional gender boundaries were ignored, and both women and men were granted equal authority to speak in meetings. (See page 138.)

longer being any abbots or priors) to only archbishops and bishops. In addition to the obvious shift in the balance of economic power away from the
Church, this change in the upper house signalled a political earthquake,
since it meant that, for the first time, there were more laymen (Lords
Temporal) than clergy.

England had now changed decisively and dramatically. Across the country lay people witnessed the dissolution of the monasteries, and the
destruction that it entailed. Monks and nuns were forced out of their
houses and quite literally dumped back into the community. The income
that had sustained them was now in the hands of the Crown or its supporters. This was considerably more dramatic than many princely Lutheran
reformations, where some monastic communities survived and were
Protestantized, but it was less radical than the reformations in Switzerland,
France and the United Provinces. It differed from these in that little
changed in the actual parish church. Monastic communities were gone and
their inhabitants with them, but the Mass was left largely intact and the
priesthood remained celibate.

Nevertheless, the issue that had turned Henry into a Protestant,
however unenthusiastic, still remained – he had no legitimate son. After
Elizabeth's birth, Anne miscarried twice, and from 1536 she began to lose
the king's favour. Henry, meanwhile, had turned his eye on Jane Seymour, a
lady-in-waiting (as Anne had been). To facilitate his marriage to Jane, Anne
was arrested and accused of using witchcraft to trap Henry into marriage, of
adultery with four men, of incest with her brother and of conspiring to kill
the king. There is little reason to believe any of the accusations. Anne's own
uncle, Thomas Howard, Duke of Norfolk, was her judge, and he seemed to
have few qualms about furthering his own ambitions by condemning Anne
and her brother to death, by stake or beheading, at the king's pleasure. Both
were eventually beheaded, as were the other four men with whom Anne was
said to have committed adultery. Howard also used his new-found favour
with the king to get Thomas Cromwell deposed (he was beheaded in 1540),
and even to get the king to marry one of his nieces, Catherine Howard (wife

number five). He himself was subsequently arrested by Edward VI and freed by Mary I, eventually becoming the premier Catholic lord in England, an honour his family still enjoys.

Henry's next marriage, to Jane Seymour, at last bore fruit when she gave birth to a son on 12 October 1537. Unfortunately, she died soon afterwards as a result of medical complications, leaving the king with one rather sickly son and two, now illegitimate, daughters (Mary and Elizabeth). He would marry three more times, but his role in the English Reformation was largely over. His most important legacies were severing the link with Rome, the destruction of the monasteries, the establishment of secular legal sovereignty over ecclesiastical affairs, the appointment of a number of committed (if quiet) Protestants, and his son, Edward VI. Edward succeeded Henry in 1547, aged nine. With Edward as a shield, his advisers and regents introduced a more thoroughgoing Protestantism to England.

Edward Seymour, Duke of Somerset, became Lord Protector and set about various political and foreign policy adventures that eventually cost him his post. However, for our purposes, the key figure is Thomas Cranmer (Archbishop of Canterbury). Both Cranmer and the Duke of Somerset were committed to creating a Protestant England. The Mass was ended and a Protestant worship service inaugurated, with Cranmer's Book of Common Prayer, published solely in English in 1549, replacing the existing Catholic Latin liturgy. The aim was to provide a moderate reformation that would unite the bulk of the population. This was supported in the same year by the Act of Uniformity. However, it failed to please more enthusiastic Protestants (such as the Scot, John Knox, who was appointed a royal chaplain) and infuriated traditionalists still attached to the Mass, if not Rome. Moreover, Somerset was never an enthusiastic persecutor, being in part fearful of antagonizing Charles V, who was still protective of his young relative, Mary, and a staunch supporter of Catholicism.

The introduction of the English Book of Common Prayer was also problematic for a very Protestant reason. Reformers regularly trumpeted the need for the Bible and worship to be in the language of the people (the vernacular). However, not everyone in England spoke English: the Western Rebellion (or Prayer Book Rebellion) started because the Cornish did not wish to leave worshipping in Latin for the language of the English. The rebellion was eventually crushed, and the acceptable language of the people in the kingdom became the single language of the majority – English. As we shall see, this same problem caused disaster for the Reformation in Ireland, where English was to be used rather than Gaelic, but not in Wales, where Welsh was used instead of English. In Scotland, a nation of two languages – Gaelic and Lowland Scots – the situation was even more out of keeping with reformation thought about the vernacular. The language adopted was English, which at least had the virtue of being 'foreign' to everyone.

When Somerset fell, he was replaced by the Earl of Warwick (later Duke of Northumberland), and the Act of Uniformity was enforced more enthusiastically, as was the use of the prayer book. Iconoclasm, almost always sanctioned if not orchestrated by the State, also occurred. The ordination of priests (who could now marry) was replaced by a government-controlled system of appointments. Dissenters were executed, and two of Henry's surviving, pro-Catholic bishops (Edmund Bonner, Bishop of London, and Nicholas Heath, Bishop of Worcester) were deposed and replaced by Protestant bishops, such as Nicholas Ridley, Bishop of Rochester, who removed the altars from the churches in his diocese and replaced them with a communion table. The Reformation had arrived in England. Its *raison d'être* may have been the sexual lusts and dynastic desires of Henry, but under Edward it became a true princely Reformation.

Unfortunately for the English Protestants, the course of reformation was not going to be smooth. In 1553 Edward died and his half-sister Mary – after some abortive attempts to stop her accession – came to the throne. She had neither forgotten nor forgiven the treatment of her mother and herself by Henry or the Protestantism that had facilitated it. She began her reign by releasing leading Catholics, such as Thomas Howard and Stephen Gardiner, Bishop of Winchester, and retroactively legitimating her mother's marriage to Henry. She then moved quickly not only to restore Catholicism, but also to secure a Catholic succession through an heir to ensure that her Protestant half-sister Elizabeth never came to the throne. This latter concern led her to marry Philip of Spain (her mother had been Philip's great aunt). This was a largely unpopular move in England, which greatly disliked all things Spanish, but it did promise the prospect of a Catholic restoration over time. More worryingly, it also suggested that England would eventually be united with Spain in the great Habsburg Empire. In the event, Philip stayed with her only a little over a year, a period that produced just one false pregnancy.

Mary was more successful in restoring Catholicism. Cardinal Reginald Pole was sent by the pope to receive England back under papal supremacy, and he became Archbishop of Canterbury. Priests who had married were told to put aside their wives or lose their livings. The Mass was restored, and, after much negotiation, most of the laws passed by Henry and Edward were repealed. Mary was forced to accept the permanent loss of monastic lands as she was in no position to confiscate them back from their new, noble owners. She also began a systematic and brutal persecution of Protestants, which led to the deaths of many, including some very influential men, such as Nicholas Ridley (see page 99). However, her reign was short-lived and became increasingly unpopular because of her ties with Spain (not helped when she allied with Spain against France, which allied with the pope, and England ended up losing its last remaining bit of France – Calais). After only five years on the throne, Mary died, and against all her plans, Elizabeth came to the throne.

Elizabeth's accession highlighted the religious complexities facing her from the outset. Pole had died almost simultaneously with Mary, leaving England without an Archbishop of Canterbury. Most of the bishops refused to participate in Elizabeth's coronation since she was a bastard not only under canon law, but also by Act of Parliament (still in force), so she had to be crowned by the obscure Owen Oglethorpe, Bishop of Carlisle, in a Latin service. He died that same year soon after being deprived of his see – crowning the queen did not save him in the coming restructuring of the

Church. Communion was celebrated by her own (Protestant) chaplain to avoid the performance of a Catholic Mass. She quickly moved to rectify the situation, beginning with the appointment of her mother's chaplain, Matthew Parker, as Archbishop of Canterbury.

The queen relied primarily on Secretary of State Sir William Cecil as well as Lord Keeper of the Great Seal Sir Nicholas Bacon for advice on how to reinstate Protestantism in her realm. The Act of Uniformity, 1559 was passed upon her accession, and it again required the use of the Protestant Book of Common Prayer in church services. Once more, papal supremacy was denied, and Elizabeth took the title Supreme Governor of the Church of England, not Supreme Head, as she and many of her advisers and public felt that the latter title was not proper for a woman, even a reigning queen. In the same year, the Act of Supremacy was passed, which forced all public officials to accept under oath her supremacy over the Church, or face severe punishment. Many bishops appointed by Mary were unwilling to accept Elizabeth's religious policy, so they were replaced. Ironically, this gave Elizabeth a relatively free hand to appoint many new, Protestant bishops. The queen also appointed an entirely new Privy Council, removing many Catholic counsellors in the process.

The result was somewhat less severe than the initial Reformation Bill submitted in 1559, and suggests that Elizabeth, at least initially, was willing to countenance a much more thorough reformation than what actually followed. That bill spoke of the Eucharist in a consubstantial manner as opposed to transubstantial, included abuse of the pope in the liturgy, banned Catholic vestments, allowed ministers to marry, banned images and confirmed Elizabeth as Supreme Head of the Church. The Bill was much resisted and altered in the House of Lords, which produced a liturgy allowing for a transubstantial understanding of the Eucharist, and denying Elizabeth the title 'Supreme Head'.

Parliament was taken out of session, and when it returned two new bills were presented. The Act of Supremacy is discussed above. The Bill of Uniformity, while legally binding, was more cautious than the initial

Reformation Bill. It removed harsh laws specifically aimed against Catholics, as long as they outwardly conformed, removed the anti-papal abuse from the liturgy and kept the wording that allowed for both a consubstantial and transubstantial understanding of the Eucharist. In a further sign that Elizabeth had taken to heart the lesson learnt from the mauling of the original Reformation Bill, she and Cecil drafted a series of royal injunctions as additions and clarifications of the two Acts, especially the Uniformity Act. Priests were to continue to wear the surplice (their main robe), and wafers rather than ordinary bread were to be used in the Eucharist.

Elizabeth's moderate reformation – especially its moderation towards what actually happened in a church service of worship – was very successful at helping the people to make yet another change in religion. However, her tolerant attitude to Catholics proved to be less successful. After the Northern Rebellion, led by Thomas Howard, was put down, the insult of a Catholic rising was further injured by the arrival of Pope Pius V's bull *Regnans in Excelsis*, which formally excommunicated the queen and declared her deposed and liable to assassination. She then began the persecution of her religious enemies, which led to a number of failed conspiracies to remove her from the throne. She also permitted the Church of England to take a more explicitly Protestant line by allowing Parliament to pass the more overtly Calvinist Thirty-nine Articles (1571), which served as a confession of faith for the Church of England (the equivalent of the Augsburg Confession for Lutherans).

As annoying as being deposed by the pope must have been, the greater threats to the English Reformation came from the active involvement of Spanish and papal money and troops in various attempts to remove the queen. Both were involved in risings (especially in Ireland), plots (some involving Mary Queen of Scots, which eventually led to her execution), and outright attacks on England (the Spanish Armada being the most notable). None of these proved successful, although the English tended to make a mental link between their new Reformation and their national identity and independence. Whenever and wherever religion became linked with identity and/or ethnicity, it proved extremely difficult to change.

This proved to be the case in Ireland, where Elizabeth and her advisers failed to follow a moderate course and, as noted earlier, ignored the humanist and reformation injunction to give religion to the people in the vernacular. As a result, Protestantism, which was clearly English-speaking, became inextricably linked with English-speaking rule in Ireland. Latin may have been just as foreign a language, but it was not the language of the invader. It seems the English experience with Irish rebellions, as well as a deep-seated conviction that the Irish were 'barbarians' and 'savages' who needed to be civilized, led to this policy, which differed dramatically from what was instituted in Wales. In Wales the state favoured the use of Welsh, and produced Bibles and liturgies in Welsh, which undoubtedly helped preserve both the language and Welsh culture to this day.

It is clear that the English Reformation was initially driven by the dynastic goals of Henry VIII, who, wanting a male heir, found it useful to replace papal supremacy with the supremacy of the English Crown. A close reading of the early legislation, limiting itself as it does to questions of temporal and spiritual supremacy, suggests that it was never Henry's intention to found a Protestant church. The original Acts sought to reverse the historic increase of papal power versus the power of secular rulers. Subsequent legislation put a decidedly Protestant spin on Henry's agenda, however. The introduction of the Great Bible in 1538 had brought the Scripture into churches in the people's language. The dissolution of the monasteries, completed by 1540, had brought huge amounts of Church land and income into the nobles' hands.

By 1549 this process of creating a new, distinctly national Church was fully under way, with the first vernacular prayer book, the Book of Common Prayer, and the enforcement of the Acts of Uniformity, which together established English (not Latin) as the language of public worship. The theological foundations for this very English Church were laid by men such as Thomas Cranmer, the principal author of the first Prayer Book, and continued under Richard Hooker and Lancelot Andrewes. Cranmer had studied in Europe and been influenced by the ideas of the reformers Calvin and Bucer. Of course, all were influenced by the ideas of humanism in general and Erasmus in particular.

During Edward VI's short reign Cranmer and others moved the Church of England significantly closer to a Protestant, Calvinist position, which was reflected in the development of the second Prayer Book (1552). This Reformed or Calvinist Protestant Reformation came to an end with Mary I, and what returned with Protestant Elizabeth was considerably less Protestant, much to the dismay of some of her more ardent Protestant subjects, especially the Puritans.

Elizabeth's solution to the problem of minimizing bloodshed and preventing more chaos over religion was the careful and moderate religious settlement evident in the 1559 Book of Common Prayer. This version of the prayer book combined elements of the Calvinistic 1552 version with the traditional Catholic liturgy that had featured in Henry's 1549 version. The prayer-book revision was buttressed by a revision of Edward's original Thirty-nine Articles of Religion (he actually started with forty-eight), plus additional rules and guidelines concerning vestments and liturgy. Elizabeth's goal was a Church with a form of worship to which everybody had to conform, but that expressed a system of belief sufficiently vague and multi-faceted to allow for many different theological tastes. The result did not please Catholics or ardent Protestants, but it did get the conformity of the majority, and, at least for the many decades of Elizabeth's reign, provided stability in a realm that had undergone four different reformations (in the late 1530s, the late 1540s, the mid-1550s and the late 1550s). Anyone born about 1510 – middle-aged when Elizabeth came to the throne – must have welcomed the calm.

The Reformation in Scotland was a briefer and much less convoluted affair than in England and Ireland. The bishops of Scotland, who were also humanistic, had already made some strides in reforming their own houses.

Initial attempts at humanistic and slightly Lutheran reform came to nothing. The Lutheran-influenced preacher Patrick Hamilton was executed in 1528. Later, in 1546, the somewhat Calvinist preacher George Wishart was burnt at the stake for heresy by Cardinal David Beaton (himself assassinated shortly after the execution of Wishart). All this contributed to complicating the situation, but things did not really change until the late 1550s. Indeed, much of what happened was greatly dependent on the foreign relations of Scotland.

Mary Queen of Scots, who acceded to the throne in her minority, had been taken to France as a child to avoid being forced to marry Henry VIII's son, Edward. In France she had been married to Francis II, who left her a widow shortly before her eighteenth birthday. From 1554 Mary's mother, Marie of Guise, who belonged to a staunchly Catholic French family and was Scotland's dowager queen, took over the regency and continued to advance French interests in Scotland. However, those Scots who favoured a Reformation found that this increasingly meant resisting ties with France, the 'auld alliance', and looking instead to England, the 'auld enemy'. In 1560 Marie died, and Mary made preparations to return to Scotland as queen. Once there, she was unable to stem the tide of Protestantism or the increasingly close relationship with England and its newly restored Protestantism under her cousin Elizabeth. Within seven years she was forced to abdicate, and then was imprisoned. She escaped, but failed in her attempt to regain the throne, and in 1568 she left Scotland for ever, seeking refuge in England and leaving her young son, James, in the care of regents. As a Catholic monarch with claims to both the Scottish and English thrones, she was a logical focal point for anti-Protestant sentiment in the British Isles. Unfortunately, this eventually led Elizabeth to the tragic conclusion that Mary alive was a luxury she could not afford. Execution swiftly followed.

Knox became the leading reformer in the land, and Protestantism was secured by ensuring that the young king, James VI of Scotland (I of England), was raised a Protestant under the careful supervision – and rough discipline – of his tutor, George Buchanan. What makes the Scottish Reformation most interesting is that it was Calvinistic, both in theology and church structure, having kirk sessions (church consistories) and general assemblies (national synods). But bishops remained in possession of their lands and titles as long as they (outwardly) conformed to the new faith. Many monastic communities were sacked, especially in the towns, but others were allowed to continue, usually under the same secular lairds who had governed them before the Reformation. The only regulations were that the Mass could not be celebrated, and no new members could be taken in. Thus, they were allowed to wither and die, but this took a while: the last reference to a monk was in the 1590s. Knox also made the astute political decision to adopt English as the official language of the Kirk, rather than either of the two vernaculars then in use (Lowland Scots and Gaelic). Thus, in many ways the Scottish Reformation appears considerably more Protestant than that in England, but behind the veneer of Calvinistic theology and liturgy were some elements of the old settlement that seem decidedly unreformed.

REFORMATION IN CENTRAL EUROPE

If the situation in Scotland seems somewhat unexpected, then that in central Europe was decidedly bizarre. The ethnic and political complexity of central and eastern Europe had allowed numerous groups to flourish. Parts of Lithuania had only been converted from paganism in the Middle Ages. The border between Orthodoxy and Catholicism ran down the centre of the region. From the fourteenth century two separate, western-looking Hussite churches had existed in Bohemia. Lutheranism made extensive headway in German-speaking areas from the Baltic to Romania. Calvinism (or Reformed Protestantism) found ready adherents in Poland and Hungary. In areas that fell under Turkish power during that period all groups were forced to tolerate one another. Muslims did not persecute other monotheists, nor did they allow them to persecute each other – in marked contrast to the treatment meted out to their co-religionists and Jews in Christian Spain. They were told to 'convert, leave or die'.

But what makes this heartland of pluralistic toleration so interesting is not the existence of the 'normal' denominations, but rather the truly strange. It is here in the centre of Europe that it is possible to get some idea of what might have happened elsewhere had Protestantism not turned so quickly and effectively to State coercion to stop believers from getting too carried away with their own priesthood, or finding their own truths in their vernacular Bibles, guided only by their consciences and the Holy Spirit. It is here that we see most dramatically both the full horror of Protestantism's propensity for schism, but also its great genius for devising new and unique social and cultural experiments. When Protestants were allowed the freedom to unite, splinter, reunite and divide again with happy abandon, the result was truly fascinating, and suggests the enormous inventiveness of the human spirit. Space does not allow for a detailed examination of each, but a few brief paragraphs on one particularly interesting example will provide a glimpse into the kaleidoscope that was the radical reformation in central and eastern Europe.

Socinianism refers to the beliefs of the Socinians, followers of Laelius Socinus and of his nephew Faustus Socinus (or Fausto Sozzini), both of whom had the rare privilege for radical reformers of dying in their beds rather than at the stake. The Socinians settled in Transylvania (under the protection of the Turks), Poland and, to a lesser extent, in the Netherlands. They were very sceptical of the value and power of reason (a power to which humanists clung so naively), and rejected both the Trinity and the divinity of Jesus. Their views were summarized in the Racovian Catechism (published 1605, but certainly written earlier), which reminds us that even radicals delighted in the process of 'confessionalization' (providing detailed explanations of what was truth and correct belief in the form of clear and precise creeds or confessions), though they tended not to enforce their confessions at swordpoint. They also believed that God's omniscience was limited to what would definitely happen and did not apply to what might happen. They believed that if God knew every possible future, free will was meaningless. In 1602 James Sienynski established a college and printing press at Raków, which published the Racovian Catechism. In 1610 a Catholic reaction began, led by Jesuits. The establishment at Raków was suppressed in 1638 after two boys pelted a crucifix outside the town, and all Socinians were eventually driven from the city by 1643.

A similar movement was known as Unitarianism. It shared with Socinianism a rejection of the Trinity, believing instead in the 'unipersonality' of the Christian Godhead, that is, the Father alone is God. Individuals who were anti-Trinitarian in any way were fiercely persecuted, and some eventually joined the Socinians in Poland and Hungary. During the course of the eighteenth century these ideas reappeared in England (see pages 157–9). Along with this fundamental doctrine about the Godhead, certain characteristics marked unitarianism: an abhorrence of coercion, little emphasis upon 'essential' matters of faith, a dislike for creeds and confessions and an approach to the Bible that was largely historical. Martin Cellarius, a friend of Luther, held unitarian views and is considered the first person to espouse them in print (in 1527); the anti-Trinitarian position of Ludwig Haetzer did not become public until after his execution for Anabaptism. Indeed, in the minds of the magisterial reformers there was always a confusion between anti-Trinitarians and Anabaptists. They were not necessarily the same, and lumping them together as 'radical reformers' is very misleading. Even the principal orthodox Italian reformer and refugee, Bernardino Ochino, in his *Dialogues* (1563), while defending the Trinity, listed objections and difficulties with the doctrine, which persuaded many of its error! Although he had worked with Calvin and served in England under Edward VI, his restless questioning eventually made him fall foul of the authorities in Zurich (where he had previously fled for refuge), and he had to flee further afield. Not surprisingly, he went to Poland, increasingly known for its toleration of all things 'religiously bizarre', not least anti-Trinitarianism and Judaism. In time even Poland became ill-disposed to his ideas, and he had to move again, this time to Moravia, another haven for marginal and radical religious groups, where he died of plague – what many in his age would have seen as a fitting divine judgement on his views.

Scattered expressions of anti-Trinitarian opinion had appeared very early in Poland. At the age of eighty Catherine, wife of a certain Melchior Vogel or Weygel, had been burnt at Cracow (1539) for heresy; whether her views embraced more than Deism (see pages 155–7) is not clear. The first synod of the Polish Reformed Church took place in 1555; by the meeting of the second synod (1556), the Church was faced with the theological challenges of Gregory Pauli and Peter Gonesius, who were aware of the works of Servetus and other anti-Trinitarians. The arrival of the Italian physician, polemicist and anti-Trinitarian Giorgio Blandrata in 1558 furnished the party with a temporary leader.

Eventually, the Polish anti-Trinitarians were expelled from the existing Reformed synod; henceforward they held their own synods as the Minor Church. Eventually, these anti-Trinitarians heard and accepted the views of Faustus Socinus, who had arrived in Poland in 1579, and melded into the wider Socinian movement. During the course of the disastrous wars in Poland–Lithuania in the seventeenth century, the Socinians became seen as Swedish collaborators. The Polish Parliament gave them the option of conforming to one of the accepted denominations – Catholicism, Lutheranism or Calvinism – or leaving the country. Being politically impotent, because their views forbade them from being magistrates, the Socinians could not even look to their noble adherents for support.

The decree came into effect in 1600. Some conformed, a large number made their way to the Netherlands, where the Remonstrants (see page 149) admitted them to membership on the basis of the Apostles' Creed; others went to the German frontier. A contingent settled in Transylvania, but did not join the theologically similar Unitarian Church, maintaining a distinct organization at Cluj until 1793. The refugees who reached Amsterdam published the *Bibliotheca fratrum polonorum* (*Library of the Polish Brethren, 1665–9*), embracing the works of Hans Krell, their leading theologian Jonas Schlichting (Szlichtyng), and their chief commentators, Faustus Socinus and Johann Ludwig Wolzogen. The title page of this collection, bearing the words *quos Unitarios vocant* (those called Unitarians) introduced the term

Unitarian to western Europe. However, the term *unitarius* seems to have been introduced by the Calvinist Péter Juhász (also called Mélius) during debates with anti-Trinitarians in 1569–71, and its first appearance in print is in a decree of the Lécsfalva Diet in 1600; it was not officially adopted by the Church until 1638.

No distinct trace of anti-Trinitarian opinion precedes the appearance of Blandrata at the Transylvanian court in 1563. He greatly influenced Ferenc Dávid, who was a religious gadfly, successively being Catholic, Lutheran, Calvinist and, eventually, anti-Trinitarian. In 1564, though, Dávid was elected by the Calvinists as 'bishop of the Hungarian churches in Transylvania', and appointed court preacher to John Sigismund, Prince of Transylvania (previously King of Hungary). His problems with the Trinity began in 1565, when he began to question the divine personality of the Holy Ghost. His emerging anti-Trinitarianism was strongly resisted by the Calvinist leader Péter Juhász, but he received support from Blandrata. John Sigismund adopted his court preacher's views, and in 1568 issued an edict of religious liberty at the Torda Diet, which allowed Dávid to remain as a bishop, but to transfer his episcopacy from the Calvinists to the anti-Trinitarians.

In 1571 John Sigismund was succeeded by Stephen Báthory, a Catholic who was considerably less inclined to toleration. Under the influence of John Sommer, rector of the Kolozsvár gymnasium (grammar school), Dávid (about 1572) abandoned the worship of Christ as a divine person in the Godhead. An attempted accommodation with Faustus Socinus made matters worse. Dávid was arrested and tried as an 'innovator'; he died in prison.

THE OUTCOME IN EUROPE

This brief excursion into the pluralism that was central European religion simply reminds us of the problems inherent in Luther's assertion of a priesthood of all believers, and the humanists' and reformers' view that the Bible's meaning was plain, simple and clear, open to both learned scholars and humble ploughmen under the guidance of the Holy Spirit. Luther, Zwingli and Calvin could not agree on the meaning of the word *is* in 'This is my body'. Learned men debated whether baptism meant 'pouring water' or 'dunking the body'; whether it was open to infants or available only to professing adults. Issues seemingly settled over a thousand years before – the 'make-up' of the Godhead, the nature of Christ as human and divine – were all open for discussion again. But by 1600 these debates had been pushed to the margins, both in discussions and, quite literally, in a geographical sense. Luther's accidental revolution had become a very real and potent revolution.

Thus, by 1600 it appeared that Europe had settled into a new religious situation. The north and northwest (except Ireland) were largely Protestant. France had a minority Protestant community, and the Holy Roman Empire (Germany) was a patchwork quilt of denominations. Switzerland was evenly divided; central and eastern Europe were pluralistically tolerant, to the disgust of Catholics and magisterial reformers alike. Italy and the Iberian peninsula were solidly Catholic, but other seemingly Catholic lands, such as the Habsburg possessions in Austria, had many Protestants. Religious violence had plagued France, Germany and the Low Countries, but a general, calm truce – more of exhaustion than principle – had settled over the Continent. This would soon change and, as we shall see in the next chapter, the first half of the seventeenth century was an orgy of denominational violence in the very heart of Europe, which eventually dragged almost every country into open warfare.

4

REAPING THE WHIRLWIND

PROTESTANT CHRISTIANS DO NOT WISH
TO BE A CHURCH IN THE SAME WAY AS
THE CATHOLIC CHURCH UNDERSTANDS ITSELF
AS A CHURCH; THEY REPRESENT A DIFFERENT
TYPE OF CHURCH AND FOR THIS REASON
THEY ARE NOT A CHURCH IN THE CATHOLIC
MEANING OF THE WORD.

CARDINAL WALTER KASPAR
PONTIFICAL COUNCIL FOR PROMOTING CHRISTIAN UNITY (2004)

ANYONE VIEWING WHAT HAD BEEN WESTERN Christendom in the first decade of the seventeenth century would have wondered where religious conflict might break out next. The nations of Scandinavia, the states of Italy, and Spain (now united with Portugal) seemed to have resolved their own internal religious settlements. Germany (the Holy Roman Empire) was religiously divided, but largely at peace, and the settlements reached in the previous century were holding. The British Isles had a number of denominational realities, but the unification of the various kingdoms under one ruling house (the Stuarts of Scotland) seemed to suggest that, in time, these would meld into a single settlement. Switzerland was divided in half, but the cantons had found a complicated yet workable solution – the two blocs sat at diets (parliaments) in different cities, and resolved pan-Confederation issues by sending delegations back and forth.

Thus, much of Europe seemed at peace. Catholicism was experiencing a period of very muscular and militant renewal as a result of the various sessions of the Council of Trent, and, with groups such as the Jesuits, was beginning to make substantial internal reforms to piety and practice. It seemed most logical to expect any problems that might erupt to be in places where Tridentine (that is, from the Council of Trent) Catholicism literally rubbed shoulders on a day-to-day basis with Protestantism – especially its more militant and muscular variety, Calvinism. This would have suggested that trouble would erupt in France or perhaps central Europe. Also, many patiently awaited the inevitable collapse of the United Provinces in the Low Countries. Not only did most Europeans think it physically impossible to run a republic on such a grand geographical scale (an issue that was a concern even into the late eighteenth century, when it troubled America's Founding Fathers), in addition, the 'toleration' of the United Provinces was noted as a weird and inevitably disastrous experiment. Any fair observer would have expected France and the United Provinces, only just having secured uneasy truces, to explode again at any moment into fratricidal civil war. Poland seemed almost perversely close to chaos as well. All such observers and expectations were proven wrong. Instead, when the situation truly deteriorated, it came in that most stable of all states, England, and that most settled and organized of all religious settlements, Germany.

THE THIRTY YEARS WAR

In 1618 the heart of Europe was plunged into bloody war that had at its core religion. It was fought almost wholly on the territory of present-day Germany, but eventually involved almost every major European power. Most bizarrely of all, it eventually pitted the forces of the Catholic Habsburgs (both in Spain and Austria) against Catholic France, and saw the beginning of the long-term decline of Habsburg power across Europe.

The Peace of Augsburg (1555) had seemingly settled the issue of religion in the empire. It confirmed the results of the 1526 Diet of Speyer, and ended the violence between the Lutherans and the Catholics in Germany. Its main provisions were that princes of the empire could choose the religion, as long as it was Catholicism or Protestantism, as they saw fit: this was known as the principle of *cuius regio, eius religio* ('whoever reigns, his religion rules'). It also allowed Lutherans living in ecclesiastical states (those ruled by a bishop or archbishop) to remain Lutheran. Lands taken from the Catholic Church by Protestants between the Peace of Passau (1552) and 1555 would not have to be returned. Any Catholic ecclesiastical leader converting to Protestantism had to renounce his realm, which put an end to the possibility that the ecclesiastical electors might convert and lead to the election of a Protestant emperor. The settlement had a number of problems: in some ecclesiastical states it left a Lutheran minority; it recognized only two denominations – Catholic and Lutheran – since the Lutherans were determined to keep the Calvinists/Reformed out of the empire; it wholly ignored any radical movements; it meant that any change in ruler might bring about a change in religion.

Moreover, some bishops had converted, but simply refused to step down from their posts. Also, Calvinism was spreading, and, to complicate matters, had converted some rulers. Finally, Tridentine Catholicism was on the march and beginning to convert Protestants back to the faith through persuasion and extremely effective educational campaigns. However, working against these causes of tension was the moderation of the Austrian Habsburgs, who still provided the empire with its emperors. Successive emperors, especially Ferdinand I and Maximilian II, but also Rudolf II and his successor, Matthias, sought to respect their Lutheran subjects and to woo them back to Catholicism rather than coerce them. They had seen the turmoil of France and England in the sixteenth century and tried to avoid the same in the empire. In particular, in their own personal lands (partially outside the empire) this meant tolerating a number of denominations, not just Lutheranism. Significant bodies of non-Catholics existed in Austria, royal Hungary (basically that part of Hungary not directly controlled by the Ottomans or under their protection in Transylvania) and Bohemia. Moreover, they were aware that the Protestant states within the empire could, and did, look outside the empire for support, if necessary, from the powerful Lutheran states of Denmark and Sweden.

This uneasy but apparently workable situation showed its first signs of cracking in the German free city of Donauwörth in 1606. The majority Lutheran population physically prevented their Catholic neighbours from holding a procession, and a violent riot resulted. It is perhaps worth reminding ourselves that magisterial Protestants were as intolerant as any Catholic state with the Inquisition could be, and that it was not just French

Catholics who could turn on their neighbours. This act of Lutheran denominational intolerance forced Maximilian, the Catholic Duke of Bavaria, to intervene to protect Catholic civil/human rights (he would not have expressed it that way – rather, he would have intervened to allow the expression of the 'one true faith'). This bit of denominational sabre-rattling was especially ominous to those states that were leaning towards Calvinism (hated by both 'official' religions of the empire). They banded together in 1608 to form the League of Evangelical (Protestant) Union under the palatine elector Frederick IV. (The palatine elector was the hereditary ruler of the County Palatinate of the Rhine, which had been elevated in 1356 from a mere county, headed by a count, to one of the Holy Roman Empire's electorates.) This led the Catholics in 1609 to form the Catholic League under the leadership of Maximilian of Bavaria as a counterweight.

When the emperor Matthias died in 1619 without male issue, his lands were inherited by his cousin Ferdinand of Styria (Austria). Ferdinand was a staunch Catholic who had been educated by the Jesuits, and he wanted to restore Catholicism in his realms. As the newly elected emperor, he had little room to move, but he had also personally inherited the throne of Bohemia. There, as king, he could act more directly and decisively. Unfortunately, Bohemia was not just Protestant: it still had a strong Hussite Church that had long ago wedded religion to ethnicity (Czech identity), and had nearly two centuries of existence alongside Catholicism. The Czechs had no intention of seeing their national religion altered. This set the stage for the first of four phases in what has become known as the Thirty Years War – the Bohemian Revolt, followed in turn by the Danish, Swedish and the French Interventions.

Matthias, aware of the complex situation, had worked hard to ensure that Ferdinand was accepted by the estates (parliaments) not only of Bohemia, but also royal Hungary, as he was heir apparent to both thrones. Many Bohemian Protestants feared this would erode their 'liberties' (promises of toleration) that had been extracted from previous kings (also Holy Roman emperors). Logically, they supported the idea of electing the elector

Frederick, a Calvinist who also happened to be married to a daughter of James VI and I of Britain. However, most imperial princes supported Ferdinand – the Catholics because he was Catholic, and the Lutherans because he was not a Calvinist. As a result, in 1617 Ferdinand was elected by the estates of Bohemia. However, when the king-elect sent two Catholic councillors to Prague in May 1618 to govern in his absence, Bohemian Calvinists seized them, subjected them to a mock trial, and threw them out of a palace window (hence the term 'defenestration'). Against the odds, they survived. Catholics said angels intervened and caught them in mid-air; Protestants said they were saved by a pile of manure. The result was that a general revolt now erupted throughout Bohemia, eventually spreading to Silesia, Lusatia and Moravia, as Protestants, largely Calvinists, squared off against their Catholic neighbours and their Catholic king.

The rebellion was largely without result, but with the death of Matthias, the Bohemians feared that Ferdinand would now be able to bring the might of the empire, as well as the help of the Spanish, against them. They naturally turned to the palatinate, and Frederick asked to be admitted to the Protestant Union. It was suggested that he might become King of Bohemia. Sadly, Ferdinand's officials made effective spies, and similar secret offers to the Duke of Savoy, the Elector of Saxony and the Prince of Transylvania were seized and published, rather undermining the Bohemian position. Protestants across the lands now securely in Ferdinand's enthusiastically Catholic grasp took the opportunity to revolt as well. Large numbers of Lutherans and Calvinists in both lower and upper Austria now rebelled. Hungary remained loyal, but the Protestant Prince of Transylvania, Gabriel Bethlen, took advantage of the situation and invaded Hungary (with the enthusiastic blessing of the Muslim Ottoman sultan).

The rebels managed to besiege Vienna and make extensive gains, helped in no small measure by the secret support of Catholic, but anti-Habsburg, Savoy. In June 1619 the siege was lifted by Austrian troops, and Bohemian documents were seized that revealed Savoy's part in the anti-Catholic rebellion. The Duke of Savoy quickly dropped his support for the Bohemian co-religionists of his Calvinist enemies in Geneva. Despite this reverse, in August the parliament of Bohemia, now officially joined by rebels in the two Austrias, deposed Ferdinand as king and elected Frederick. This quickly spread the conflict. With the loss of much of Hungary to the Protestant Transylvanians, the situation looked very bleak indeed for the Catholics under Ferdinand – there was no question that the Calvinists would extend to any captured Catholic lands the liberties they were so enthusiastically defending.

Imperial and Habsburg politics now intervened and widened the situation, while also seriously threatening the Bohemians. The Spanish persuaded Protestant Saxony, bribed by the offer of controlling Lusatia at the end of hostilities, to intervene on the Catholic side. Spanish forces in the southern Netherlands tied down the armies of the Protestant Union. Finally, the emperor transferred the electoral title from the palatinate to the Duke of Bavaria in return for convincing the Catholic League to intervene. One immediately sees the weakness of the Augsburg idea of *cuius regio, eius religio* – it was entirely dependent on the whims of individual rulers and dynasties that had considerably more concerns than what denomination their subjects practised. This allowed Austrian and Catholic League forces to defeat the rebellion in the two Austrias, and then, united, to move against Bohemia. On 8 November 1620 imperial forces decisively defeated Frederick and the Bohemians (augmented by no small number of Scots fighting for his Stuart wife) at the Battle of White Mountain. This string of victories allowed Ferdinand to rescind various liberties granted in Austria and Bohemia, and begin the aggressive re-Catholicization of these lands.

The League of Evangelical Union disintegrated, and Frederick was deposed and declared an outlaw, fleeing into exile in the Netherlands, Denmark and Sweden. His state was dismembered and given to various Catholic rulers, thus opening the now Calvinist palatinate to the forces of Tridentine Catholicism. The Spanish, sensing that the time was ripe to renew their war to reconquer the United Provinces, took much of the palatinate, which allowed their forces to outflank the Dutch along a much longer front. This first phase of warfare ended when Bethlen signed the Peace of Nikolsburg (31 December 1621) in return for lands in royal Hungary. With the capture (by siege) of Mannheim and Heidelberg in 1622, and Frankenthal in 1623, the palatinate came under Spanish Catholic control. Some campaigning continued near the Dutch border, but on 6 August 1623 imperial forces under Johann Tserclaes von Tilly clashed with Frederick's sole remaining fighting force under Christian of Brunswick and destroyed 80 per cent of the army (over 10,000 men). Defeated, in exile, and under pressure from his father-in-law, James VI of Scotland and I of England, Frederick abandoned his claims and accepted defeat. This seemed to settle the crisis, though it left the empire's Protestants very weakened, and a strong, united Catholic force seemingly free to move decisively, once and for all, against the Protestants.

This implicit threat led Christian IV of Denmark, a Lutheran and, as Duke of Holstein, an imperial nobleman, to intervene. Denmark was wealthy and strong during this period; the only other European country with a comparably strong financial position was, ironically, Bavaria. Christian was also helped by the French first minister Cardinal Richelieu, together with the Dutch and English, who, united by fear of an outright Habsburg victory, agreed to subsidize the war. Christian raised a mercenary army of 20,000 men and invaded. Ferdinand II turned to a wealthy mercenary leader and Bohemian nobleman, Albrecht von Wallenstein, who pledged his large army (variously reported at between 30,000 and 100,000 soldiers) to Ferdinand in return for the right to plunder any captured territories. Christian was surprised by the appearance of Wallenstein's troops, and, faced with the additional forces under Tilly, he had to withdraw. The situation only worsened for Christian: England was in the first throes of its struggles between Crown and Parliament; a brief revolt by the Huguenots (see pages 80–2) threw France into temporary turmoil; Sweden was occupied by war with Poland; Protestant Brandenburg and Saxony had no stomach for ending the precarious truce in the eastern part of the empire. By 1626 imperial forces had defeated what was left of the forces against them.

Unable to defeat Denmark outright, the emperor negotiated the Treaty of Lübeck (1629). Christian IV abandoned his support for the Protestants, but kept Denmark intact.

At this moment, Ferdinand, flushed with victory and scenting the chance to make extensive gains against Protestantism, overreached himself. The Catholic League persuaded him to take back the Lutheran holdings that were, according to the Peace of Augsburg, rightfully the possession of the Catholic Church, but had not been handed back. The Edict of Restitution (1629) listed them: two archbishoprics, sixteen bishoprics and hundreds of monasteries. It appeared to all Protestant observers that this was but the beginning of a campaign – backed by the large armies under Tilly and Wallenstein – to conduct the re-Catholicization that everyone could see was beginning in Austria and Bohemia. This was almost certainly Ferdinand's ultimate goal, as it had been of Charles V, but he was also a politician and emperor, and as much as he disliked Protestantism, he was coming to fear Wallenstein. He dismissed him in 1630, which seriously weakened the imperial forces just as another Protestant state, Sweden, decided (as had Denmark, with disastrous results) to act before it was 'too late'.

Gustavus II Adolphus, like Christian IV before him, rushed to aid the German Lutherans, and to strengthen Sweden's influence in the German states around the economically important Baltic Sea. Gustavus feared the increased power of the Habsburg position after the defeat of Denmark. He was also subsidized by Richelieu and the Dutch, the latter hoping to relieve pressure against themselves from the Spanish forces in the southern Netherlands and the occupied palatinate. From 1630 to 1634 Swedish troops drove the Catholic armies back and regained most occupied Protestant lands.

Having dismissed Wallenstein, Ferdinand was entirely dependent on the Catholic League. At the Battle of Breitenfeld (1631) the Swedish forces defeated the Catholics under Tilly, who was killed in battle the next year. Sweden and the Protestants were now in the ascendancy. With Franco-Dutch aid, and their forces swollen by mercenaries who switched sides after

Breitenfeld, the Swedes appeared unstoppable. With defeat looming, Ferdinand turned to Wallenstein and his army once again. Forced into a confrontation at a time and place of Wallenstein's choosing, the Swedes joined battle at Lützen in 1632. Although they held the field at the end of the battle, Gustavus Adolphus lay among the dead. Bereft of their genius, the Swedes and their allies were beaten two years later, in September 1634, at the First Battle of Nördlingen. A few months before the battle, though, Ferdinand had begun to fear that Wallenstein was about to switch sides, so had him assassinated. Although the battle was still won, without Wallenstein and Gustavus Adolphus, tactical driving force was lacking on both sides, and peace seemed the obvious next step. The result was the Peace of Prague (1635), which ended the fighting. Subsequent negotiations agreed that the implementation of the Edict of Restitution could wait for forty years, and allowed Protestants to secularize Church states they had held in 1627 (this cost them dearly in the south and west, since the empire had made extensive gains there by 1627). In addition, the German armies of both sides were amalgamated into a single, imperial army, though Protestant Saxony and Catholic Bavaria retained practical control of their contingents in this new army. Foreign alliances were forbidden, and anyone who joined the rebellion against the emperor after 1630 (when the leading Protestant states had taken fright at imperial power and joined the Swedes) was granted an amnesty.

France, however, was horrified at the newly strengthened imperial position. Joining with the Dutch and the Swedes, who had been cut out of Germany by the negotiations after Prague, the French moved against the Habsburgs, who now controlled almost every state bordering France. Spain quickly retaliated and invaded. The combined imperial and Spanish forces ravaged Champagne and Burgundy, and threatened Paris in 1636, before being pushed back by French forces. The deaths of Richelieu and Louis XIII in 1643 left a minor (Louis XIV) on the throne, and his chief minister, Cardinal Jules Mazarin, had little stomach for continued warfare, even though the defeat of the Spanish at Rocroi in the same year had relieved the French position. He therefore opened negotiations for peace. On the battlefield in Germany, both sides now fought for the best position before peace. In 1645 Swedish forces defeated the imperial army at the Battle of Jankau, near Prague, and French troops defeated the Bavarians in the Second Battle of Nördlingen. This latter defeat convinced Bavaria to leave the war, and on 14 March 1647 Bavaria, France and Sweden signed the Truce of Ulm. The following year the combined forces of Sweden and France defeated the imperial army in two decisive battles, Zusmarshausen and Lens. This reduced imperial possessions to Austria. The emperor had no choice but to begin negotiations in earnest. The result, in 1648, was the Peace of Westphalia.

AFTERMATH OF THE THIRTY YEARS WAR

The war changed the face of European power politics. The reality of Spain's military and political decline was apparent to all. Totally occupied with the fighting in France, the empire and the Low Countries, Spain was ill prepared for revolts at home in Portugal (united to Spain since 1580) and Catalonia. Unable to control both and maintain its forces elsewhere, Spain had to recognize Portuguese independence in 1640. It also had, finally, to accept the independence of the United Provinces in 1648. The German states all came out of the war more powerful in relation to the empire. This meant that the heart of Europe was occupied by a weak and splintered political unit for centuries to come. The result was that France emerged from the war as the single dominant military and political power on the Continent, and the Habsburgs lost out to the Bourbons.

The peace treaty not only ended the war, but it also ended the way in which states related to one another and to their citizen—subjects. Boundaries were established and new states came into being. Whereas many regions had been subjected to overlapping jurisdictions (secular and ecclesiastical, for example), it now became the norm that individuals of a respective nation were subjected first and foremost to the laws and whims of their own respective government, rather than to those of neighbouring powers (religious or

secular). The war had other consequences too: large-scale religious warfare ceased; mercenaries who had caused so much destruction, especially
through pillage, were almost wholly replaced by State-paid, State-controlled
national armies; many began to see that the close interrelationship of
churches and states had greatly complicated the war and increased its ferocity. Many now began to suggest that religion should be mostly an individual
matter, and states (even with established churches) should stop being so
involved in and identified with any one religion, or any religion at all.
Experience not only with religious warfare, but also State-directed religious
coercion, underpinned demands in the eighteenth century for the disestab-
lishment of religion, and the separation of Church and State – an idea
enshrined in the American constitution of 1789.

THE RISE OF PURITANISM

As mentioned earlier, the growing crisis in the British Isles meant that the
British government had to drop its involvement in the wars racking
Germany from the 1620s onwards. Although the Elizabethan settlement
had brought stability and peace to the English situation, there had always
been a band of Protestants who wanted the State to go further in
Protestantizing the English Church. In 1603 the accession of the Scottish
house of Stuart to the English throne created a union of crowns that had
two differing Protestant settlements. North of the border, English
Protestant enthusiasts, or Puritans, were able to behold with jealous eyes
what they considered to be the thoroughly Protestant Presbyterian Kirk of
Scotland (they perhaps failed to note not only the enduring presence of
bishops, but also the enthusiasm of James VI/I, and later Charles I, for
those bishops). On the other hand, the Stuarts, who certainly preferred
the episcopal structure, arrived in England to find a Church firmly under
royal power, a situation that rather appealed to them. It was, however,
these Puritans and their clashes with Charles that would eventually lead to
a civil war that proved not only as bloody as the Thirty Years War, but also
managed to produce religious alliances as peculiar as Catholic France

funding Lutheran Sweden to liberate the Calvinist palatinate from Catholic Spain.

Puritans did not originally call themselves by that name; it was, along with Precisemen and Precisions, a term of abuse used by other Protestants. In the manner of most Protestant groupings during that period, who had an enormous assurance of their own righteousness and rightness, they simply called themselves 'the godly'. Thus, the word 'Puritan' described a type of religious belief and practice rather than a particular religious sect or denomination. As Patrick Collinson has suggested (*The Elizabethan Puritan Movement*, 1967), 'Puritanism had no content beyond what was attributed to it by its opponents.' Puritans knew and recognized themselves as members of particular churches or movements; they did not unite together under this name. Thus, one can safely speak of Anglicans or Presbyterians or Dissenters as Puritans, secure in the knowledge that they would almost certainly have condemned one another to prison!

In practice, though, this often disparate group was united by the conviction that the Elizabethan settlement had subordinated politics to 'true, godly religion' (by which they normally meant something Presbyterian and Calvinistic), and had allowed for the retention of too many 'superstitious' (that is, Catholic) practices. Among these were the vestments worn in the service of worship, the placement of the altar at the east end of the church (bearing in mind that most Puritans abhorred the concept of an altar in favour of a communion 'table'), the use of wafers instead of normal bread at Communion, and they endlessly debated the method in which Communion was received (standing, kneeling or seated).

Many of these Puritans had become even more convinced of the need for change when they were in exile under Mary Tudor. During their time overseas, Protestants such as Thomas Cartwright, Walter Travers and Andrew Melville had come into close contact with the magisterial reformers in Geneva and Emden (Germany). Having seen what they wanted, they returned to find that they did not get what they desired; instead they got Elizabeth's religious *via media* (middle way). However, although influenced by Calvinism, Puritans were not united on every issue of doctrine. This reflects the origins of the movement, which developed through several phases. They did share a belief that the Church had become corrupted by superstitious practices and by contact with pagan civilizations, particularly that of Rome. Most importantly of all, they deplored the involvement of politics and politicians (that is, non-Puritan rulers) in the Church.

As a result, they all argued for a restructuring and 'purification' of Church practice and belief through biblical supremacy. They also shared, to one degree or another, a belief in the priesthood of all believers. However, they radically differed on Church organization. In addition (a problem noted earlier), it was not exactly clear who would have the final word on what the Bible meant or how a believer was to exercise his (let alone her) priesthood. Put simply, as a group, the Puritans wanted the Church of England to resemble more closely the Protestant churches of Europe, especially the Church of Geneva. They objected to ornaments and rituals, such as vestments, church organs and genuflection, which they said were idolatrous, mere 'popish pomp and rags'. They also rejected the power of ecclesiastical courts, while favouring consistorial discipline (which, to someone on the sharp end, looked much like an ecclesiastical court with lay members). They refused to accept completely all the ritual directions and formulas of the Book of Common Prayer. Its imposition by force of law and government-sponsored inspections designed to ensure conformity sharpened Puritanism into a definite opposition movement.

By the end of Elizabeth's reign the movement was coalescing around support for one of two types of Church organization: Presbyterianism, which had a hierarchy of councils – sessions and synods – above the 'parish' church, or Congregationalism, in which each individual congregation was in control of its own affairs. As the bishops were the leaders in the imposition of the prayer book, the one form of government Puritans came most to dislike was episcopalianism, where the hierarchy was capped and controlled by bishops, even though Calvin had argued that there was no intrinsic problem with bishops, and many Lutheran (and a few Reformed) churches retained bishops. Initial opposition often used satire; for example, the *Martin Marprelate* series (1588–9) lampooned the government and the Church's hierarchy, especially the bishops.

The government was not slow to respond to the Puritan attacks. The theologian Richard Hooker wrote *Of the Laws of Ecclesiastical Polity* (1593) to counter arguments in favour of Presbyterianism. In particular, he said that he wrote to refute the views of 'brothers of the Geneva Church' and to support the developing Anglican *via media*. Hooker, like other conformists, did not reject the Puritans as Christians; rather, he would probably have agreed with the views of Matthew Hutton, Archbishop of York, who wrote:

> The Puritans (whose phantasticall zeale I mislike) though they differ
> in Ceremonies & accidentes, yet they agree wth us in substance of
> religion, & I thinke all or the moste p[ar]te of them love his
> Ma[jes]tie, & the p[re]sente state, & I hope will yield to conformitie.
> But the Papistes are opposite & contrarie in very many substantiall
> pointes of religion, & cannot but wishe the Popes authoritie & popish
> religion to be established.

However, the more forcefully and explicitly the established Church defended and explained itself, the more difficult the situation became for many Puritans (on their way to becoming separatists and Dissenters). The question was whether they should continue in outward conformity with a distasteful religious regime, or take the separatist and illegal step of withdrawal from the State Church? Each new controversy led to a fresh round of schisms, and therefore laid the ground for the patchwork of denominations that all draw their inheritance from Puritans within the Church of England who longed for a Calvinistic reform.

Many, in particular, looked to the model in Scotland. When James VI of Scotland became James I of England he appointed several known Puritans to powerful positions within the Church of England. This tended to balance somewhat the anti-Puritanism that was taking root in the episcopacy and increasingly identifying all things Puritan with all things Presbyterian. Nevertheless, James was not a Puritan, and regarded them with great suspicion; indeed, he viewed the Puritan movement as potentially dangerous to royal control of the Church. In particular, his experiences with the Kirk had made him deeply suspicious of Presbyterians and their 'controllability'. His authorization of the King James Bible can therefore be seen partly as an attempt to reinforce Anglican orthodoxy against the Geneva Bible. The latter was popular among Puritans, and was laced with anti-royalist translations and potentially revolutionary notes and marginalia.

Even the production of a vernacular Bible was a matter of debate and concern, not only because of the notes, but also because of the translation. For example, some Bibles chose to translate *episcopos* as 'bishop', while others translated it as 'elder'. The former suited the bishops of the Church of England, the latter the Presbyterians of the Kirk. Similarly, the Greek word *baptizein* could be transliterated into English as 'baptize' (in effect, a foreign word that meant whatever it was said to mean), or it could be translated into English as 'dunk' or 'immerse' (the Greek word being used for the process of immersing cloth in dye to colour it). The former suited proponents of infant baptism, while the latter would later prove very appealing to those who supported adult believers' baptism. Thus, even the vernacular word chosen was not without debate, and that was before men such as Luther and Zwingli chose to argue over what 'is' might mean!

Many Puritans, especially under Charles I, came to the conclusion that separation was the only option. The result was the rise of the Dissenter. Since Dissenters effectively excluded themselves from numerous careers that required official and explicit conformity to the Anglican settlement, many found themselves forced into a number of new industries and trades. For example, they tended to dominate the import/export business, and were eager to colonize the New World, which had the advantage of being far from governmental oversight. As their transatlantic trade with America flourished, many Dissenters in England grew quite wealthy. Meanwhile, the artisan classes became increasingly Puritan (though not necessarily separatist) thanks to the Puritan emphasis on preaching and evangelizing.

The French aristocrat, philosopher and historian Alexis de Tocqueville suggested in *Democracy in America* (1835, 1840) that the Pilgrims' Puritanism was the very thing that provided a firm foundation for American democracy, and in his view, these Puritans were hard-working, egalitarian and studious. The idea of economic discipline having a religious basis was echoed in the work of sociologist Max Weber (see pages 259–61), but both de Tocqueville and Weber argued that this discipline was not a force of economic determinism, but one factor among many that should be considered when evaluating the relative economic success of Puritanism. Others have suggested that some opposing tendencies within Puritanism – for example, a desire to create a just society and a moral fervour for bringing that society into existence – were not always likely to produce a free and wealth-producing culture, but might instead lead to something very narrow and intolerant.

In sum, the central tenet of Puritanism was God's supreme authority over human affairs, as expressed in the Bible (as they interpreted it, of course). This meant that they sought both individual and corporate conformance to the teaching of the Bible, and that they pursued moral purity down to the smallest detail, as well as ecclesiastical purity to the highest level. This led them, for instance, to support widespread literacy so that everyone could read the Bible. On a personal level, the Puritans emphasized that each person should be continually reformed by the grace of God to fight against sin. A humble and obedient life should be the goal of every Christian. This reliance on the Bible, and also on the Church fathers, produced some interesting results. For example, St John Chrysostom, a favourite of the Puritans, spoke eloquently against theatre, and the Puritans adopted his view when attacking this aspect of the decadence (as they saw it) of English culture. In New England this emphasis upon continual purity and determined focus on godliness led to bans on plays, maypoles and games of chance, all of which were considered immoral and a distraction from the important and vital quest for godliness. However, contrary to their present-day image (or the views of their supposed heirs), Puritans were not opposed to drinking alcohol in moderation or to enjoying their sexuality within the bounds of marriage as a gift from God, though they did publicly punish drunkenness and sexual relations outside marriage.

In terms of Church worship, the Puritans believed it should be strictly regulated by what is commanded in the Bible. They condemned as idolatrous or superstitious (often both) many worship practices, regardless of their age – indeed often because of their age. Like most of the Reformed churches on the Continent, Puritans wanted a minimum of what they saw as ritual or decoration, and preferred that worship focus almost wholly and totally on the preaching of God's Word. They also tended (as did Zwingli) to disapprove of music in church, quite often limiting it to the singing of the psalms.

Although they strongly disapproved of any system, such as Erastianism, that placed the Church under State control, they did not want separation of Church and State. Rather, they believed that the State had a divine obligation to work in cooperation with the Church (in practice, guided by the Church) to maintain and promote godliness, to protect and reward virtue, including 'true religion', and to punish wrongdoers. Although conforming and dissenting Puritans favoured a priesthood of all believers, one of the wrongs they expected the State to punish was anyone reading the Bible and coming to a radically different interpretation from their own. Many Dissenters, as their clashes with the State religion and the Crown grew, argued that any assertion of the divine right of kings was heresy. This, for obvious reasons, put them on a collision path with Charles I, who had learnt well from his father that kings ruled by divine right.

This desire to create not only a godly Church, but also a godly society peopled by godly citizens under the watchful eye and firm hand of godly magistrates, eventually led to a clash with the king, who had no intention of relinquishing his control of the Church, and was in any case motivated by an entirely different aesthetic of worship. The result was eventually open conflict that would result in the execution of Charles and the establishment (for the only time in its history) of a British republic.

Traditionally, this conflict has been known as the English Civil War. However, this is misleading as there was actually a series of interlocking wars and campaigns (1639–51) in England, Scotland and Ireland. Most present-day historians tend therefore to refer to all these conflicts collectively as the Wars of the Three Kingdoms. These were the outcome of tensions between the king and his subjects over religious and civil issues. Religious disputes centred on whether religion was to be dictated by the monarch or chosen by subjects, but guided and somewhat constrained by the wider 'godly' community. The related civil question was to what extent the king's rule was constrained by parliaments – in particular, his right to raise taxes and armed forces without parliamentary consent. The wars were also national in content as the Scots and Irish rebelled against English domination of the three kingdoms. With the victory of the English Parliament over the king, the Irish and the Scots, ironically, helped to determine the future of Britain as a constitutional monarchy with power centred on London. The Wars of the Three Kingdoms occurred at the same time as a number of similar conflicts elsewhere: the Fronde (France) and the rebellions of the Netherlands, Catalonia and Portugal (see page 123). This period can therefore be seen as one of general crisis in Europe, in which smaller conservative units within society resisted the centralizing tendencies of absolutist monarchs and their bureaucracies.

Indeed, the list of such rebellions on the Continent chimes much more obviously with the situation in the British Isles when one considers the host of sub-wars that actually united to comprise the Wars of the Three Kingdoms: the Bishops'/Prayer Book Wars (1639 and 1640), the Irish Rebellion (1641), the First English Civil War (1642–6), Confederate Ireland (1642–9), the Scottish Civil War (1644–5), the Second English Civil War (1646–8), the Cromwellian conquest of Ireland (1649) and the Third English Civil War (1650–1). It might seem logical to call these collectively the British Civil War, but this would be difficult for two reasons. First, the three kingdoms did not unite into a unit called 'the United Kingdom of Great Britain and

Ireland' until 1800. Second, many Irish historians are loath to group the nations under the name of a political unit that still exists and to which Ireland no longer belongs. This would be similar to avoiding calling the various colonial and Indian wars of eighteenth-century North America the 'American' wars or, worse, wars of the United States.

CLASHES BETWEEN CROWN AND CHURCH

James VI/I began the process of annoying his subjects as early as 1584, when he started appointing new bishops to dioceses in Scotland. The General Assembly protested, so he had to compromise: the bishops remained, but they left the Church to the Presbyterian ministers and the General Assembly. However, once in England, James tried again to impose episcopalianism in Scotland. He stopped the General Assembly from meeting, and appointed even more Scottish bishops. In 1618 he went further, holding a General Assembly and pushing through Five Articles that were episcopalian – and largely ignored by the Kirk and its ministers. In 1625 he was succeeded by his son Charles I, who was less skilful or restrained, and was crowned in St Giles' Cathedral, Edinburgh, in 1633 in an Anglican service. Opposition to his attempts to enforce Anglican practices reached a flashpoint when he introduced a Book of Common Prayer. The Kirk denounced both, and the Prayer Book was ignored or greeted with violence when anyone tried to use it. Charles's confrontation with the Scots came to a head in 1639, when he tried and failed to force them by military means. The clashes over the role of bishops and the introduction of the Prayer Book led to the Bishops' Wars in 1639, and again in 1640. By the end of the two campaigns, Charles faced a Scotland radicalized by his attacks, and declaring in their National Covenant that episcopacy was contrary to God's Word and that kings ruled by consent and contract, not divine right. Facing defeat in battle in 1640, Charles had to accept the situation in Scotland and, more importantly, was forced to recall the English Parliament because the wars had ravaged the treasury and he needed money – if, for no other reason, because he owed the Scots £300,000 in reparations.

On 3 November 1640 the English Parliament reconvened for what became known as the Long Parliament. In 1628 Charles had been forced to call on Parliament to pay for his role in the opening phases of the Thirty Years War. Parliament had voted the money, but had also got extensive concessions from the king in the form of a Petition of Right. Charles had found the experience so distasteful to his ideas about divine right that he endeavoured to reign without Parliament. This he managed to do until 1640. However, in the interim, leading Englishmen had seen the excessive lengths to which Charles would go to raise money without Parliament, and the innovative ways in which he could erode their perceived rights. It is hardly surprising, then, that when Parliament was presented with his request for money to fund his campaigns in the Bishops' Wars, the members first refused and declared themselves in permanent session. It then proceeded to present the king with an even longer list of grievances, which, unlike the Petition of Right, included complaints about religious practices. It was clear that Parliament had no intention of doing anything the king wanted until these grievances were addressed.

The conduct of Charles's lord deputy in Ireland, Thomas Wentworth, did not help the situation in England or Scotland. He had infuriated the Irish Catholics by repeated moves to confiscate their lands and grant them to Protestant colonists from England and Scotland. He had also angered them by enforcing new taxes, but denying Roman Catholics full rights as subjects. What made this situation really dramatic was his plan, in 1639, to offer Irish Catholics the reforms they had been looking for in return for their raising and paying for an Irish army to put down the Scottish rebellion. The army was to be officered by Protestants, but the image of an Irish Catholic army enforcing 'absolutist' divine-right rule horrified and angered both the Scottish and English Parliaments. Both threatened to mount invasions against Wentworth and Ireland.

Alienated by Protestant, English-speaking domination, and frightened by the threats coming from the English and Scottish Parliaments, a small group of Irish conspirators launched the Irish Rebellion, claiming that they were supporting the king's rights. The rising was marked by attacks, and even massacres, on the Protestant 'plantations' in Ireland. Rumours spread in England and Scotland that the killings had the king's approval and were a practice for planned moves against England and Scotland by the king leading Irish troops. As a result, the English Parliament refused to pay for a royal army to put down the rebellion, and instead raised their own armed forces. The king did the same, which meant that there were now two armies in England supposedly raised to put down an Irish uprising.

The actual details of the wars that followed need not detain us for long – rather, it is the religious aspects that are important and interesting. Nevertheless, some historical framework is useful. The two armies theoretically poised to invade Ireland simply fell to fighting each other as civil war broke out in England. The Scottish Covenanters, as the Presbyterians called themselves, sided with the English Parliament, joining the war in 1643; they were crucial in Parliament's victory. The royalist forces (often called Cavaliers as opposed to the parliamentary Roundheads) were eventually defeated by the New Model Army (the military force organized by Cromwell and the other parliamentarians), and the financial power of London, which backed Parliament. In 1646 Charles I surrendered. After failing to come to a compromise with Parliament, he was arrested and executed in 1649. This was the ultimate expression of the ideas about monarchy and 'contractual' government that first surfaced (coupled with religion) in the French Wars of Religion (see page 84).

In Ireland the rebel Catholics formed their own government (Confederate Ireland), hoping to aid the king in return for religious toleration and political autonomy. Troops from England and Scotland fought in Ireland, and Irish Confederate troops mounted an expedition to Scotland in 1644 that touched off the Scottish Civil War. Initial royalist victories in 1644–5 were reversed with the end of the First English Civil War and the return of the Scottish Covenanters' armies. After the end of the Second English Civil War, the victorious parliamentary forces, now under Oliver Cromwell, invaded Ireland and crushed the royalist–confederate alliance in 1649. At this point, though, the conservatism of some Scots – and their anger at having a Stuart king's head removed by the English (just as his grandmother's had been) – led to a split between England and Scotland. The Scots were unwilling to move towards a republic, and, as a result of the Bishops' Wars, had already secured a constitutional relationship with their king. Consequently, they crowned Charles's son as Charles II. Cromwell embarked on the conquest of Scotland in 1650–51. By the end of the wars, the Three Kingdoms were a unitary state called the English Commonwealth, in theory a republic, but in practice more of a military dictatorship.

What was really radical, though, was the religious situation that began to develop. As with the initial phases of the Reformation a century before, the turmoil of the wars allowed many people to think new ideas and to experiment with new practices. Moreover, the religious settlement in the Commonwealth was also experimental. Although there was wide religious freedom, this was not extended to Catholics. The Church of England (that is, a State Church) was abolished, along with the House of Lords and the Parliaments of Ireland and Scotland. Members of the House of Commons were sent home and not recalled, thus disappointing many who had hoped for a fairly democratic republic with male suffrage. In Ireland almost all lands belonging to Irish Catholics were confiscated as punishment for the rebellion of 1641; harsh penal laws were also passed against this community. Thousands of Parliamentarian soldiers were settled in Ireland on confiscated lands. Indeed, both Ireland and Scotland were occupied by the New Model Army during the Commonwealth interregnum.

SURVIVORS OF THE RESTORATION

As interesting as these political and constitutional arrangements were, they did not survive the royal restoration. What did survive were the religious ideas and groups that came into being during the chaos of the wars and the freedoms of the Commonwealth. Three of these groups can be examined for a taste of the variety of opinion that bloomed in the mid-seventeenth century. First, the very radical Levellers and Diggers, who were largely political in interest but not without some fascinating ideas about how to organize a 'Christian' society. Second, the Quakers emerged as a group dedicated to individual experiential religion and that largely rejected much 'orthodox', traditional Christian doctrine. In examining this group, one man, William Penn, will serve as an example not only of a Quaker, but also of what Quakerism might have meant had it made an impact at the more powerful and wealthier levels of society. The third group gives us a chance to see what happened to Puritanism not only after its 'defeat' with the restoration of the monarchy, but also when freed almost entirely from authority by that great liberator – a big, wide body of water. The Pilgrims took Puritanism to North America, turning their backs on what they considered an old world largely incapable of redemption, to build anew God's kingdom in virgin land. Cotton Mather, one of the earliest and most prolific writers and thinkers in North America, is examined later to provide a window into the mindset of these religious colonists (see page 146).

THE DIGGERS

The instigator of the Diggers was Gerrard Winstanley, who founded the group in 1649 (when Charles I was deposed and beheaded) as the True Levellers. This name came from their belief in Christian communism – the levelling or sharing of property – based on a reading of Acts 2: 42, 44–5 and 4: 32–7. (It has to be said that the vast majority of Protestants and Catholics did not interpret these passages this way.) The group wanted to reform the existing social order in favour of a simple agrarian lifestyle based upon small, egalitarian, rural communities. Once they put their ideas into practice and started to cultivate common land, they became universally known as 'Diggers'. Their radical reading of the Bible was not unique in mid-seventeenth century England. Indeed, it highlights the inherent problem in giving all Christians a Bible, telling them to read it and then to be guided by it in the light of their own consciences under the inspiration of the Holy Spirit. The result can be the pacifism of 'turn the other cheek' or the coercion of 'thou shalt not suffer a witch to live'.

The group was influenced by radical writings in the 1640s, which called for a democracy based on suffrage for each head of household. They tended to oppose so-called Fifth Monarchy Men, who wanted a theocracy (in effect, these were very radical Puritans who wanted to ensure England was godly in time for Christ's return in 1666). Winstanley and fourteen others published a pamphlet in which they called themselves the True Levellers to distinguish their ideas from the Levellers, who were identical to any outside observers. Their ideas developed a worldview that stressed an interrelationship between humans and nature, and acknowledged the inherent connections between people and their surroundings. So far, so Mennonite. What set the Diggers apart was the democratic, even anarchist aspect of their beliefs. They dreamed grandly and were not content simply to exist in quiet, self-contained communities. They argued that when the common people of England had formed into self-supporting communes, there would be no place in society for the ruling classes. The lack of any 'profit motive' (that is, no one to hire to work their fields or pay rent to them for use of their property) would eventually force the ruling elite to join the communes or starve.

In 1649 the government learnt that the Diggers had started farming common land and removing enclosing walls, ditches and hedges on St George's Hill at Weybridge in Surrey. Fearing something sinister, the local New Model Army commander was sent to investigate. He interviewed Winstanley and decided that the group was more likely to starve than start a revolt, and suggested that the local landowners who had complained should consider using the courts instead of the army. The landowners decided that simple intimidation (beatings and arson) would be quicker. Eventually the Diggers were tried and condemned as Ranters.

The Ranters were a truly bizarre group, which may not even have existed. Their central idea was pantheism (that God is in every creature). They denied the authority of the Church and the Bible, refused to recognize any priests or ministers, and instead called upon men to 'hearken to the Jesus within'. Ranters were often associated with nudity, which they may have used as a form of social protest, as well as a symbolic expression of abandoning earthly goods.

In any case, the Diggers lost the case and moved on before the army could evict them. Some of the evicted Diggers moved a short distance to Little Heath. Eleven acres (about five hectares) were cultivated, six houses built, winter crops harvested, and several pamphlets published. After some initial indifference and support, they were again moved on. A few other colonies tried to form, but in the end the movement never amounted to more than a couple of hundred people, and disappeared by 1651 as a result of the concerted efforts of the army, the courts and local landowners. However, although they were few in number, the Diggers highlight yet again the amazing ability of radicalism to take root in a society and use the Bible as its theoretical underpinning. Anyone who thinks that the Bible is by nature a conservative, pro-capitalist document would do well to consider the example of the Diggers.

QUAKERS

The Religious Society of Friends, commonly known as Quakers because of their habit of shaking or quaking when moved by the Spirit, began in England during the civil-war period as a result of disaffection with the main Protestant sects or denominations. Traditionally, the Dissenter and weaver's son George Fox has been seen as the founder of the movement, though perhaps it would be more accurate to describe him as its most famous early exponent. Its opposition to violence of any variety means that the Society of Friends is considered one of the so-called 'peace churches' – those denominations committed to non-violence and pacifism. Most (Hutterites, Amish, Mennonites) of these denominations have their roots in the radical reformation of the sixteenth century, though some, like the Friends, arose in the seventeenth century and others, such as Jehovah's Witnesses, are nineteenth century in origin. Although Quakers have never been numerous worldwide, they have had a disproportionate impact in some areas, such as

Pennsylvania (particularly Philadelphia), Birmingham (England) and Greensboro (North Carolina).

Quakerism arose during the Commonwealth, when the Church of England was banned and religious 'liberty' allowed, as a breakaway group from Puritanism. The general response to this new religion reminds us that Cromwellian religious toleration was not only withheld from Catholics, but also from certain Protestant groups. Quakers were imprisoned and beaten in both the British Isles and the British colonies. In the Massachusetts Bay colony, Quakers were banished on pain of death. Some Quakers were even executed for their beliefs; most famously, Mary Dyer was hanged in Boston Square when she returned from permanent banishment. In addition, Quakers were effectively banned, by various required religious oaths (called tests), from sitting in the Westminster Parliament from 1698 to 1833.

Unlike other groups that emerged within Christianity, the Religious Society of Friends has tended towards having little hierarchical structure and no creeds. Most Quakers would agree that their faith does not fit within traditional Christian categories, but is an expression of another way of experiencing God. The various branches have widely divergent beliefs and practices, but the central concept to many Friends may be what is variably called the 'inner light', 'the God within', 'the inward Christ', or 'the spirit of Christ within'. Early Friends, though, more often used terms such as 'truth', 'the seed' and 'the pure principle', expecting that each person would be transformed as Christ formed in them. George Fox and the other early Quaker preachers believed that direct experience of God was available to all people without mediation – namely, ministers, sacraments, or even the Bible. Much of Quaker thought was based on trying to hear what God was saying and allowing the Spirit freedom inside a person. As the Quaker writer and son of a Puritan magistrate Isaac Penington wrote in a letter dated 1670: 'It is not enough to hear of Christ, or read of Christ, but this is the thing – to feel him my root, my life, my foundation.'

In this sense, then, it is appropriate to stress the mysticism of Quaker thought. However, this is not medieval mysticism, which tended to be

solitary. Quaker mysticism was communal, largely expressed through meetings where the Friends gather to listen to God. In addition, Quakers did
not follow their mystical revelations into withdrawal from the world – quite
the opposite. Action, they believed, led to greater spiritual understanding
for both the individual and the entire meeting. This mystical connection
resulted in something truly radical for a group arising from Protestantism –
a downplaying of the Bible. Robert Barclay, one of the greatest writers and
thinkers of the Society of Friends, wrote that the Bible was only 'a declaration of the fountain, and not the fountain itself, therefore [it is] not to be
esteemed the principal ground of all Truth and knowledge, nor yet the
adequate primary rule of faith and manners'. Fox also rejected the authoritative nature of the Bible, as well as established ecclesiastical structures in
replying to Protestant ministers defending both. Fox said that he 'was
commanded to tell them God did not dwell in temples made with hands.
But I told them what it was, namely, the Holy Spirit, by which the holy men
of God gave forth the scriptures, whereby opinions, religions and judge-
ments were to be tried; for it led into all Truth, and so gave the knowledge
of all Truth.'

In effect, Quakers believed they had solved the conundrum that had
faced Protestantism since its outset – how to avoid conflict over interpretation of an authoritative text, in this case the Bible. Early Friends believed
that Christ would never lead them in ways that contradicted the Bible, so
making the Bible subordinate to the Spirit prevented conflicts among
Quaker leaders and their understanding of the Bible. It is an interesting
solution, but not one that has appealed to most Protestants, let alone most
Protestant leaders. Needless to say, this did lead to conflict, and in time the
various groups of Friends subdivided into a spectrum ranging from 'evangelical' Friends, who accepted the Bible's authority, to those who believed
that revelation continued and could lead in directions seemingly at variance
with the Bible.

Perhaps most interesting of all was how Quakers believed that their
faith should be practised and their God worshipped. Early Friends did not

believe in relying upon outward rites and sacraments, believing that holiness can exist in every activity: all life was sacred. They experienced baptism by the Holy Spirit as an inward, transforming experience, and knew communion with Christ in the midst of gathered worship in 'watchful' silence. Thus, they did not perform baptism as a rite of membership. Friends believed that any meal with others could be a form of communion, and therefore had no Eucharistic ritual. Having said that, there was also no ban on participating in or practising such rites as long as they did not become an obstacle to personal, mystical communion with God.

This simplicity extended from worship to life. Quakers traditionally wore plain clothes in order to address three concerns: the vanity and superiority associated with fanciness, the conformity associated with wearing the latest fashions, and the wastefulness of frequently buying new styles and other adornments. At one time this practice of plainness allowed other people to identify (and persecute) Quakers easily. In time many Friends saw an attachment to plainness as a type of holier-than-thou vanity and abandoned it. Plainness in speech addressed other concerns: honesty, class distinction and vestiges of paganism. These principles were put into practice by affirming rather than swearing oaths (based on Matthew 5:34), setting fixed prices for goods (a novelty in the seventeenth century, when haggling was much more common), avoiding the use of honorific titles (especially galling in a status-conscious society), using numbers rather than names for the days of the week and the months of the year (both were pagan in origin), and using familiar forms for the second-person pronoun (this produced the extensive retention of the informal 'thee/thou', which English abandoned in favour of the universal use of the formal 'you' – this is why the King James Bible addresses God as 'thee': it is how seventeenth-century people addressed their closest friends and relatives – a courtesy Friends extended to everyone). Just as shocking as refusing to recognize distinctions of class, Friends ignored traditional gender boundaries. Both women and men were granted equal authority to speak in meetings for worship. Fox's wife, Margaret Fell, was as vocal and literate as her husband, publishing several Quaker tracts.

It is not perhaps surprising to find that Quakerism had little appeal to the elite in seventeenth-century England. Refusing to acknowledge status or gender, and addressing everyone, prince, pauper or pet, in the same way was less than enticing. Moreover, the threat of persecution was very real indeed. Nevertheless, William Penn stands out as an example of a wealthy, socially prominent Quaker. The son of an admiral, Penn came from a distinguished Anglican family, but became a Quaker at the age of twenty-two. His father, who held an extensive estate in Ireland, had hoped his son might gain preferment in Charles II's newly restored court, but instead William was imprisoned in 1668 for writing a tract (*The Sandy Foundation Shaken*) that attacked the doctrine of the trinity.

Worse was to follow. Penn was expelled from Christ Church, Oxford, for being a Quaker, and was arrested several times. At his most famous trial Penn pleaded to see a copy of the charges laid against him, as was his legal right, but the judge, the Lord Mayor of London, refused. Despite heavy pressure from the judge to convict, the jury returned a 'not guilty' verdict. The Lord Mayor then jailed Penn again (for contempt of court) and had the jury arrested too. The members of the jury, fighting their case from prison, managed to win the right for all English juries to be free from the control of judges, and to assess not just the facts of the case, but also the law itself (in the US legal system this is called 'jury nullification'). Penn decided that England could provide no safe haven for Quakers, so, along with some others, gained a land grant to half of what is now New Jersey. He drafted a charter (or constitution) for the soon-to-be-founded colony, which guaranteed free and fair trials by jury, freedom of religion, freedom from unjust imprisonment, and free elections. This original land grant was greatly extended when Penn negotiated with Charles II over the repayment of a loan made to Penn's father in 1681. Penn originally called this new colony Sylvania (wooded), but the king added 'Penn' to the front to honour the admiral. The freedom of religion in the colony of Pennsylvania (complete freedom of religion for everybody who believed in God) brought not only English, Welsh, German and Dutch Quakers to the colony, but also

Huguenots fleeing the revocation of the Edict of Nantes by Louis XIV, Mennonites, Amish and Lutherans from Catholic German states (as the re-Catholicization of many imperial and Habsburg lands continued apace – see pages 119–23).

Penn even visited his colony (literally his because his family owned it under royal charter until the American Revolution) from 1682–4. After the building plans for Philadelphia (city of 'Brotherly Love') had been completed, Penn explored the interior. He befriended the local Indians, even, according to tradition, signing a treaty with them to ensure they were paid fairly for their lands (£1200). Penn even learnt several different Indian dialects in order to communicate without interpreters. He introduced laws saying that if a European did an Indian wrong, there would be a fair trial with an equal number of people from both groups deciding the matter (similar to the provisions of the Edict of Nantes in cases involving Catholics and Huguenots). His measures in this matter proved successful. Even though later colonists did not treat the Indians as fairly as Penn and his first group of colonists had done, later settlers and Indians remained at peace in Pennsylvania much longer than in the other English colonies. Unsurprisingly, the French writer Voltaire (among others) not only praised the 'Great Treaty', but noted its irony as well: it was 'the only treaty between [Indians and Europeans] that was *not* [author's emphasis] ratified by an oath, and that was never infringed'. It is worth noting, though, that this liberality did not extend to Africans: Penn owned and traded in slaves.

While Pennsylvania was settled with almost every hue of the denominational spectrum, colonies to the south were being founded with the Anglican Church established by law. Here the prejudices and legal restrictions of England were replicated, but in some, such as Maryland (founded by Caecilius Calvert, Lord Baltimore, a Catholic member of the Irish peerage), even Catholics were tolerated. To the north, however, the ultimate losers of the civil wars, the Puritans, were getting a chance to build their own utopia. In effect, the North American colonies provided various religious denominations with the chance to compete in proving just how 'right' they were by building a truly 'godly' (as each would see it) society in an area unfettered by the history and complexity of Europe. The Pilgrims and other Puritan settlers of New England were especially convinced that they would be successful in constructing a 'city set on a hill' that would become a 'light unto the world'.

PILGRIMS

Early settlers of the Plymouth Colony in New England are commonly known as 'Pilgrims' or 'Pilgrim Fathers'. Their leadership came from a religious congregation that had fled a volatile political environment in the east Midlands for the relative calm of Holland. Being separatist Puritans, they had concluded that their differences with the Church of England were irreconcilable and that their worship had to be organized independently. Concerned with losing their cultural and linguistic identity, the group later arranged with English investors to establish a new colony in North America. Established in 1620, it would ultimately succeed in becoming the second English colony (after Virginia). The Pilgrims' story, often embellished, has become a central theme in American historical and cultural identity.

With the increasing anti-Puritanism of the Church of England under first James, then Charles I (and William Laud, Archbishop of Canterbury), many Puritans, especially non-conforming separatists, found living in England untenable. As William Bradford recorded in *Of Plymouth Plantation*, his chronicle of the earliest years of the new colony:

> But after these things they could not long continue in any peaceable condition, but were hunted & persecuted on every side, so as their former afflictions were but as flea-bitings in comparison of these which now came upon them. For some were taken & clapt up in prison, others had their houses besett & watcht night and day, & hardly escaped their hands; and ye most were faine to flie & leave their howses & habitations, and the means of their livelehood.

The community had mixed fortunes in Holland, and some members became embroiled in the debates between Calvinists and Arminians (see page 148). All decided, though, that they needed to move. One major motivating factor was that everyone could see that hostilities were soon to be resumed between Spain and the United Provinces (see pages 147–8 and 150).

After various false starts, the *Mayflower* finally reached land in November 1620. Hoping to sail further south, the ship was forced to turn back by bad weather and anchor in present-day Provincetown Harbor. In one of the first exploratory trips on land an artificial mound was found near the dunes, which the explorers partially uncovered and found to be a native grave. Further along, a similar and more recent mound was found and opened. Grave goods, including baskets of maize were found, which the colonists took and placed in an iron kettle they also found, intending to use the stolen corn as seed for planting. Further along, after taking more corn, they found a pair of native dwellings. Nobody was home, so the colonists went through the owners' belongings and stole 'some of the best things'. They attributed the find to 'God's good providence'. House-breaking, grave desecration and the theft of grave goods served as an interesting if chilling harbinger of things to come in the relationship between European Christians and the natives of the region.

In fact, local people had already had a chance to familiarize themselves with their new Christian neighbours, as Englishmen had already visited the site for fishing. In the Cape Cod area relations were poor following a visit several years earlier. Twenty people from Patuxet, the place that would presently become New Plymouth, and another seven from Nausett had been captured and carried to Spain to be sold as slaves into Spanish Catholic hands. Ironically, one of the Patuxet abductees, Tisquantum, became an ally of the Plymouth colony. The Pokanoket people, who also lived near by, had developed a particular dislike for the English after one group came in, captured numerous people, and shot them aboard their ship. Moreover, there had already been reciprocal killings at Martha's Vineyard and Cape Cod. More importantly, the vast majority of the local inhabitants had already died as a result of the introduction of smallpox, leaving much of the land 'vacant' for new settlement. Or, as the writer Cotton Mather put it, smallpox had cleared the land 'of those pernicious creatures to make room for better growth' – another example, the Puritans believed, of 'God's good providence'. Thus, the Puritans found a land to occupy and to begin the arduous task of building a New Jerusalem and a New Israel.

Cotton Mather, in addition to being famous for persecuting witches, was also a great exponent of this 'experiment'. He provided much of the theological and theoretical rationale for the work being conducted in New England and the building of this new society of the 'godly'. At fifteen he received his bachelor's degree from Harvard College (later University), followed three years later by his master's. The author of nearly five hundred books and pamphlets, Mather's prolific output made him one of the most influential religious leaders in the colonies. He struck a 'moral tone', demanding that second- and third-generation Puritans return to the theological roots of Puritanism. His writings form one of the more important bodies of documents in colonial American history, as they reflect a particular tradition of seeing and understanding the significance of place, especially coupled with God's providence – nothing happens by accident. As a Puritan thinker and social conservative, Mather drew on the figurative language of the Bible to explain his views. In particular, his review of the Puritan colonial experiment in New England sought to explain signs of his time as predicting the success of the venture. He began, or rather popularized, the tradition of seeing success as a sign of God's blessing on the colonial (later American) venture.

As a result, the experiences of these early Puritan settlers, both intellectual and physical, became elevated in the subsequent American way of thinking about its appointed place among other nations. God's hand was seen in the historical experiences of the godly in New England. Most Christian groups tended to read current events and history with a view to understanding God's will. However, convinced that they had been saved from persecution as a 'godly' remnant and settled (planted like seed) in 'good soil', the Puritans of New England were convinced that they had a special mission from God not only to build, but also to maintain this new godly society. As they prospered and grew, they were further convinced that theirs was the 'right' path, for surely God would not bless error, only godliness. Further success, by which they usually meant wealth, comfort, happiness and bountiful food, simply deepened this conviction. Profoundly convinced that God actively took part in the affairs of this world (their descendants as Deists would soon reject this view – see page 155), their Calvinism allowed them no other interpretation of their successes.

ARMINIUS V. GROTIUS

It is perhaps worth while to end this chapter by returning to one other great Calvinist experiment in building a godly society. The Dutch also flourished during the seventeenth century, and many interpreted this as a sign of God's favour. However, the United Provinces in the Low Countries was not a godly, separate society; rather, it was a culture that tolerated (albeit to the annoyance of the Calvinist ministers of the national Church) Catholics, Anabaptists and Jews. Interestingly, few if any Calvinists – seeing God's blessing in the material and military successes of the republic – ever felt that God was rewarding religious toleration. Rather, the continued existence of the 'ungodly' in their midst was seen by the Calvinists as simply an impediment to greater divine blessings and the ultimate explanation for every natural disaster or military setback in the years when war resumed with Spain. Even worse (as we shall see), the very foundations of Calvinist thought – predestination, a doctrine enthusiastically shared by Luther – were challenged from within. It seems, therefore, most appropriate to end this chapter by considering how Dutch Calvinism turned on itself in the very midst of Dutch success against Catholic Spain.

During the period of the Twelve Years Truce, beginning in 1609, the Dutch not only enjoyed the freedom to make money, which they did quite enthusiastically, but also the time to engage in theological debate and schism, which they did very successfully, tinged with politics. Two factions emerged in the Dutch camp along political and religious lines. On one side were the Arminians, followers of Jacobus Arminius, a leading theologian, supported by major merchants and thinkers, such as Johan van Oldenbarnevelt (Land's Advocate of Holland), and on the other side was Hugo Grotius, the great philosopher of law. The Arminians tended to be favoured by well-to-do republican merchants, who found aspects of the Calvinist doctrine of predestination problematic. They were opposed by the more radical Gomarists, named after Franciscus Gomarus, a leading theologian, who supported Prince Maurice of Nassau. In 1617 the conflict escalated when the republicans got the Sharp Resolution passed because this allowed cities to persecute the Gomarists. (The Arminians may have disliked Calvinist predestination, but they seem not to have minded Calvinist coercion.) Prince Maurice accused van Oldenbarnevelt of treason, had him arrested and, in 1619, executed. Hugo Grotius, who had been arrested with van Oldenbarnevelt, managed to escape. The slumbering frictions between the new merchant–regent class and the more traditional military nobility had come to a violent eruption. Fortunately for the Dutch, the resumption of war with Spain in 1622 put an end to the threat of an equally violent civil war.

But Arminianism was more than just a religious cover for political action, and its impact, especially on Wesley and Methodism (see pages 164 and 168) strongly supports this. Indeed, it was almost certainly the case that for those involved the religious issues were much more important than any related political matters. Arminius questioned many of the beliefs that were seen, by about 1600, as foundational or fundamental to Calvinism and even Lutheranism. His views seem at first to be traditionally Protestant: humans are naturally unable to make any effort towards salvation; salvation is possible by grace alone; works are not the cause, nor do they contribute to salvation. So far so good, but then Arminius went down an entirely different path from Calvin or Luther: God's election is conditional on faith in Jesus; the atonement of Jesus (His death on the cross) was potentially for all people; God 'allows' His grace to be resisted by those unwilling to believe; salvation can be lost, as it is conditional upon continued faith.

Arminius held that the traditional understanding of divine sovereignty, omnipotence (all-powerful), omniscience (all-knowing), election (how a person is chosen to be saved or damned) and predestination (things happen as God knows they will happen) made God the author of sin. Arminius died before his views could be tested before a Dutch national synod, but his supporters presented their case as Five Articles of Remonstrance (hence they are often known as Remonstrants). Prince Maurice of Nassau sided with their Calvinist opponents, who alleged that the Remonstrants were simply resurrecting a type of Catholic 'works' salvation'. Maurice systematically removed Arminian magistrates from office and called a national synod at Dordrecht. This Synod of Dort excluded Arminian delegates, but had Calvinist representatives from other countries. In 1618 it condemned Arminius and his followers as heretics. It also codified Calvinist theology with its famous Five Points of Calvinism in response to the Five Articles of Remonstrance. Arminians across Holland were removed from office, imprisoned, banished and sworn to silence. Twelve years later Holland officially granted Arminianism protection as a religion, although animosity between Arminians and Calvinists continued.

In English the Five Points of Calvinism are known by the acronym TULIP, an amusing recognition of their Dutch origin. The early magisterial reformers, while they might have decried the emphasis placed on these five issues, would almost certainly have agreed with the basic beliefs they expressed. The first affirmed Total depravity – that people are fallen as a result of Adam and Eve's sin in all their parts and are therefore unable to do anything towards their own salvation. The second is that election, or being chosen by God to be saved or damned, is Unconditional – in other words, God simply chooses and there is no reason other than his own choice. The third declares that Christ did not actually or potentially die on the cross for everyone; rather, his act of atonement was Limited to those already elected or chosen. The fourth view was that when faith arises as a result of grace, the gift of faith is Irresistible: a person cannot refuse the gift. A fallen person is dead in their sin and called to new life – an analogy is made with Christ calling Lazarus back to life – being dead, Lazarus was not able to accept or refuse the call; he simply rose from the dead. The final point is that once a person is chosen, atoned and called, that person will **P**ersevere in faith until death. A live, chosen, saved person stays alive, chosen and saved because he is sustained in grace entirely by God's action and will not lose salvation because of anything he does or can do. As we shall see below, it was not just Arminius who thought that these ideas made God the author of sin or allowed some 'Christians' to think they could do whatever they wanted without becoming damned.

The debate about Arminianism continued, but the Spanish invasion of 1622 turned Dutch attention to the more vital issue of national survival. The Dutch had some early successes, capturing key fortifications along the border. However, they overreached themselves when they moved further into the southern (Spanish) Netherlands in an attempt to take Antwerp and Brussels. While the local population may have loathed the Spanish at the end of the sixteenth century, the Catholics had been as busy Catholicizing the population in the south as the Calvinists had been Protestantizing the north during the truce. The result was that the Dutch were rather surprised to find that their fellow Netherlanders did not welcome 'liberation' from Catholic Spain by an army of iconoclastic Calvinists. Forced to withdraw, it was now the turn of Spain to try to strike the decisive blow. In 1639 Spain sent an armada bound for Flanders, loaded with 20,000 troops to defeat the northern 'rebels'. However, the armada was decisively defeated at the Battle of the Downs on 31 October. This victory had historic consequences far beyond the Dutch Revolt, as it permanently broke the back of Spanish sea power.

The result of the warfare from 1622 to 1639 was a stalemate more or less along the pre-existing border. On 30 January 1648 the war ended with the Treaty of Münster, part of the wider, pan-European Peace of Westphalia, which ended the Thirty Years War. The Dutch Republic was recognized as an independent state, and retained control of the limited territories (parts of Flanders, Brabant and Limbourg) taken in the later stages of the war.

Along with the Restoration of Charles II, the conclusion of the Dutch Revolt and the Thirty Years War brought an end to large-scale religious warfare in Europe.

AN UNEASY PEACE

By the end of the seventeenth century, religion had ceased to be a significant motivating factor in European power politics. For over a century religious warfare had swept across Europe, touching almost every state except Italy (which had enough warfare of the purely secular variety), Spain (which had just united after centuries of religious warfare against the Muslim Moors) and Norway. Although religion played a part in much of this violence, it was also clear that religion, when dominated by the State, was more likely to become simply a tool of the State. It is necessary to recall only the number of Catholic states that supported the Protestants during the Thirty Years War and vice versa. In that, the radicals appeared to have been right – submission to and reliance upon the coercive power of the State simply returned Christianity to the disastrous path it had taken when it had allowed itself to become enslaved to the Roman state under Constantine.

It was also clear that over a century of warfare had not diminished the ability of religion to excite and motivate Europeans. Tridentine Catholicism was deep in the splendour of the baroque, and Catholic charity was flourishing in the hands of numerous new monastic and semi-monastic orders. Protestantism showed no signs of losing its ability to reinvent itself in any number of new and interesting subdivisions. While magisterial Protestantism had wedded itself to the interests of the elite – and this very often meant merchant, proto-capitalist elites – radical Protestantism constantly evidenced an enthusiasm for dramatic social experimentation. The sociologist Max Weber (see pages 259–61) stressed the supposed capitalistic 'background beat' to Protestantism, but radicals remind us that there was also a Protestantism that wanted to hold property and raise children in common, to eschew wealth for simple living and contented poverty, to avoid any entanglements with big government in favour of small-community (male-dominated) democracy, and to reject the State's offer of power and coercion in return for the power of persuasion and example.

The big questions remained. To what extent would Protestantism be a religion of the wider community and its institutions, a faith permeating and directing the lives of all citizens? Would it rather be a faith of a committed few living their own lives, disciplining themselves, in the midst of an unbelieving world? Was Protestantism to be a faith that stressed creeds, catechism and confessions, or abandoned concern over doctrine to focus on the practical issues of poverty and injustice? Would the believers, exercising their priesthood, be allowed to read their own Bibles and, led by the Spirit and answering to their own consciences, work out for themselves their own salvation? Over a century of warfare may have convinced most Europeans that violent coercion was unworkable, but it was not clear what this would mean in practice for Europe's competing beliefs.

5

GREAT
AWAKENINGS

I HAD BELIEVED THAT [CONNECTICUT WAS] THE
LAST RETREAT OF MONKISH DARKNESS, BIGOTRY,
AND ABHORRENCE ... I JOIN YOU, THEREFORE,
IN SINCERE CONGRATULATIONS THAT THIS DEN
OF THE PRIESTHOOD IS AT LENGTH BROKEN UP,
AND THAT A PROTESTANT POPEDOM IS NO
LONGER TO DISGRACE THE AMERICAN HISTORY
AND CHARACTER. IF BY RELIGION WE [MEAN]
SECTARIAN DOGMAS ... THEN ... THIS WOULD
BE THE BEST OF ALL POSSIBLE WORLDS, IF THERE
WERE NO RELIGION IN IT. BUT IF THE MORAL
PRECEPTS, INNATE IN MAN ... IF THE SUBLIME
DOCTRINES OF ... DEISM TAUGHT US BY JESUS OF
NAZARETH ... CONSTITUTE TRUE RELIGION, THEN,
WITHOUT IT, THIS WOULD BE ... INDEED, A HELL.

THOMAS JEFFERSON
IN A LETTER TO JOHN QUINCY ADAMS (1817)

AFTER A CENTURY OF RELIGIOUS WARFARE, EUROPE
settled into peace divided into opposing denominations. With the notable
exception of France, states across the Continent now had single, official,
State-supported denominations. In the Netherlands, though, the official
Church was not able to rely on State coercion to enforce conformity.
Likewise, Switzerland was divided into two denominational camps, with
some shared territories enjoying both. In central Europe re-Catholicization
was continuing apace. In some areas, such as Bohemia, this was done with
the support of the coercive power of the State; in others, such as Poland,
Catholic missionary organizations and, in particular, the excellent educational system supplied to children (mostly boys) by groups such as the
Jesuits were having great success in converting 'the next generation' back to
the old faith.

Just as importantly, though, the experience of violent, catastrophic
religious warfare had made many suspicious of State involvement and had
deeply shocked even more. The various denominations learnt to coexist,
whether within communities or in terms of high-powered political manoeu-
vring. Individuals got on with their lives, some seeking (through various
'awakenings') a deeper, more personal (less State-driven) faith, and others
turning away from an approach to religion (traditional, denominational
Christianity) that had become tainted with the blood of victims of
inter-denominational violence. Since denominationalism was to become

intricately linked with the new philosophical outlook of the day (Enlightenment), the most obvious place to begin this discussion is with Deism. Nevertheless, while Deism attracted some of the greatest minds and most prominent leaders of the day, the common people – especially Protestants who could not turn to the semi-monastic movements that exploded in baroque Catholicism – yearned for a faith that was vibrant, alive and personal: a faith that belonged to them, not the State. In Lutheran lands this would produce Pietism; in the English-speaking world Methodism. These two movements combined with a general renewal of spirituality in many Calvinistic denominations to produce the First Great Awakening (as the renewal movements were called in North America). Later, a second period of spiritual renewal, the so-called Second Great Awakening, would produce not only a rekindling of many of the communal ideas of the radical reformation, but would also lead to an explosion of new denominations, with dramatic consequences for Protestant society and culture (as we shall see in Chapter 6).

DEISM

A movement, not a denomination, Deism was a religious offshoot of the Enlightenment, the philosophical movement of the eighteenth century that advocated Reason as the basis for ethics and government (among other things) rather than revealed, objective truth. Its general tenets were a denial of the Trinity and the divinity of Christ. It also tended to reject the historical accuracy of biblical miracles, regarding them as allegorical or mythical. It also denied the active involvement of God in history, thereby denying Providence as most traditional Calvinistic Protestants would have understood it. God was the Great Creator or the Prime Mover responsible for creating the natural world, but that same God thereafter made no direct interventions in his creation. The most common metaphor for explaining this Deistic view was that God was like a clockmaker. He had made the entire workings of the clock and set it running, but from that point onwards the clock simply ran (the metaphor collapses when one asks who winds the clock periodically to keep it running). Although it can be said to be a type of Unitarianism or Socinianism (see pages 107–10), in reality it was a new movement. One thing is clear: by any normative definition of Protestantism or Christianity, adherents of Deism were not orthodox – not Christian.

Indeed, Christians and Deists of the period considered each to be a distinct 'religion', although they shared a common text, the Bible – understood and used very differently, and a common way of discussing their faiths. It is worth noting one of the easiest ways of distinguishing adherents to both groups. Christians regularly talked about Christ, especially Jesus, while Deists confined themselves to discussing God (they regarded Jesus as an exemplary human being). An awareness of the difference between a Christian and a Deist, as well as the importance of language, can be seen in Thomas Jefferson's comments about George Washington when he retired to Mount Vernon:

> Dr. Rush told me (he had it from Asa Green [chaplain to Congress]) that when the clergy addressed General Washington, on his departure from the government, it was observed in their consultation that he had never, on any occasion, said a word to the public which showed a belief in the Christian religion, and they thought they should so pen their address as to force him at length to disclose publicly whether he was a Christian or not. However, he observed, the old fox was too cunning for them. He answered every article of their address particularly, except that, which he passed over without notice.

It was certainly clear to Jefferson that Washington was not a Christian, but at the same time had no great desire to offend the Protestant, Christian sympathies of the assembled ministers. Washington's own views on denominationalism (and, indeed, ethnicity, race and immigration) are even more apparent in a letter he wrote in 1784 when seeking suitable workmen for some repairs at Mount Vernon: 'If they are good workmen, they may be of

Asia, Africa, or Europe. They may be Mohometans, Jews or Christians of any Sect, or they may be Atheists.' This highlights a Deist's indifference to confessional distinctions.

While most Deists simply avoided organized religion (as Washington did – he never attended Communion services lest his unwillingness to receive the bread and wine occasioned comment), others took the more distinctive and 'normative Protestant' step of forming yet another denomination. Many more Deists organized themselves into societies, mostly gnostic, in believing that study could lead to greater enlightenment and access to secret (arcane) and hidden (hermetic) knowledge. Freemasonry, which counted many of the Founding Fathers among its membership, is the best example of this type of group. However, for those who desired a more traditional approach to Deist ideas, there was the formation of English-speaking Unitarianism.

UNITARIANISM

Between 1548 and 1612 we find a string of anti-Trinitarians executed (or saved by recantation) littering the English landscape. These had some connection with Continental Socinianism. Thus, in 1609, we see the dedication of a Latin version of the Socinian Racovian Catechism to James VI of Scotland and I of England: the two men responsible for the publication were burnt. In 1648 denial of the Trinity was made a capital crime under the Commonwealth established after the English Civil War, but it was not enforced; indeed, Oliver Cromwell intervened to save two condemned Socinians (Paul Best and John Biddle) from the stake. In London, Biddle led Socinian conventicles in 1652–4 and 1658–62. In addition to his own writings, he reprinted (1651) and translated (1652) the Racovian Catechism, and the *Life of Socinus* (1653).

This movement, calling itself Unitarian, came into the open in 1705 when Thomas Emlyn, while leading a London parish of the Church of England, became the first preacher to describe himself as Unitarian. This was contrary to the Toleration Act, 1689, which excluded from livings in the Church all who preached or wrote against the Trinity. This emergence of English Socinianism, under the name of Unitarianism, was coupled with the reappearance (since the early Church) of Arianism or semi-Arianism, which denied Jesus any divinity. Samuel Clarke's *Scripture Doctrine of the Trinity* (1712) introduced Arian concepts to a wider audience.

Unitarian ministers and congregations began to appear not just in the established Church, but also in dissenting chapels with defections from the General Baptists, the Presbyterians and the Congregationalists. They did not necessarily unite denominationally, but were connected by a shared rejection of the historic doctrines of the ancient creeds of the Church. The leading figures in stressing the Arian, human-alone Christology (doctrine of Christ) were mostly Congregationalists, such as Nathaniel Lardner, Caleb Fleming, Joseph Priestley and Thomas Belsham. The formation of a distinct Unitarian denomination in England dates from the secession (1773) of Theophilus Lindsey from the Anglican Church. The (Protestant) Church of Ireland had already seen a break under Dr William Robertson, who has been called 'the father of Unitarian nonconformity'.

A rapid number of defections led to an amendment of the Toleration Act in 1779, substituting belief in Scripture (whatever that might mean) for belief in the Anglican (explicitly Trinitarian) Thirty-nine Articles. In 1813 laws making anti-Trinitarianism a crime were repealed, long before legal restrictions on Catholics were removed. English Unitarianism produced some remarkable scholars, such as John Kenrick, James Yates and Samuel Sharpe, but few very popular preachers, with the notable exception of George Harris. It educated its clergy at Manchester College, Oxford, the Unitarian Home Missionary College (founded in Manchester in 1854), and the Presbyterian College in Carmarthen, Wales. It is best remembered for being the spiritual home of the Chamberlain family of politicians (Joseph, Austen and Neville) and the Courtauld family of industrialists. Unitarianism seems never to have made much of an impact during this earlier period in Scotland, though it is worth noting that Thomas Aikenhead was executed in Edinburgh as late as 1697 for blaspheming the Trinity.

The growth of anti-Trinitarianism (Unitarianism), as well as its less well-organized partner Deism, saw the first widespread departure from 'orthodox' Christianity since the early Church. Although there had been (as we have seen) many groups with similar views, they were never numerous or influential. This changed as the twin impact of the after-effects of State-sponsored religious warfare and Enlightenment philosophy led many educated people to consider the very basic tenets of Christianity. Protestantism had finally begun to show not only a propensity for schism, but even for producing non-Christian religion. It now became possible to believe in a God who was not the traditional Triune (Trinitarian) God of Christianity.

Indeed, it is worth noting this ability of Luther's 'accidental revolution' not only to lead to great diversity (through schism), but also into non-orthodox Christianity. Socinianism is but one example; later periods would see the appearance of Christian Scientism and Jehovah's Witnesses. The most extreme example, though, has to be the development of Mormonism, which many Christians would consider polytheistic (having more than one God). Finally, Luther set in motion a train of events that could also lead to agnosticism and atheism, or what would appear to be either in the eyes of Christian and Protestant believers – for example, Deism. By stressing the responsibility of individual believers to interrogate the Bible and themselves, the possibility arose that the result would be a near total loss of faith.

Many people, however, chose to respond to the appalling example of coercive, violent religion and its reliance upon the power of the State by turning their Protestantism within. Just as many medieval Christians had responded to the disasters of the plague and the shocking example of Christianity riven by multiple popes by developing a new, personal, often internalized and mystical faith (the *devotio moderna*), Protestants during the late seventeenth and eighteenth century turned to a closer, individual union with God and a more mystical, devotional system.

The result was the First Great Awakening, which might be regarded as a general spiritual movement among Protestants in response to established churches that had became almost departments of state, staffed more by civil servants than ministers. During the early eighteenth century, Protestantism, especially in the English-speaking world, was witness to a dramatic explosion in personal devotion to religion. Before examining exemplary manifestations of these religious awakenings (Methodism and Pietism in this chapter, and a more detailed analysis of the results of the Second Awakening in Chapter 6), it would be most useful to sketch the two awakenings.

THE FIRST GREAT AWAKENING

Historians have traditionally applied the term 'First Great Awakening' to a religious movement among American colonial Protestants in the 1730s and 1740s. It made religion intensely personal to the average person by creating a deep sense of spiritual guilt and redemption. Although normally applied to the North American context, the awakening was part, as the historian Sydney Ahlstrom put it, of a 'great international Protestant upheaval' that also created Pietism in Germany and the Evangelical Revival and Methodism in England. Pietism aside, the awakening had its most dramatic and lasting impact in North America, so we shall begin in the colonies. In America the awakening (or 'revival' in later terminology) brought Christianity to the slaves and was a fundamentally crucial event in New English history as it challenged not only the authority of the then established Church (Calvinist Puritan Congregationalism), but also the State that defended it, and the culture and society it had created. Indeed, everywhere the awakening incited rancour and division between those who favoured religion as it had 'always' been practised and believed, and those who longed for something new and a return to the perceived halcyon days of sixteenth-century Protestantism.

In the end, though, these traditionalists failed, and the awakening had a dramatic effect. It largely reshaped the Congregational and Presbyterian denominations (New England and New Jersey), Dutch Reformed (New York and other mid-Atlantic colonies), German Reformed denominations (Pennsylvania), and helped create the Methodist and Baptist denominations.

(In the southern colonies the awakening was more likely to create these churches than to affect the 'mainstream' denominations.) The awakening had much less of an impact on the Anglican (Episcopal) and Quaker religions, which explains why it is usually seen as a New English movement; the Quakerism of Pennsylvania, the Catholicism of Maryland and the Anglicanism of the southern colonies were largely untouched. Unlike the Second Great Awakening, which began about 1800 and reached out to the unchurched, the First Great Awakening focused on people who were already church members. It changed their rituals, their piety and their self-awareness.

The revival first began with Jonathan Edwards (see pages 171–5), a well-educated Congregationalist minister from Northampton, Massachusetts, a firm Calvinist who was nevertheless convinced that individuals needed an immediate, personal religious experience. The Methodist preacher George Whitefield (see pages 169–71), visiting from England and also a Calvinist, continued the movement, travelling across the colonies and preaching in a dramatic and emotional style. The new style of sermons (dubbed Revivalistic Sermons), and the way people practised their faith, breathed new life into religion in America. Rather than passively listening to intellectual discourses in a detached manner, people became passionately and emotionally involved in their religion, often more so than many preachers had anticipated. People began to study the Bible at home, which effectively decentralized the means of informing the public on religious matters, and was akin to the individualistic trends present in Europe during the Protestant Reformation. The chaotic results were also very similar.

Those attracted to the message of the itinerant preachers called themselves the 'New Lights'. It is interesting to note that this group did not seem to find the connection with newness or novelty quite as horrifying as the sixteenth-century Protestants had done. Those early reformers were keen to stress that they were 'returning' to the Christianity of the early, apostolic Church. These New Lights called those who were 'agin 'em' the 'Old Lights'. Some historians see the First Great Awakening as the first true

American event (rather overlooking the fact that it was part of a pan-Protestant movement), and, as such, represented a step towards a common American value system. It might be argued, however, that it actually demonstrated the extent to which the colonies were 'plugged' into a wider European culture. The historian Jon Butler challenged the notion (in his *Awash in a Sea of Faith: Christianizing the American People*, 1990) that there was in fact a First Great Awakening across the thirteen colonies. According to Butler, there were a number of local revivals, but they lacked the sort of overarching associations and connections required to form a true national or international movement. That the movement embraced staunch Calvinists and decided Arminians is but one example of the point Butler and others have made.

THE SECOND GREAT AWAKENING

Also known as the Great Revival, the Second Great Awakening consisted of several kinds of activity distinguished by locale and expression of religious commitment, which suggests, as noted by Butler (above), that it may have been a number of revivalist movements occurring at the same time. In New England the renewed interest in religion inspired a wave of social activism among 'Yankees' (originally a term of derision, it normally applies to New Englanders, in particular, or northerners more generally). In western New York the spirit of revival encouraged the emergence of new Restorationist and other denominations. It was also one of the influences on the Holiness Movement (see pages 186–91). In the west, especially in Kentucky and Tennessee, the revival greatly increased the size and, indeed, the number of Methodist and Baptist denominations, and introduced into America a new form of religious expression – the 'Scottish camp meeting'. Across the new Republic, the revival created an explosion of new denominations.

The New England Congregationalists (whose grandparents would have experienced the last years of the First Awakening) set up missionary societies to evangelize the settlers in the west, who were largely without churches. Members of these societies not only acted as apostles for the faith, but as educators and exponents of eastern, urban culture as well. Publication and education societies promoted Christian education, most notably the American Bible Society (founded 1816). Social activism, inspired by the revival, gave rise to abolition groups, as well as the Society for the Promotion of Temperance, and began efforts to reform prisons and care for the disabled and mentally ill people. Those touched by the revival often believed in the perfectibility of people (see the Holiness Movement, page 188), and stressed not only their own moral improvement, but also that of their neighbours and their society in general.

In the Appalachian region, the revival most often took the form of the camp meeting – a religious service of several days' length, with many preachers often preaching to different parts of the large crowds at the same time. Pilgrims (and the way settlers streamed to these meetings had much in common with the great pilgrimages of the Middle Ages) in thinly populated areas looked to the camp meeting as a refuge from the lonely life on the frontier, and the even more important chance to save their souls. The sheer exhilaration of participating in a religious revival with hundreds, perhaps thousands of people inspired the dancing, shouting and singing associated with these events.

The first camp meeting took place in July 1800 at Creedence Clearwater Church in southwestern Kentucky. A much larger one was held at Cane Ridge, Kentucky, in 1801, attracting thousands of people. Numerous Presbyterian, Baptist and Methodist ministers participated. It was this event that stamped the organized revival (still associated with the work of Billy Graham and similar evangelists) as the major mode of church growth for denominations such as the Methodists and Baptists. This great revival quickly spread throughout Kentucky, Tennessee and southern Ohio, and each denomination had assets that allowed it to thrive on the frontier. The Methodists developed and expanded their very efficient organization of travelling ministers, known as 'circuit riders', who sought out people in remote frontier locations. These circuit riders were largely drawn from settler families, which helped them to establish a rapport with the frontier folk they hoped to convert.

METHODISM

The most important movement to come out of the First Great Awakening was the very same Methodism that so dramatically increased as a result of the Second Awakening. However, Methodism came into being not in the colonies, but in Britain. Its great missionary vision, though, meant that it rapidly spread throughout Britain's eighteenth-century empire. Reaching out to those who were rather overlooked by the established (Anglican) Church, it originally appealed especially to workers, poor farmers and slaves. Theologically, it was Arminian (see page 148), emphasizing that all people could be saved, and Low Church in liturgy (that is, lacking in ritual and, especially, clerical dress and formal prayers, such as the heavily prescribed Book of Common Prayer used in the Church of England).

The Methodist revival began in eighteenth-century England. It was started by a group of men, including John Wesley and his younger brother Charles, as a movement within the Church of England, focused on Bible study, a 'methodical approach' to that study, mutual 'confession' and Christian living. The term 'methodist' was originally a pejorative nickname given to a small society of students at Oxford, meeting between 1729 and 1735, for the purpose of mutual improvement. They were accustomed to take Communion every week, to fast regularly and to abstain from most forms of amusement and luxury.

The early Methodists reacted against the perceived apathy of the Church of England. They used open-air preaching, recalling the large outdoor sermons of the Dutch Revolt, as well as presaging the camp meetings of the Second Great Awakening, and established Methodist societies wherever they went. They were notorious for their enthusiastic, emotional sermons, and were often accused of fanaticism. Members of the established Church feared that the new doctrines promulgated by the Methodists, especially the need for the constant and sustained action of the Holy Spirit upon the believer's soul, and the individualistic practices they built into their 'method' would produce ill effects upon weak minds. An early critic of the movement wrote that Methodists had 'the natural Tendency of their Behaviour, in Voice and Gesture and horrid Expressions, to make People mad'. Later critics from more well-heeled denominations were no less unkind in suggesting that Methodists were simply 'Baptists who can read'. In one of his paintings William Hogarth attacked Methodists as 'enthusiasts' full of 'Credulity, Superstition [now no longer a term that automatically meant 'Catholic'] and Fanaticism [which was still meant to recall the dangerous enthusiasm of the Anabaptists]'.

Traditionally, Methodism has believed in the Arminian view of free will, as opposed to predestination. This distinguishes it, historically, from Calvinist traditions, such as Presbyterianism. However, in strongly Calvinist areas, such as Wales, Calvinistic Methodism developed. For his part, though, Wesley was not a systematic theologian; however, Methodist ministerial students and trainee local preachers do study his sermons for his theology. In reality, the popular expression of Methodist theology is to be found in the hymns of John's brother, Charles. Since enthusiastic congregational singing was part of the movements springing up during the early eighteenth century, Wesleyan theology took root and spread through hymns in a number of different denominations (recalling the effective use made of hymns as a tool of theology among Lutherans). Methodism has historically insisted that personal salvation always involves Christian mission and service to the world. Or, as Wesley's Covenant Prayer, still said annually by most Methodists, put it:

> Christ has many services to be done. Some are easy, others are
> difficult. Some bring honour, others bring reproach. Some are
> suitable to our natural inclinations and temporal interests, others are
> contrary to both ... Yet the power to do all these things is given to
> us in Christ, who strengthens us ... I am no longer my own but
> [Christ's]. Put me to what you will, rank me with whom you will;

put me to doing, put me to suffering; let me be employed for you
or laid aside for you, exalted for you or brought low for you; let me
be full, let me be empty, let me have all things, let me have nothing;
I freely and wholeheartedly yield all things to your pleasure and
disposal.

Scriptural holiness, an idea uniquely stressed by Methodists, entailed
more than personal piety; love of God was always linked with love of neighbour and a passion for justice. For example, disputes over slavery placed the
Church in difficulty during the first half of the 1800s (in the very midst of
the Second Awakening), with northern church leaders reluctant to take a
stand, fearing a split with the south. However, the Wesleyan Methodists
(later the Wesleyan Church) and the Free Methodist churches broke off
under the leadership of staunch abolitionists. (Free Methodists were especially active in the Underground Railroad, the system of safe houses that
helped runaway slaves from slave states to Canada.) Finally, in a much larger
split (1845), the churches of the slaveholding states left the Methodist
Episcopal Church and formed the Methodist Episcopal Church, South. The
northern and southern branches were eventually reunited in 1939, when
slavery was no longer an issue. However, race continued to be an issue, and
some southerners (conservative in theology and segregationist) opposed the
merger and formed the Southern Methodist Church in 1940.

This brief overview of the two awakenings and the rise of Methodism
can be usefully expanded by an examination of the lives of three of the great
figures of the First Awakening. They can serve as excellent examples of the
impact of this religious revival on the individual, as well as its ability to span
enormous theological divides.

JOHN WESLEY

Three distinct phases in John Wesley's life were key to the development of
Methodism. The first was at Oxford University, where he was involved in
the so-called Holy Club; the second, while he was parish priest in Savannah,

Georgia (Wesley remained in the established Church throughout his life); the third in London, after he returned to England. In 1720 Wesley entered Christ Church, Oxford, and received his Master of Arts degree in 1727. He was ordained deacon in 1725, and elected fellow of Lincoln College the following year. He was his father's curate for two years, then returned to Oxford to fulfil his functions as a fellow. During his early years, John had enjoyed a deep religious experience, but this waned during his school years and even more so at university. As one biographer wrote, Wesley went to Charterhouse 'a saint and left a sinner'.

Leading Wesley scholars point to 1725 as the date of his conversion to 'Christianity' in the sense of a personal saving experience. In the year of his ordination he read Thomas à Kempis, one of the great authors of the late medieval *devotio moderna*. Wesley resolved to keep God's law, inwardly and outwardly, as sacredly as possible. He pursued a rigidly methodical and abstemious life, studied the Scriptures, and performed his religious duties diligently, depriving himself so that he would have alms to give. He devoted himself to a godly life, and began to seek after holiness of heart and life. Thus, it was no surprise that when, in 1735, a clergyman 'inured to contempt of the ornaments and conveniences of life, to bodily austerities, and to serious thoughts' was wanted by Governor James Oglethorpe to go to the province of Georgia, Wesley responded, accompanied by his brother and follower, Charles, and remained in the colony for two years.

While in Georgia, Wesley began to develop the traits that later became associated with Methodism. For example, he began the first Sunday school. However, he left the colony, convinced he had failed, and under suspicion that he was radically altering the 'religion' of the established Church. Specific charges were brought against him, especially on account of his unusual liturgical 'experiments'. A journal entry in 1735 reported that Wesley spent three hours 'revising' the Book of Common Prayer — not normally the job of a parish priest. One of his parishioners reportedly told Wesley, 'The people ... say they are Protestants. But as for you, they cannot tell what religion you are of. They never heard of such religion before. They do not know what to make of it.' During the sixteenth century and much of the seventeenth, this sort of comment would have been rather quickly followed by the words 'sentenced to be burnt at the stake'.

Wesley returned to England depressed and beaten. It was at this point that he turned to the Moravians, a German sect, whom he had encountered three years earlier on his way to Georgia. At one point during the voyage a storm came up and broke the mast off the ship. While the English aboard panicked, the Moravians calmly sang hymns and prayed. This experience led Wesley to believe that the Moravians possessed an inner strength that he lacked. His 'Aldersgate Experience' of 24 May 1738, at a Moravian meeting in Aldersgate Street, London, in which he heard a reading of Luther's preface to the Epistle to the Romans (he would later write, 'I felt my heart strangely warmed') is but one of many experiences in Wesley's journey of faith. A few weeks later he preached a remarkable sermon on the doctrine of present, personal salvation by faith, which was followed by another (decidedly Arminian sermon) on God's grace 'free in all, and free for all'. He allied himself with a Moravian society in Fetter Lane, London, and in 1738 went to Herrnhut (Saxony), the Moravian headquarters in Germany, forming a historic link between Methodism and the great radical movements of the early Reformation and, indeed, the Hussites before. Late in 1739 Wesley broke with the Moravians, feeling that they had fallen into heresies (most magisterial reformers would have said they had always been guilty of this), especially Quietism (a Christian philosophy focused on self-lessness leading to 'self-annihilation' – in the spiritual sense – and 'absorption into the Divine'), and decided to form his own followers into a separate society. 'Thus,' he wrote, 'without any previous plan, began the Methodist Society in England.'

Apart from his concerns about heresy, Wesley was convinced that the Moravian Church had failed in its duty to call sinners to repentance, that many of the clergymen were corrupt, and that souls were perishing in their sins. Wesley regarded himself as commissioned by God to bring about revival in the Church, and no opposition, or persecution, or obstacles could prevail against the divine urgency and authority of this commission. Unwilling that people should perish in their sins, and unable to reach them from church pulpits, he began field-preaching. Seeing that he and the few clergymen cooperating with him could not do the work that needed to be done, he was led, as early as 1739, to approve of lay preaching: men and women who were not episcopally ordained were permitted to preach and do pastoral work. Thus, one of the great features of Methodism, to which it has largely owed its success, was adopted by Wesley in answer to a necessity.

The doctrines that Wesley emphasized in his sermons and writings were first, prevenient grace – the gift of God that allowed a person the freedom to choose or reject the offer of salvation (this got around the problem noted on page 150 in the analogy with Lazarus dead in the tomb as sinners are dead in sin: Wesley said God gave just enough life to allow someone to decide to leave the tomb or not); other doctrines were present, personal salvation by faith, the witness of the Spirit and sanctification. He defined the witness of the Spirit as 'an inward impression on the soul of believers, whereby the spirit of God directly testifies to their spirit that they are the children of God' (assurance). Sanctification he spoke of (in 1790) as the 'grand *depositum* which God has lodged with the people called Methodists'. Wesley taught that sanctification was obtainable instantaneously by faith at any point between justification and death. It was not 'sinless perfection', but he believed that those who are 'perfect in love' are not troubled by sin.

GEORGE WHITEFIELD

Although a friend and co-worker in this great revival movement, George Whitefield remained a Calvinist and rejected Wesley's Arminian ideas. In contemporary accounts he, not John Wesley, was spoken of as the supreme figure and even as the founder of Methodism. His fame as a preacher was such that he has been called by some historians 'the first modern celebrity'. Raised the son of a widow who kept an inn at Gloucester, he was educated at the Crypt School in that city and then Pembroke College, Oxford. Being poor, Whitefield did not have the means to pay for his tuition, so he entered

Oxford as a servitor, the lowest rank of student. In return for free tuition, he was assigned as a servant to a number of higher ranked students. His duties included waking them in the morning, polishing their shoes, carrying their books and even doing their coursework. While at Oxford, he joined the Holy Club with the two Wesleys. His genuine piety led the Bishop of Gloucester to ordain him in 1736 before the canonical age of 25, and his humble origins undoubtedly influenced his views.

Whitefield's legacy was particularly felt in North America. In an age when crossing the Atlantic Ocean was a long and hazardous undertaking, he visited the continent seven times, making thirteen crossings in total. He preached nearly every day for months to large crowds of sometimes several thousand people as he travelled throughout the colonies, especially New England. It is estimated that throughout his life he preached more than 18,000 formal sermons, and if less formal occasions are included, that number might rise to more than 30,000. In addition to his work in America and England, he made fifteen journeys to Scotland, two to Ireland, and one each to Bermuda, Gibraltar and the Netherlands. But his connection was strongest with the American colonies. The Old South Presbyterian Church in Newburyport, Massachusetts, was built for his use, and he requested to be buried under the pulpit of this church: his tomb remains there to this day.

Despite his great efforts at changing the religious culture of his time, Whitefield was a man of his age. For example, his great works in Georgia (including the establishment of Bethesda Orphanage, which still exists to this day) did not include abolitionism. Originally, Georgia's charter did not permit slavery, but in 1749 there was a movement to introduce it there, which Whitefield supported. He subsequently owned slaves who worked at the orphanage. Indeed, it is worth remembering (as will be discussed at greater length later) that the issue of slavery was one that divided Protestants. Many, indeed most, in the eighteenth century used the Bible, especially the curse laid on Noah's son Ham (Genesis 9:24–7 and 10:6–12) as 'proof' that God had eternally damned Africans to servitude.

Whitefield's greatest gift, though, was his role as an outdoor preacher.

In this he was a harbinger of the great revival camp meetings of the nineteenth century and the later evangelists of the twentieth century. He first took to preaching in the open air, with remarkable results, at Bristol, which at that time was a centre of vice in all its worst forms. He was also the first to provide spiritual succour to the colliers who lived near that city and were largely 'unchurched'. Twenty thousand workers crowded to his sermons, and the white runnels caused by the tears that ran down their coal-blackened cheeks showed how visibly they were affected. Whitefield was known for his powerful voice and his ability to appeal to the emotions of a crowd. Unlike most preachers of his time, he spoke extemporaneously rather than reading his sermon from notes. Strong men were moved to hysterical convulsions by the force of his sermons. Wesley saw these physical reactions as manifestations – evident 'signs of grace'. Whitefield, though, ever the traditional Calvinist, considered them to be 'doubtful indications'.

There is no small irony in the consequences of Whitefield's work. He was a Calvinist, yet the movement that arose from his efforts with the Wesleys was Arminian; the Calvinistic version of Methodism never really prospered. His dislike and distrust of the 'physical manifestations' his sermons caused was to no avail. His style of preaching became the norm in American evangelicalism, and with it an emphasis upon a 'response' from the hearers. This stress on a demonstrable, experiential, frequently emotional response became the norm. As with so many aspects in the history of Protestantism, this is yet another example of the 'law of unintended consequences' – or, rather, Luther's 'accidental revolution' bearing truly bizarre fruit.

JONATHAN EDWARDS

This move away from a very creedal and 'intellectual' form of traditional Protestantism rooted in the magisterial tradition was also an unintended, and undoubtedly deeply distasteful, consequence of the work of Jonathan Edwards. Known as one of the greatest and most profound American evangelical theologians, his work is very broad in scope, but he is often associated with his defence of Calvinist theology and the Puritan heritage. A prodigy from an early age, Edwards was trained for college by his father and his elder sisters, all of whom received an excellent education. At the age of ten he wrote a semi-humorous tract on the immateriality of the soul. (He must certainly have been gifted to combine theology and humour.) Two years later his interest in natural history led him to write a remarkable essay on the habits of the 'flying spider'. He entered Yale College in 1716, just short of his thirteenth birthday. In the following year he became acquainted with the philosopher John Locke's *Essay Concerning Human Understanding*, which influenced him profoundly. During his college studies, he kept notebooks labelled 'The Mind', 'Natural Science', which included a discussion of atomic theory, and 'The Scriptures', laying the foundation for a planned, extensive work on natural and mental philosophy. He even drew up rules for its composition. Thus, even before his graduation in September 1720, as valedictorian and head of his class, he seems to have had a well-formulated philosophy. As a philosopher and theologian he would make a most unlikely 'evangelist'.

As with so many other reformers we have examined, Edwards had a life-changing experience. However, in keeping with his Calvinism, his experience took a number of years. The period 1720–6 figures prominently in his diaries and also in his 'Resolutions' – rules he devised to regulate his own conduct and personal devotion. He had long been an eager seeker after salvation, and was not fully satisfied as to his own conversion until an experience in his last year at college (which he failed to discuss at length), when he lost his feeling that the election of some to salvation and of others to eternal damnation was a 'horrible doctrine'. Rather, he now saw predestination as 'exceedingly pleasant, bright and sweet'. He took a great and new joy in the beauties of nature, and delighted in the allegorical interpretation of the Song of Solomon. Balancing these mystic joys is the stern tone of his 'Resolutions', in which he is almost ascetic in his eagerness to live earnestly and soberly, to waste no time, and to maintain the strictest temperance in eating and drinking.

At this point it seemed most likely that Edwards would become a leading controversialist fighting off the advancing Arminianism of groups such as the Methodists. At Boston in 1731 he preached the 'Public Lecture' (published as *God Glorified – in Man's Dependence*). This was his first public attack on Arminianism. The key argument was God's absolute sovereignty in the work of redemption. God may have originally created man to be holy, but as a result of the fall, it was of His 'good pleasure' and 'mere and arbitrary grace' that any man was now made holy. God might deny this grace without any disparagement to any of His perfections. Edwards was deflected from this path of theological dispute when, in 1733, a religious revival began in Northampton, Massachusetts, and reached such intensity (in the winter of 1734 and the following spring) as to threaten the business of the town, which was coming to a standstill. In six months nearly three hundred were admitted to the Church. The revival gave Edwards an opportunity to study the process of conversion in all its phases and varieties, and he recorded his observations with psychological minuteness and discrimination in *A Faithful Narrative of the Surprising Work of God in the Conversion of Many Hundred Souls in Northampton* (1737). A year later, he published *Discourses on Various Important Subjects*, the five sermons that had proved most effective in the revival, and of these none, he tells us, was so immediately effective as that on the *Justice of God in the Damnation of Sinners*, from the text, 'That every mouth may be stopped'. Another sermon, published in 1734, on the *Reality of Spiritual Light* set forth what he regarded as the inner, moving principle of the revival, the doctrine of a special grace in the immediate and supernatural divine illumination of the soul.

Although he was no supporter of emotionalism and experientialism, Edwards was convinced of the reality of what he felt was God's work in New England. As he watched the revival growing, he became acquainted with Whitefield (the personal connections between the leading figures of the First Great Awakening are reminiscent of the contacts among many of the sixteenth-century reformers). In 1741 Edwards preached probably his most famous sermon (*Sinners in the Hands of an Angry God*) in Enfield,

Connecticut. Conservative leaders of his established Congregational church were increasingly concerned by the emotional 'extremism' they thought characterized the revival.

In 1741 Edwards published in its defence *The Distinguishing Marks of a Work of the Spirit of God*, dealing particularly with the phenomena most criticized – the swoonings, outcries and convulsions. These 'bodily effects', he insisted, were not distinguishing marks of the work of the Spirit of God one way or another (following Whitefield rather than Wesley in this conclusion). So bitter was the feeling against the revival in the more strictly Puritan churches that in 1742 he was forced to write a second apology, *Thoughts on the Revival in New England*, in which he argued that the great moral improvement of the country was evidence of God's hand in the revival. In the same pamphlet he defended an appeal to the emotions, and advocated preaching terror when necessary, even to children, who in God's sight 'are young vipers'. He considered 'bodily effects' incidental to the real work of God, but his own mystic devotion and the experiences of his wife during the awakening (which he recorded in detail) made him think that the divine visitation (salvation) quite often overpowers the body. In reply to Edwards, the Unitarian Charles Chauncy anonymously wrote *The Late Religious Commotions in New England Considered* (1743). He argued that the only measure of the divine nature of the revival was the resulting changed conduct of the converts. The general convention of Congregational ministers in the province of Massachusetts Bay protested 'against disorders in practice which have of late obtained in various parts of the land'.

Eventually Edwards fell out with not only his fellow ministers, but also his own congregation. He was banned from his pulpit, preaching his farewell sermon in May 1755. Despite offers from as far afield as Scotland and Virginia, Edwards chose to work with Native Americans, not only to save them, but also to protect their interests against those of the more rapacious European settlers. He later accepted the post of president of Princeton, where he would die from the after-effects of a smallpox inoculation. His greatest legacy was his voluminous body of philosophical and theological works, although these are now largely forgotten. What has proved more enduring, though rarely ever associated with him specifically, is the increasing role of emotion in American Protestantism. He would never have accepted that physical and psychological manifestations were essential marks of salvation, but these became strongly associated with the First Great Awakening. They would come into their own in the Second Great Awakening, and remain to this day an enduring feature of American evangelicalism.

PIETISM

While religious revival was sweeping British North America, similar movements were afoot elsewhere. In particular, Pietism was having an impact in Lutheran areas of Europe. Beginning in the late seventeenth century, it is arguably the first movement in this general move towards a Protestant *devotio moderna* in the eighteenth century. It inspired Wesley and Methodism, but was also instrumental in the Brethren movement. It combined the Lutheran emphasis on Biblical doctrine with the Reformed, and especially Puritan, emphasis on individual piety, and a vigorous Christian life. While this was the fundamental combination, the emphasis was decidedly on a pious, godly life.

The movement arose from a general sense that the Lutheran Church specifically and Protestantism more generally were moribund, and that what was needed was a revival of practical and devout Christianity. The successes of baroque Catholicism and its flowering of lay charitable and devotional movements, as well as the setbacks after the Thirty Years War, certainly contributed to a sense of malaise and that all was not well with Protestantism. This resulted in many voices calling for change. For example, proto-Pietist Lutheran theologian Heinrich Müller described the font, the pulpit, the confessional and the altar as 'the four dumb idols of the Lutheran Church' and Theophilus Grossgebauer of Rostock, echoing the prophets of the Old Testament, raised what he called 'the alarm cry of a watchman in Sion'.

The name 'Pietist', much as 'Methodist' had once been, was a term of ridicule applied to adherents of the movement by its opponents. The Lutheran Church had continued Melanchthon's work constructing an intellectual backbone for the evangelical Lutheran faith. By the seventeenth century the denomination remained a creed-based, theological and sacramental institution, that retained many of the liturgical traditions of Roman Catholicism. In the Reformed Church (which was represented in Germany), the influence of John Calvin had not only produced doctrinal differences from Lutheranism, but also a strong emphasis on the daily life and behaviour of the believer. The Presbyterian structure gave the people a share in church life, albeit limited and prescribed, that the Lutherans lacked, but it involved a dogmatic legalism that, the Lutherans believed, imperilled Christian freedom and fostered self-righteousness.

The direct originator of the movement was Philipp Jakob Spener. Born at Rappoltsweiler in Alsace, he was given a strong religious upbringing by a devout godmother, who used books of devotion such as Johann Arndt's *True Christianity*. Spener was convinced of the necessity of a moral and religious reformation within German Lutheranism. He studied theology at Strasburg, where the professors at the time (especially Sebastian Schmidt) were more inclined to 'practical' Christianity than to theological disputation. Just as importantly, he later spent a year in Geneva, where he was greatly influenced by the strict moral life and rigid ecclesiastical discipline he saw there. He was also captivated by the preaching and the piety of the Waldensian professor Antoine Léger, and the converted Jesuit preacher Jean de Labadie.

During a stay in Tübingen, Spener read Grossgebauer's *Alarm Cry*, and in 1666 he entered upon his first pastoral charge at Frankfurt, with a deep conviction that a devout Christian life within evangelical Lutheranism was being sacrificed to rigid orthodoxy. Pietism, as a distinct movement in the German Church, began when Spener started holding religious meetings at his house (*collegia pietatis*), during which he repeated his sermons, expounded passages of the New Testament, and induced those present to join in conversation on religious questions. In 1675 he published his *Pia desideria* (*Earnest Desires for a Reform of the True Evangelical Church*), the title of which gave rise to the term 'Pietists'. In this publication he made six proposals as the best means of restoring the life of the Church:

- An earnest and thorough study of the Bible should take place in private meetings called *ecclesiolae in ecclesia* (mini-churches within the Church).
- A Christian universal priesthood should be encouraged, in which the laity share in the spiritual government of the Church.
- Knowledge of Christianity should be attended by the practice of it as its indispensable sign and supplement.
- Those who disagree doctrinally should be treated with sympathy and kindness instead of merely didactic, and often bitter, attacks on them.
- Theological training at universities should be reorganized to give more prominence to the devotional life.
- A different style of preaching should be developed to replace pleasing rhetoric and implant Christianity in the inner or new man.

This work produced a great impression throughout Germany, and although many orthodox Lutheran theologians and pastors were offended by Spener's book, its accusations and demands were too well justified and self-evident to be denied out of hand. A large number of pastors immediately adopted Spener's proposals.

In 1686 Spener accepted an appointment to the court-chaplaincy at Dresden, which allowed him a wider though more difficult sphere of labour. In Leipzig a society of young theologians was formed under his influence for the learned study and devout application of the Bible. Three magistrates belonging to that society commenced courses of expository lectures on the Scriptures of a practical and devotional character, which were zealously frequented by both students and townsmen. The lectures aroused, however, the ill will of the other theologians and pastors of Leipzig, and Spener and his supporters had to leave – to found the University of Halle. The theological chairs in the new university were filled according to Spener's proposals. The main difference between Lutheran Pietism and orthodox Lutheranism arose from the Pietists' conception of Christianity as consisting chiefly in a change of heart and consequent holiness of life. Orthodox Lutherans rejected this viewpoint as a gross over-simplification, stressing the need for participation in the institutional life of the Church and for sound theological underpinnings. Put simply, religion had to be more than an experience or a feeling.

Spener's stress on the necessity of a new birth and a separation of Christians from the world led to exaggeration and fanaticism among some Pietists (akin both to the extremism that marked some developments from the two awakenings in North America, as well as earlier in the sixteenth-century Reformation). Many Pietists soon maintained that the new birth must always be preceded by agonies of repentance and that only a 'regenerated' theologian (one who could claim an emotional experience) could teach theology. All Pietists shunned common worldly amusements, such as dancing, the theatre and public games. Opponents said that this was just a new version of justification by works. In addition, the *ecclesiolae in ecclesia* also weakened the power and meaning of the traditional institutions of the Church.

As a distinct movement, Pietism was strongest by the middle of the eighteenth century. Its very individualism helped pave the way for the German Enlightenment (*Aufklärung*) that would take the Church in an altogether different direction. However, Pietism also contributed to the revival of biblical studies in Germany, and to religion becoming once again an affair of the heart and of life, not merely of the intellect. It also gave a new emphasis to the role of the laity in the Church, more restricted than Luther's original emphasis on a priesthood of all believers after the rise of various forms of Anabaptism. As one historian put it succinctly, and rather controversially: 'It was the last great surge of the waves of the ecclesiastical movement begun by the Reformation; it was the completion and the final form of the Protestantism created by the Reformation. Then came a time when another intellectual power took possession of the minds of men.'

LATER AND LONG-TERM EFFECTS OF
THE GREAT AWAKENINGS

Through its impact on the Moravian Church, which had become moribund, Pietism would have (as we have seen) a direct impact on Wesley. Count Nicolaus Ludwig von Zinzendorf, Spener's godson and a pupil in the Halle Orphanage, was key to the revival of the Moravians. Finally, Pietism led to the establishment of Lutheran (and Protestant) missions around the world. In the twentieth century Dietrich Bonhoeffer of the (anti-Nazi) German Confessing Church also considered Pietism to have had an important impact, but he saw this in less positive terms. He called Pietism the last attempt to save Christianity as a religion, but Bonhoeffer denounced the basic aim of Pietism, to produce a 'desired piety' in a person, as unbiblical.

No matter what Bonhoeffer thought, those caught up in the Great Awakenings of the eighteenth century were convinced of two things. First, they believed that God was moving in their midst to do wonderful things. Second, they never doubted that they were calling Protestantism back to its sixteenth-century roots, and thereby to the Church of the Apostles. In so doing, they (with God's help) were able to see off the great threat to the faith coming from the Enlightenment. The philosophical awakening of the same century had buffeted Christianity with a spectrum of dangers, ranging from outright atheism through anticlericalism to agnosticism and secularist indifference. Having weathered these storms, many faithful would have thought Protestantism stronger and more vibrant in the opening decades of the nineteenth century than it had been at any time since the late sixteenth century.

However, this optimism would have overlooked a number of important aspects of the Great Awakenings. The Deism of many leaders was certainly not Protestantism; indeed, it was not Christianity. Men such as Washington and Jefferson spoke much of God, but they were not advocating adherence to the God of Methodism or Pietism. Indeed, it is not really clear that they would have advocated adherence to any God or creed. To some extent one can see Deism as the triumph of Socinianism in taking the minds and hearts of many leaders of the day. However, although this faith may have appealed to the educated, it was not a faith for the masses. Or, to put it more accurately, it was not a faith to force on the masses. Socinianism, and its later descendant, Deism, shared with other radical reforms an emphasis upon free thinking and an unwillingness to coerce. In the end, Deism faded away, leaving behind a number of Unitarian denominations, mostly in the English-speaking world.

The more enduring denominations of the age, though, in thinking they were simply restoring Protestantism, were rather downplaying the substantial changes that they had introduced. Mostly noticeable was the triumph of Arminianism by the beginning of the nineteenth century. It would be unfair to see this as a return to some form of 'works' salvation', just as it was unfair to categorize sixteenth-century Catholicism as a system based on works. Both, though, insisted that there must be some measure of involvement by the individual in the salvation process. This involvement did not 'earn' salvation (it was not a bribe), and it in no way obliged God to save the individual (He could not be forced to save 'by contract'). Nevertheless, for Methodists, and those influenced by their thoughts (see pages 164–75), 'by faith alone' meant something very different from what Luther and Calvin intended.

Just as importantly, the emphasis upon the individual and an individual experience (often emotional) would have been equally alien and probably abhorrent to the magisterial reformers. They had seen emotive experientialism, and it looked like Müntzer and Münster. The process of denominalization (developing clear, precise creeds) and catechizing the faithful (teaching them theology in some detail) was just as alien and probably just as abhorrent to the revivalists of the Great Awakenings. Edwards and Whitefield were fighting a rearguard action in espousing Calvinism, and by their very methods crucially undermining their own efforts. Protestantism came out of the Great Awakenings stronger and more vibrant, but also much more emotional and experiential. It had also developed a very keen awareness, even ideology, of the individual and the individual's role in salvation and God's work on Earth. As we shall see, these new ideas and emphases would have a dramatic impact on Protestantism during the course of the nineteenth and early twentieth century.

6
CREATING A JUST SOCIETY

IF [ONE CLASS] OWNS A LARGE PART OF THE NATIONAL WEALTH ... THIS CLASS WILL ... SEE TO IT THAT THE VAST POWER ... OF GOVERNMENT SERVES ITS INTERESTS. AND IF ... ANOTHER CLASS ... IS ECONOMICALLY DEPENDENT AND HELPLESS ... IT WILL [NOT] BE ALLOWED AN EQUAL VOICE IN SWAYING POLITICAL POWER. [ONE CANNOT HAVE] ECONOMIC INEQUALITY AND POLITICAL EQUALITY. AS OLIVER CROMWELL WROTE ... 'IF THERE BE ANY ONE THAT MAKES MANY POOR TO MAKE A FEW RICH, THAT SUITS NOT A COMMONWEALTH' ... [OR] LINCOLN ... '[A] REPUBLIC CANNOT BE HALF SLAVE AND HALF FREE. THE POWER OF CAPITALISM OVER THE MACHINERY OF OUR GOVERNMENT, AND ITS CORRODING INFLUENCE ON THE MORALITY OF OUR PUBLIC SERVANTS [IS VISIBLE TO ALL].'

WALTER RAUSCHENBUSCH
CHRISTIANITY AND THE SOCIAL CRISIS (1907)

THE END OF THE EIGHTEENTH CENTURY AND THE opening decades of the nineteenth were a watershed in European history. Anti-clericalism and distaste for theology were features not only of the Enlightenment and Deism, but also of many of the revivalist and reform movements that swept across Europe (especially the English-speaking world) during that period. The Enlightenment and Deism stressed a very intellectualized approach to reality that placed a great premium on the power of human reason. This was very different, though, from the positive view of reason espoused by humanism in the sixteenth century. For humanism, reason was a tool that could be deployed in developing a better understanding of God's revealed truth. Many Enlightenment thinkers used reason to demolish the very concept of revealed religion, and Deists saw reason as a direct means of understanding the divine without recourse *through* revealed truth (that is, the Bible). The mind became not only an organ for understanding revealed truth, but one that was capable of uncovering concealed truth as well. Divine revelation, if it existed at all, was not necessarily needed.

The revivalist movements did not reject revealed truth, but they placed a much greater emphasis on the 'lived' experience of the faith. Creeds and confessions took second place to the more practical realities of a personal relationship with God through the Spirit. As Deism was different from humanism, these revivalist movements were not, for the most part,

Anabaptist or mystical. They still relied heavily on the Bible as revealed truth, but stressed that what was being revealed was Jesus, the Saviour of sinners, rather than a system of theological beliefs and 'truths'. For them, the heart was the key organ in religion. Luther, Calvin and the other magisterial reformers wanted to put the Bible into the hands of every humble labourer so that it could be read, studied and believed; the revivalists wanted the same labourers to hear the Word so that it would enter their hearts and effect a change in behaviour (but not necessarily a change of denomination).

What both reformers and revivalists shared, though, was an emphasis upon the individual. This individualism was then coupled with an acute sense (which would have been understood by the Anabaptists) that society had to change not just its systems of worship. New groups arose in this new age, questioning exactly what, in practice, it meant for their society and culture when St Paul said 'in Christ there can be no male and female' (Galatians 3:28). If there was to be 'neither Jew nor Greek', could there be 'black and white'? If there was to be 'neither bond nor free', could slavery be tolerated? How could a person treat someone as they would like to be treated – Christ's 'Golden Rule', as found, for example, in Matthew 7:12 – and stand by while children were worked to death in mines and factories? Even if one rejected the communal ownership of property in the early Church (see pages 49–50), which created so many 'communist' Anabaptist groups, could one ignore poverty and the obligations to love a neighbour as much as one loved one's self (for example Matthew 19:19)?

But this was not another outburst of Anabaptism or radical reformation. The groups that arose in the nineteenth century out of the Enlightenment and the Great Awakenings did not want to separate from the world. Some did, but the majority saw their role as renewing society and religion. Many were millenarian in believing that Christ's return was imminent and the world about to end. Even a short list of the movements and denominations that came into their own during this period (or soon thereafter) gives some idea of the enormous energy that was being unleashed in Protestantism, and the extent to which even the Enlightenment and Deism had failed to dampen people's enthusiasm for religion – or the ability of Protestantism to divide: the Shakers (1720s), Swedenborgianism (1780s – the great American tree-planter John 'Johnny Appleseed' Chapman was a member), the Restoration Movement (c.1800), Plymouth Brethren (1820), Millerites (1830), the Latter-day Saints (commonly called Mormons) (1830), Disciples of Christ (1840s), Seventh Day Adventism (1860s), Pentecostalism (1860s), the Salvation Army (1865), Christian Scientism (1879) and Jehovah's Witnesses (1917). Not since the first decades of Protestantism had so many new denominations and movements burst into existence.

Although the specific beliefs and structures of each of these are almost endlessly fascinating, it is necessary to focus on general trends and those wider movements that radically altered Western society. Coming out of the eighteenth century, the Holiness Movement would stress the individual experience of salvation. Abolitionism challenged societies over the continued existence of race-based slavery. Later in the century the Social Gospel Movement would unite fairly conservative theology with a firm commitment to social change and egalitarianism. Finally, running though many of these other groups was the impact of the liberalism that had flourished in the eighteenth century and that, in the nineteenth, began to take shape not only as a philosophical mindset, but also as a political and religious movement.

THE HOLINESS MOVEMENT

One movement that can be seen to underpin many of the numerous denominations that came into being is the Holiness Movement. It took a radically new approach to what actually happened after salvation. While Luther stressed salvation, and many magisterial reformers and Anabaptists looked at the impact of salvation in a community or communal setting, the Holiness Movement focused on the individual and the 'working out' of their salvation. However, this movement marked a decided break with the past in rejecting the notion that depravity, inherited from Adam and Eve, was a necessary condition of man, or an essential part of his character. Depravity, it believed, could be overcome and eradicated by God's power: the carnal nature of man could be cleansed, indeed removed, through faith by the power of the Holy Spirit if people's sins are forgiven. The results or blessings of this new state included spiritual power and an ability to maintain purity of heart (that is, thoughts and motives that were uncorrupted by sin or sinlessness). This idea is typically referred to in Holiness churches, which exist to this day, as 'entire sanctification', though most scholars and theologians prefer the term 'Christian perfection'.

In general, the Holiness Movement sought to promote a Christianity that was personal, practical and life-changing. Three key concepts of the movement were regeneration by grace through faith (in that sense, clearly Protestant), Christian sanctification (in the sense meant by those in the movement, most definitely not traditional Protestantism) and the assurance of salvation by the witness of the Spirit (similar to the Calvinists' 'perseverance of the saints', but considerably more assured – the believer actually knows that he or she is saved, rather than having a general assurance that an elect person will be saved). While the last two views are unique to the Holiness Movement, the first concept shows that the movement can be said to be at one with traditional Protestantism.

However, even the first concept was not understood in a traditional Protestant sense. Rather, salvation by grace through faith tended to take on a more personal and emotional, that is, more mystical, quality than in other segments of Christianity. Many participants in the Holiness Movement were devout churchgoers who felt that they had not had a personal 'salvation experience' and believed that they needed to do so. This was very much in keeping with the new way in which Protestantism operated as a result of the First and Second Great Awakenings (see pages 159–60). The second concept referred to another type of personal experience after regeneration. Saved people dedicated their lives to God and received the ability to lead a more holy life. Some Holiness groups taught that this experience could lead to a truly and completely sinless life, while others taught that a person became gradually more holy, without necessarily ever becoming completely holy. This second experience was given various names in different denominations: 'second touch', 'second blessing', 'filling with the Holy Spirit'. The third concept referred to an innate or experiential knowledge (feeling) within people who have been regenerated that regeneration has actually happened to them personally. This was described as an 'assurance of salvation'.

In part, the movement began as a recapturing of ideas already found in Wesley's doctrine of Christian Perfection. In 1836 a Methodist woman, Sarah Worrall Lankford, started the Tuesday Meeting for the Promotion of Holiness in New York City. The following year, another Methodist, Timothy Merritt, founded a journal called the *Guide to Christian Perfection* to propagate and promote the Wesleyan idea that a Christian could live without committing serious sin (note, not entirely without any sin). That same year Lankford's sister, Phoebe Palmer, experienced what she called 'entire sanctification'. She began leading the Tuesday Meeting for the Promotion of Holiness, which at first only women attended. Later, however, Methodist bishops and ministers also began to attend. She eventually became editor of the journal (then called *Guide to Holiness*), and in 1859 published *The Promise of the Father*, advocating holiness and also supporting women in ministry.

The most important male to attend these early meetings was Thomas Upham. The meetings led him to the study of various mystics and mystical movements, for example, Johann Arndt, a forerunner of German Pietism (see pages 176–9). He also turned to Catholic mystics such as Jeanne-Marie Bouvier de la Motte-Guyon, an advocate of Quietism, which insisted on 'intellectual stillness' and interior passivity as essential conditions of perfection. It argued that man's highest perfection consisted of a psychic 'self-annihilation' and subsequent absorption of the soul into the divine, even during the present life. In this way, the mind withdrew from worldly interests passively to contemplate God. Although of interest to Upham, it is easy to see why Quietism was proscribed as heresy in very explicit terms by the Roman Catholic Church.

As other men became involved, the Holiness Movement began to spread. Two men affiliated with the movement founded Oberlin College, Ohio – Asa Mahan, the college president, and Charles Grandison Finney, a very successful evangelist and famous hymn-writer – promoted the idea of Christian Holiness. In 1836 Mahan experienced what he called 'baptism by the Holy Ghost'. He believed that this experience (note the stress on a personal experience) had cleansed him from both the desire and inclination to sin. Finney immediately saw that this 'second experience' could provide a solution to a problem he observed during his evangelistic revivals. Many people were claiming to experience conversion (that is, an initial experience of being saved), but then slipping back into their old ways of living. He began to preach that a filling with the Holy Spirit could help converts to continue in their Christian life.

The movement now began to gain important adherents from other denominations. A Presbyterian called William Boardman promoted the idea of Holiness through his evangelistic campaigns and his book *A Higher Christian Life* (1858). That same year, the Quaker Hannah Whitall Smith had a personal conversion experience. Two years later she claimed that she had found the 'secret' of the Christian life, which, she said, was complete devotion to God and, at the same time, God's transformation of one's soul. Her husband, Robert Pearsall Smith, had a similar experience at the first 'official' Holiness camp meeting in Vineland, New Jersey, in 1867. The Holiness Camp Meeting movement was begun by two Methodist ministers who subsequently founded the National Camp Meeting for the Promotion of Holiness, commonly known as the National Holiness Association (now called the Christian Holiness Association). After Smith had received the 'blessing', he and his wife became lay leaders in the organization.

At these camp meetings, people were encouraged to repent their sins, accept Christ as their Saviour, and commit their lives to holy living. As many as 20,000 people at a time participated in some meetings. Eventually, though, Smith disgraced himself at the height of his ministry by an adulterous affair, and his wife continued her spiritual journey and died a universalist, believing the universalist idea that, eventually, all souls will be saved. The Holiness Movement came close to truly great success when it almost captured the greatest evangelist of the day. In 1871, as a result of some soul-searching and the prayers of two Methodist women who attended one of his meetings, the great revivalist preacher Dwight L. Moody had what he called an 'endowment with power'. He never officially joined the Holiness Movement, but he did spread some of its ideas.

In the 1870s the Holiness Movement spread to Britain, where it was called the Higher Life movement (from Boardman's book *A Higher Christian Life*). Higher Life conferences were held at Broadlands and Oxford in 1874, and at Brighton and Keswick in 1875. The Keswick Convention soon became the British headquarters for the movement. From its English base the movement would spread to Scotland, and in 1886 found the Faith Mission. In 1874, the year after he left a Presbyterian church in Ontario to take a charge in New York City, the movement also had an impact on Albert Benjamin Simpson, who would later found the Christian and Missionary Alliance (1887).

Although the Holiness Movement did not appear to have a dramatic impact on society and culture, it left a lasting influence in the effect it had on the formation of a number of important movements for religious and social change during that period. Indeed, these groups are numerous, and include the Wesleyan Church, the Free Methodist Church (the church of this author's maternal grandparents), the Church of the Nazarene, the Salvation Army, the Christian and Missionary Alliance, the Church of God (Holiness), the Conservative Holiness Movement, and the World Gospel Mission. In addition, the Pentecostal movement traces its origins to the Holiness Movement. It is not surprising, though, that the movement seems not to have had a wide and dramatic impact. It was fundamentally a personal and individual movement. As such, it might be easy to discount it, but that would be a mistake. Its genius and lasting impact lies in the stress placed on personal experience and feeling (emotion) as validators of truth. Believers know (that is, they feel) they are saved. They experience (again, feel) God working in their hearts and saving their souls. Much of this had its roots in the evangelism of the Second Great Awakening, but it was the enthusiasm and fervour of the Holiness Movement that sustained and spread it to the extent that its rhetoric (and this is its lasting legacy) is now the main way of discussing salvation among most American evangelical Protestants.

This subtle but important legacy of the Holiness Movement is almost wholly overlooked, in marked contrast to that of the abolitionist movement. One might argue that Abolitionism was a one-issue movement, but, as with the Holiness Movement, its progress and fate has shaped not only America, but also the world. Its legacy may initially seem the more important and dramatic of the two, but anyone who has heard the powerful emotional and experiential appeal of a modern evangelical sermon would do well to remember the Holiness Movement.

ABOLITIONISM

Begun in Britain during the eighteenth century, Abolitionism was a political movement that sought to abolish the practice of slavery and the world-wide slave trade. It eventually became a global movement that was largely successful in achieving its goals. In fact, the trade in slaves had been made illegal in England as early as 1102, but the last form of enforced servitude did not disappear until the beginning of the seventeenth century. (In Scotland mineworkers and their families continued to be sold along with the mines they worked until the late eighteenth century.)

Despite this legal situation, the eighteenth century still saw black slaves being brought to Britain as personal servants by their owners. They could not be bought or sold in Britain, but their legal status, and that of slavery in Britain, was not clear. However, in 1772 the case of a runaway slave named James Somerset forced a legal decision. His owner, wanting to return Somerset to his possessions in Jamaica, kidnapped him. While in London, however, Somerset had been baptized, and his conscientious godparents issued a writ of habeus corpus, which forced the State to decide Somerset's status. On 22 June 1772 the Lord Chief Justice, William Murray, Lord Mansfield, rendered his verdict on whether Somerset, as property, could be 'moved', or, as a person in a society that did not recognize slavery, could be abducted.

The state of slavery is of such a nature, that it is incapable of being introduced on any reasons, moral or political; but only positive law [man-made law as it stood], which preserves its force long after the reasons, occasion, and time itself from whence it was created, is erased from memory: it's so odious, that nothing can be suffered to support it, but positive law. Whatever inconveniences, therefore, may follow from a decision, I cannot say this case is allowed or approved by the law of England; and therefore the black must be discharged.

Unfortunately for slaves throughout the empire (and miners in Scotland), the ruling applied only in England. However, it did immediately emancipate nearly 15,000 slaves in England, and also laid down that slavery contracted in other jurisdictions (such as the American colonies) could not be enforced in England.

In that sense not only did Lord Mansfield engage in that conservative bugbear of 'judicial activism', but he also preceded and totally disagreed with the decision of the Taney Supreme Court (see pages 201–2), which held that the civil contract of servitude was binding throughout all the States. (It was the legal concept embodied in this contract that segregationist opponents of interracial marriage in northern states before the 1960s, and of gay marriage in Massachusetts today, wished to ignore.) Fortunately for Somerset, Mansfield argued that the issue in deciding such cases involving human beings was not positive law, but rather a healthy dose of common sense (reason) and human decency. He did not really care what problems came from his decision: he simply ruled that Somerset had to be set free.

After reading of the Somerset case, a black slave in Scotland, Joseph Knight, left his master, John Wedderburn. As a result, a similar case was brought in Scotland, helped by the author James Boswell and the lexicographer Samuel Johnson, who argued that 'no man is by nature the property of another'. That same year, 1776, Thomas Jefferson wrote that all men were free while almost certainly benefiting from being waited on by one of his slaves. The result was the same, but the reasoning fundamentally different.

The Scottish bench declared that Knight was free on the basis of 'natural rights', declaring that 'we [the judges] sit here to enforce right not to enforce wrong'. They also made clear that chattel slavery did not exist under the law of Scotland (nevertheless, there were native-born Scottish slaves until 1799, when the coal miners noted above gained emancipation). Lord Mansfield in England freed Somerset despite positive law, while the judges in Scotland freed Knight because they refused to make a judgment they considered fundamentally 'wrong'. In both cases, to the benefit of the many slaves in Britain, the judiciary was well in advance of the legislature.

A few years later the issue of slavery began to take shape as an imperial issue. By 1783 an anti-slavery movement was beginning among the British public. Dr Beilby Porteus, Bishop of Chester and later of London, used his 1783 Anniversary Sermon for the Society for the Propagation of the Gospel in Foreign Parts (the Church of England's foreign mission body) to issue a call to the Church to cease its involvement in the slave trade and to formulate a workable policy to draw attention to and improve the conditions of the slaves on the Church's plantations in Barbados, which were helping financially to sustain the work of the Church!

That same year the first English abolitionist organization was founded by a group of Quakers, and succeeding generations of them remained active and influential throughout the life of the movement. On 17 June 1783 the issue was formally brought to government by Sir Cecil Wray, MP, when he presented a Quaker petition to Parliament. In May 1787 the Committee for the Abolition of the Slave Trade was formed to stop the Atlantic slave trade and the trafficking of slaves in all British colonies and among other countries. The leaders of the committee were members of the Clapham Sect, a group of evangelical reformers who met in Clapham, and Quakers. Since Quakers could not become MPs, William Wilberforce was persuaded to become the leader of the parliamentary campaign. Like many other abolitionist groups, the committee wanted to repatriate the slaves, that is, return them to Africa, regardless of how many generations removed from Africa they might be. Thus, one particular project of the abolitionists was the establishment of Sierra Leone as a settlement for former slaves.

Eventually, enormous public and political pressure were brought to bear, supported by extensive literature and emotive images. Consequently, the government was forced to act. On 25 March 1807 the Abolition of the Slave Trade Act was passed. This Act imposed a fine of £100 for every slave found aboard a British ship. The intention was to eradicate the slave trade within the British Empire. However, the trade continued, and the Act had one appalling consequence: captains in danger of being caught by the Royal Navy would often throw slaves into the sea to reduce the fine. To stop this practice, in 1827 Britain declared that participation in the slave trade was piracy and punishable by death.

However, this Act did not free slaves already held in the empire – it merely stopped British participation in the international trade. In the 1820s the abolitionist movement again became active, this time campaigning against the institution of slavery itself. The Anti-Slavery Society was founded in 1827. Many of the campaigners were the same as had previously campaigned against the slave trade. On 23 August 1833 the Slavery Abolition Act completely outlawed slavery in the British colonies. A year later, on 1 August 1834, all slaves in the British Empire were emancipated, though they were to remain indentured (servants) to their former owners in an apprenticeship system that was not finally abolished until 1838. In addition, the substantial sum of £20 million was paid in compensation to plantation owners in the Caribbean. From 1839, the British and Foreign Anti-Slavery Society worked to outlaw slavery in other countries, and this organization continues today as Anti-Slavery International.

The situation in France was fairly similar. French colonies in the Caribbean used slaves in the labour-intensive and physically brutal production of sugar. The slave trade had been regulated by Louis XIV's 1689 *Code Noir*. The institution of slavery was first repealed following the Haitian Revolution (1791) led by Toussaint l'Ouverture. The rebels forced the First Republic (1792–1804) to repeal slavery on 4 February 1794. The Abbé Henri Grégoire (elected Bishop of Blois under the Revolutionary Civil

Constitution of the Clergy, and later refused the last rites by the Archbishop of Paris because he would not retract his oath to this constitution) and the Society of the Friends of the Blacks, founded in 1788 and led by Jacques Pierre Brissot, who was guillotined during the Revolution, were part of the abolitionist movement, which had laid important groundwork in building anti-slavery sentiment in Paris before the Revolution and the Haitian Revolt. Sadly, slavery was re-established under Napoleon only to be abolished for a second time under the Second Republic (1848–52) on 27 April 1848 by the Schoelcher Decree. Although not slaves, Africans were indentured to mines, as well as to forestry and rubber plantations, in French-African colonies for decades thereafter.

Abolition occurred at various times across continental Europe, and in most cases was less the result of religious sentiment (which played a key role in France and Britain, and later in America) than Enlightenment and liberal thought. For example, between 1843 and 1855 some 250,000 Roma (gypsies) were freed after five centuries of slavery in Romania. Most promptly left the country for western Europe and America. Peter the Great abolished Russian slavery, but serfdom remained: serfs could not be personally sold, but, as with the Scottish miners, were 'property' attached to a specific place. On 3 March 1861, well before Lincoln's Emancipation Proclamation, Tsar Alexander II freed the serfs.

Abolitionism in America actually predated the Revolution. In Philadelphia on 14 April 1775 the first American abolition society – the Society for the Relief of Free Negroes Unlawfully Held in Bondage – was established, primarily by Quakers, whose religious views led them to object strongly to slavery as much in the North American colonies as in Britain. The Revolution and British occupation of Philadelphia caused the society to lapse, but it was re-formed in 1784, with the statesman Benjamin Franklin as its first president. The membership remained heavily Quaker, however.

Although the Revolution temporarily stopped the work of the society, the ideas released by the Revolution caused individuals and groups in every state to turn to the issues of slavery and abolition. The main organs agitating for abolition in the northern states were the Quakers, the Pennsylvania Antislavery Society and the New York Manumission Society – even though New York was almost the last northern state to pass an abolition law. The Constitutional Convention (1787) postponed federal control of the slave trade (unlike other forms of interstate commerce) until 1807.

All the states north of Maryland began gradually to abolish slavery between 1781 and 1804, by which time all states had abolished or severely limited the slave trade. Indeed, Rhode Island, as a colony, was the first to achieve this, in 1774; Virginia had also attempted to do so before the Revolution, but the English Privy Council had vetoed the Act. She and all the others eventually did so in 1786, the exception being Georgia, which complied in 1798. Northern emancipation Acts typically provided that slaves born before the law was passed would be freed at a certain age. This allowed slavery to linger; in New Jersey a dozen 'permanent apprentices' were recorded in the 1860 census. The first state to abolish slavery outright was Massachusetts, where a court decision (again, judicial activism in evidence) in 1781 interpreted the Massachusetts Constitution of 1780, which asserted in its first article, 'All men are created free and equal', for the abolition of slavery. This was later explicitly codified in a second version of the Massachusetts Constitution written by the future second US president John Adams.

By the 1820s and 1830s the American Colonization Society had become the main organization working for abolition. It had broad nationwide support, with leaders such as Henry Clay, founder of the Whig Party and a senator. It created an American colony (Liberia) in Africa and assisted thousands of blacks, both ex-slaves and free-born, to emigrate or repatriate. Although conditions were horrific and many died, enough survived to ensure that their descendants were able to dominate the country until the 1980s. Increasingly, though, other abolitionists rejected the idea of 'return', and the society began to founder.

With the 1840s a radical change was introduced into the American approach. William Lloyd Garrison, a leading journalist and social reformer, who later campaigned for temperance and women's rights, demanded 'immediate emancipation, gradually achieved'. By this he meant that slave owners should immediately 'repent' (note the religious rhetoric) and establish a system of emancipation. Indeed, Garrison frequently used religious language when denouncing slavery: 'I accuse the land of my nativity of insulting the majesty of Heaven with the grossest mockery that was ever exhibited to man.' Obviously, his views were also influenced by Enlightenment ideas about the universality of human rights: 'Our country is the world, our countrymen are all mankind. We love the land of our nativity, only as we love all other lands. The interests, rights, and liberties of American citizens are no more dear to us than are those of the whole human race. Hence we can allow no appeal to patriotism, to revenge any national insult or injury.'

Abolitionism in general had a strong religious base, including Quakers and, in the northern states, people who had been converted by the revivalist fervour of the Second Great Awakening during the 1830s. Indeed, belief in abolition contributed to the breaking away of some small denominations (such as the Free Methodist Church) from the larger denominations that were unwilling to confront the issue directly.

Abolitionists were also moved to try to influence the next generation through education. In response to the unwillingness of the oldest northern colleges (Harvard, Yale and Princeton) to support abolition, alternative colleges (Bates in Maine and Oberlin in Ohio) were founded. Indeed, northern abolitionists largely combined their rejection of slavery with a general desire to change society. Thus, most supported the temperance movement, public schooling, and prison- and asylum-building and reform. Interestingly, though, they tended to split completely over the issue of women's rights.

Despite its very obvious Protestant roots and rhetoric, Abolitionism actively recruited Catholic supporters. Daniel O'Connell, the Roman Catholic leader of the Irish in Ireland, supported the abolition of slavery in the British Empire and in America. As a major activist in securing Catholic emancipation (the removal of the legal discrimination against Roman Catholics in Great Britain and Ireland), he was one of William Lloyd Garrison's models. Garrison recruited him to the cause of American Abolitionism, and O'Connell, the black abolitionist Charles Lenox Remond, and Theobald Mathew, a temperance priest, organized a petition with 60,000 signatures, urging the Irish of America to support abolition. O'Connell also spoke up for abolition in America.

However, the Repeal Associations that O'Connell had established to argue for an end to the Act of Union (1800) between Ireland and Great Britain were largely pro-slavery. It may seem strange to find whites arguing for their own freedom while supporting the enslavement of blacks. Some have suggested that this happened because many Irish immigrants feared the competition of free black labour. Others have said Irish-Americans did not care to have their liberty lumped together with black emancipation. Finally, the overwhelmingly Protestant membership and rhetoric of Abolitionism may have offended others. However, this would imply that Irish-Americans were somehow unique in their views. Southern slaveholders who disliked the British were happy to support Irish emancipation, and, lest we forget, the Founding Fathers often held and sold slaves while espousing the high ideals of the Enlightenment about the rights of all men.

The reality is that Irish-Americans (the main body of Catholics in America) were as split as their Protestant fellow Americans. Thus, radical Irish nationalists – those who broke with O'Connell over his refusal to contemplate the violent overthrow of British rule in Ireland – were split on the issue of slavery. John Mitchel, who spent the years 1853–75 in America, was a passionate propagandist for slavery, and three of his sons fought in the Confederate Army. On the other hand, his former close associate Thomas Francis Meagher served as a Union brigadier-general.

The Roman Catholic hierarchy, largely based in slave-holding Maryland, supported slavery while advocating the spiritual equality of blacks – blacks could be full Catholics, but not full Americans. The Bishop of New York denounced O'Connell's petition as a forgery, and, if genuine, an example of unwarranted foreign interference. The Bishop of Charleston declared that while Catholic tradition opposed slave trading, it had nothing against slavery (which was true enough of both Catholicism and Protestantism). No American Catholic bishop supported abolition before the Civil War; even during the war, they freely participated in the Mass with slave-owners. One historian ruefully observed that 'ritualistic' churches separated themselves from heretics rather than sinners; he observed the same acceptance of slavery among Episcopalians and Lutherans. Indeed, one Episcopal bishop was a Confederate general. Of course, the existence of the *Southern* Baptist Convention, which came into being over the issue of northern abolitionism, would suggest that even 'non-ritualistic' churches could be pro-slavery.

In the United States, however, Abolitionism always combined Protestant rhetoric with the language of the American Revolution and its key documents: the Constitution and, more frequently, the Declaration of Independence. This same reliance on sacred texts (the Bible) and secular texts (of American history) is a recurring theme in American social reform. This stress in American ideology (with or without the Bible) underlies Garrison's assertion:

> I am a believer in that portion of the Declaration of American
> Independence in which it is set forth, as among self-evident truths,
> 'that all men are created equal; that they are endowed by their
> Creator with certain inalienable rights; that among these are life,
> liberty, and the pursuit of happiness'. Hence, I am an abolitionist.
> Hence, I cannot but regard oppression in every form – and most
> of all, that which turns a man into a thing – with indignation and
> abhorrence. Not to cherish these feelings would be recreancy to
> principle. They who desire me to be dumb on the subject of slavery,
> unless I will open my mouth in its defense, ask me to give the lie to
> my professions, to degrade my manhood, and to stain my soul. I will
> not be a liar, a poltroon, or a hypocrite, to accommodate any party,
> to gratify any sect, to escape any odium or peril, to save any interest,

to preserve any institution, or to promote any object. Convince me that one man may rightfully make another man his slave, and I will no longer subscribe to the Declaration of Independence. Convince me that liberty is not the inalienable birthright of every human being, of whatever complexion or clime, and I will give that instrument to the consuming fire. I do not know how to espouse freedom and slavery together.

This is the stuff of revivalist preaching, but the text is Jefferson the slave-holder, not John the Evangelist.

The institution remained solidly supported in the South, however, and that region's customs and social beliefs evolved into a strident defence of slavery, especially the stronger the anti-slavery stance developed in the North. Although most northerners were anti-slavery, the majority had little sympathy with Abolitionism. Indeed, many northern politicians and leaders, including Abraham Lincoln, Stephen Douglas (the Democratic presidential nominee in 1860), John C. Fremont (the Republican nominee in 1856), and Ulysses S. Grant married into slave-owning southern families, seem-ingly without any qualms. Basically, being opposed to slavery was not neces-sarily the same as Abolitionism, which was, as a principle, far more than the wish to limit the extent of slavery: abolitionists wanted slavery abolished. Most northerners, on the other hand, accepted that slavery existed in the South and that the Constitution did not allow the federal government to intervene there, but they did not want it to spread. Where there was general support for emancipation, it was to be gradual and compensated.

One significant segment of northerners was united in support of imme-diate abolition. The abolitionist movement was strengthened by the activi-ties of free African-Americans, especially in the 'black' churches, who argued that the old biblical justifications for slavery (regularly rehearsed by almost all southern, and not a few northern, ministers and priests) contra-dicted the New Testament. However, African-American activists and their writings were rarely heard outside the black community. This changed with the rise of Garrison, who was much influenced by the arguments coming from the free black community. He was also instrumental in discovering the ex-slave Frederick Douglass, who eventually became a prominent activist in his own right. Eventually, Douglass would publish his own, widely distributed Abolitionist newspaper, the *North Star*.

In the early 1850s the American abolitionist movement split into two camps over the issue of the United States Constitution, which institutionalized an acceptance of slavery in the way in which seats were apportioned for the House of Representatives: slaves counted, but not as 'full' people. This issue arose in the late 1840s after the publication of *The Unconstitutionality of Slavery* by Lysander Spooner. The Garrisonians publicly burnt copies of the Constitution, called it a pact with slavery, and demanded its abolition and replacement. Another camp, led by Spooner and, eventually, Douglass, considered the Constitution to be an anti-slavery document. Using an argument based upon Natural Law (the idea that an order has been divinely established and is inherent in all humans and known to them through the voice of conscience) and a form of social-contract theory articulated strongly in the sixteenth century, especially in France (see page 84), they said that slavery existed outside the Constitution's scope of legitimate authority and should therefore be abolished.

Much of this argument came to the fore with the decisions being handed down by the Supreme Court under Chief Justice Roger B. Taney – interestingly, the first Roman Catholic to hold the post – who had in earlier years referred to slavery as 'a blot on our national character'. In three key decisions the court made it clear that the Constitution was fundamentally dedicated to the preservation of the rights of slave-owners and the maintenance of slavery. In most cases the Taney court favoured the power of the State and opposed federal intervention. However, when it came to slavery, the judicial activism of the court was staunchly on the side of the federal government forcing states to accept slavery (as a civil contract of another state).

In *Prigg* v. *Pennsylvania* (1842) the court held that the Constitutional prohibition against state laws that would emancipate any 'person held to service or labor in [another] state' barred Pennsylvania from punishing a Maryland man who had seized a former slave and her child, then taken them back to Maryland without seeking an order from the Pennsylvania courts permitting the abduction (the exact opposite of the decisions in Britain half a century earlier). The Taney court extended this rule ten years later in *Moore v. Illinois* (1852) to hold that 'any state law or regulation which interrupts, impedes, limits, embarrasses, delays or postpones the right of the owner to the immediate possession of the slave, and the immediate command of his service, is void'. Five years later Taney wrote the decision for the court in the Dred Scott case (1857) that declared any restrictions imposed by Congress on the spread of slavery into the territories, such as those found in the Missouri Compromise (which had ensured that states would be admitted in pairs – one slave, the other free) to be unconstitutional. Taney's language in interpreting the meaning of the Constitution was solidly based on what, he asserted, the framers of the Constitution intended when it was written. His explanation of the court's ruling was clear: African-Americans, free or slave, could not be citizens of any state because the drafters of the Constitution had viewed them as 'beings of an inferior order, and altogether unfit to associate with the white race, either in social or political relations, and so far inferior that they had no rights which the white man was bound to respect'.

Abolitionism, although rooted in religion and American constitutional thought, was also entwined with ideas about class consciousness. The artisan republicanism of Robert Dale Owen and Frances Wright contrasted starkly with the politics of prominent elite abolitionists, such as the industrialist Arthur Tappan and his evangelist (again, note the role of religion) brother Lewis. While the former pair opposed slavery on the basis of solidarity among 'wage slaves', such as factory workers, with 'chattel slaves', the Tappans strongly rejected this view, opposing any suggestion that northern workers were slaves.

In the end the situation was not settled by the judiciary or legislature as it was in Britain, but rather, as in the French Empire, by force of arms. The election of Lincoln on a Republican platform opposed to any extension of slavery into any territories that might become states threatened, in time, to tip the balance of power in the Senate, until then equally divided between senators from free and slave states. The South responded by anticipating what they thought would be inevitable – abolition. They seceded. The outbreak of hostilities shifted the debate from slavery to the future existence of the nation as an intact union. Only after a string of federal victories, and in the face of possible European recognition of the rebel states, did Lincoln declare the emancipation of slaves (on 1 January 1863) in states still in rebellion (that is, *not*, for example, Maryland, which had not left the Union). Slavery itself was not totally and universally abolished until the Thirteenth Amendment was ratified (1865). Even then, in time (as we shall see in the next chapter) states were able to use the Constitution's separation of federal and state power to strip black American citizens of most of their political rights and introduce segregation via the Jim Crow laws.

THE SOCIAL GOSPEL MOVEMENT

Like Abolitionism, the Social Gospel movement had an explicit religious undertone. Unlike Abolitionism, though, it was (and to a certain extent continues to be) aimed at a whole range of perceived social evils. From its beginnings in the late nineteenth century and into the early twentieth century it expressed a 'Christian concern' about a range of issues: poverty, alcohol, drugs, crime, racism, slums, hygiene, education and militarism. Although the movement has largely disappeared, its principles continue to inspire newer movements, such as Christians Against Poverty. In contrast to many groups inspired by the Holiness Movement, Social Gospellers did not expect an imminent return of Christ or the end of the world. Rather they believed human effort could usher in the coming new Kingdom of God on Earth and, as a result, the return of Christ. (The technical description of this belief is 'post-millennial'.) They believed the Second Coming could not and would not happen until humankind rid itself of social evils by human effort – in effect, until humans made the planet fit for the Messiah's earthly kingdom. For the most part, they rejected pre-millennialist theology (which was – and is – predominant in the southern United States). This teaches that the Second Coming of Christ is imminent and that Christians should devote their energies to preparing for it rather than focusing on the concerns of this world, which, in any case, could not be solved merely by human agency or action. Their millennial views are very similar to those shared by so-called Christian Reconstructionists, except that Social Gospel leaders were in the main politically and religiously liberal (in contrast to the Reconstructionists, who tend to be politically libertarian but religiously fundamentalist). As such, the Social Gospel movement arose from Christian Modernism, and competed with the anti-Modernist movements of evangelicalism and fundamentalism.

In modern times this movement has all but withered as times have changed, many perceived evils have been 'dealt with' (by laws, though not always in reality), and conservative religions have come to dominate the agenda. However, in the United States prior to the First World War, the Social Gospel was the religious wing of the progressive movement, a muscular and militant form of Protestantism aimed at combating injustice, suffering and poverty. During the Depression and the New Deal of the 1920s–30s, Social Gospel ideas apparent in the work of Harry Hopkins (a chief adviser to Roosevelt, and architect of the WPA (Works Progress Administration) and Lend Lease programme) and Mary McLeod Bethune (a daughter of former slaves, who was in Roosevelt's Office of Negro Affairs or, the 'black cabinet') focused the Social Gospel spotlight on racism. Bethune had been largely responsible for getting the Red Cross to integrate in 1917, and had worked tirelessly, if vainly, for federal anti-lynching legislation.

During the Second World War the movement became moribund, but was reinvigorated by the work of civil-rights leaders (see pages 226–33). With extensive legal gains in the 1960s and 1970s, and the rise of conservatism generally and evangelicalism/fundamentalism more specifically, the movement has all but lapsed in America. However, the Social Gospel movement is still influential in Canada's United Church, and in the Anglican

Church in England, where the Social Gospel has found expression in pacifism. A key figure in this Canadian expression of the Social Gospel was Margaret S. McWilliams, the first president of the Canadian Federation of University Women (1919), president of the Women's Canadian Club (1922), president of the Manitoba Historical Society (1944–8), and Winnipeg's second female alderman (1933–40). She is most remembered, though, for her writings, which promoted the ideas of the Social Gospel: *Manitoba Milestones* (1928), *If I Were King of Canada* (1931) and *This New Canada* (1948). The Social Gospel also remains influential among Christian socialist circles in Britain in the Church of England and Methodist and Calvinist movements. In Catholicism liberation theology (largely repudiated by recent popes) has similarities to the Social Gospel.

Despite later conservative critiques, especially from those with a strong theological agenda in rejecting post-millennialism as a motive for action, the Social Gospel movement was the prime motivational factor in much of Protestantism for many of the decades around 1900, and its efforts led to truly important and lasting reforms and improvements in society. This combination of religion and social reform was succinctly expressed by one Presbyterian: 'The great ends of the church are the proclamation of the gospel for the salvation of humankind; the shelter, nurture, and spiritual fellowship of the children of God; the maintenance of divine worship; the preservation of truth; the promotion of social righteousness; and the exhibition of the Kingdom of Heaven to the world.'

In other words, Protestant Christianity was meant to be as much about eliminating poverty and prejudice (that is, radically altering the way society worked and individuals interacted in it) as it was about preaching to convert sinners. Religion was not just changing the pattern of behaviour of a single, individual convert; it was also changing the pattern of behaviour in the entire culture towards its members and other cultures.

In the decades straddling 1900 many Protestants were disgusted by poverty and the appalling conditions in slums and tenement housing. The Social Gospel movement provided a religious rationale for action to remove those evils. Activists within the movement hoped that by public-health measures, as well as enforced schooling to develop talents and skills among the poor, the quality of their physical and moral lives would improve. A key goal was the reform of labour laws, especially the abolition of child labour and limitations on the working hours of mothers. By 1920, American Social Gospellers were crusading against the twelve-hour day for men at US Steel, and those who might be inclined to mock the Social Gospel Movement for pie-in-the-sky idealism would do well to pause when leaving work after an eight-hour shift to recall that they have much for which to thank the movement.

In some cases, the Social Gospellers were moved to take direct action to improve conditions, rather than await government legislation. For example, reformers inspired by the movement opened settlement houses, most notably Hull House in Chicago, operated by Jane Addams (for her efforts she became the first American woman to earn the Nobel Peace Prize). These houses helped the poor (especially immigrants) improve their lives by offering services such as daycare, education and health care to needy people in slum neighbourhoods.

The Social Gospel movement in the United States was parallel to the Christian Socialism movement in Britain at about the same time. The two movements coalesced in Canada, where they were especially influential. Many ministers became active in the socialist movement in the form of the Cooperative Commonwealth Federation (CCF) and later the New Democratic Party. For example, Tommy Douglas, a Baptist minister, was leader of the CCF from 1942, and the premier of Saskatchewan from 1944 to 1961, where he headed the first socialist government in North America. He oversaw the introduction of universal public medical coverage in Canada, and during the period 1961–71 he led the New Democratic Party at the federal level.

The Social Gospel was greatly influenced by the fictional works of the Congregational minister and committed Christian Socialist Charles Sheldon. His catchphrase in the face of perceived social evils, 'What would

Jesus do?', had a tremendous and lasting impact on the way American Protestants expressed and understood their religion (just as the Holiness Movement introduced an emphasis upon individual experientialism and 'feeling'). His works *In His Steps* (1897) and *The Reformer* (1902) had a direct impact on one of the leading early theologians of the Social Gospel in the United States.

WALTER RAUSCHENBUSCH

Rauschenbusch, as one of the most articulate religious exponents of the movement, is worthy of some close examination. He was the son of a German preacher who taught at the Rochester Theological Seminary in upstate New York. There he was raised on the conservative Protestant doctrines of his time, including biblical literalism and substitutionary atonement, both of which we have encountered in various guises from the sixteenth century onwards. But when he himself attended the seminary, those teachings were challenged. He learnt of the 'Higher Criticism' (a form of critical academic analysis, prominent among Christian modernists, that treated Biblical texts as 'mere' historical documents); this eventually led him to conclude that traditional 'ideas about the inerrancy of the Bible [were] untenable'. He also began to doubt substitutionary atonement: 'it was not taught by Jesus; it makes salvation dependent upon a trinitarian transaction that is remote from human experience; and it implies a concept of divine justice that is repugnant to human sensitivity'. However, these changes to his beliefs did not shatter his faith or lead him away from the Church; rather, these challenges reinforced his faith.

It was this new, altered and reinforced faith that gave a theological structure to the ideas of the Social Gospellers. Rauschenbusch said that Christianity's goal was to spread God's kingdom not through 'fire and brimstone', revivalist (emotive) preaching, but by living a 'Christlike' life (example). Rauschenbusch rejected substitutionary atonement, arguing that Christ died (as an example) 'to substitute love for selfishness as the basis of human society'. More dramatically, but very much in the tradition of many 'radical' Protestant groups we have already seen, he wrote that 'Christianity is in its nature revolutionary.' Admittedly, he meant Protestant Christianity. For him, the kingdom of God was 'not a matter of getting individuals to heaven, but of transforming the life on earth into the harmony of heaven'; his goal was to create heaven *on* Earth.

Rauschenbusch's ideas and work flew in the face of mainstream Protestantism in the late nineteenth century. The large Protestant denominations were largely allied with, and financially dependent on, the social and political establishment, in effect supporting the domination of 'robber barons' (powerful, often philanthropic industrialists, such as Andrew Carnegie and John D. Rockefeller), income disparity, and the use of child labour. Those large but poor denominations (rural and frequently southern versions of Baptists and Methodists) tended to ignore or dislike the Social Gospel, not for its agitation against social ills, but because it was perceived as being modernist and liberal. Moreover, it has to be said that the Social Gospel tended to focus on urban ills, not the problems of the rural poor. The large, wealthy, urban-based denominations did not see a connection between their ministries and the issues of social injustice, inequality and poverty, but Rauschenbusch saw his duty as a minister and student of Christ to act with love by trying to improve social conditions. These ideas were to prove extremely influential on as diverse a group as Mahatma Gandhi, Martin Luther King Jr and Archbishop Desmond Tutu.

This led him to direct action. In 1892 Rauschenbusch and some friends formed a group called the Brotherhood of the Kingdom. Its charter declared that 'the Spirit of God is moving men in our generation toward a better understanding of the idea of the Kingdom of God on earth', and that their goal was 'to re-establish this idea in the thought of the church, and to assist in its practical realization in the world'. In a pamphlet, Rauschenbusch wrote: 'Because the Kingdom of God has been dropped as the primary and comprehensive aim of Christianity, and personal salvation has been substituted for it, therefore men seek to save their own souls and are selfishly indifferent to the evangelization of the world.'

ABOVE

17 *Lead Mining at Leadhills* by David Allan (1744–96). A key goal of many Social Gospellers and other 'liberal' Christians was the reform of labour laws, especially the abolition of child labour and limitations on the working hours of mothers. (See page 206.)

LEFT

18 *George Whitefield* (1769) by John Greenwood, after Nathaniel Hone. It is estimated that throughout his life, Whitefield preached more than 18,000 formal sermons. He visited America seven times and made 15 journeys to Scotland, two to Ireland, and one each to Bermuda, Gibraltar, and the Netherlands. (See page 169.)

ABOVE
19 *Signing the Declaration of Independence* (c. 1817)
by John Trumbull. In scenes reminiscent of Scots
signing their National Covenant, America's
Founding Fathers declared their independence
from Britain on 4 July 1776. However, these
same men often held and sold slaves while
espousing ideals about the rights of men.
(See page 199.)

OPPOSITE TOP
20 *Cross-section of a slave ship* by Jacques-Henri
Bernardin de Saint-Pierre (1737–1814). The
Abolition of the Slave Trade Act imposed a fine
for every slave found aboard a British ship. One
appalling consequence was that captains would
often throw slaves into the sea to reduce the fine.
(See page 194.)

ABOVE
21 *Benjamin Franklin* (c. 1785) by Joseph Siffred
Duplessis. In 1784, the Quaker Society for the
Relief of Free Negroes Unlawfully Held in
Bondage was reformed after the American
Revolution with Benjamin Franklin as its first
president. (See page 195.)

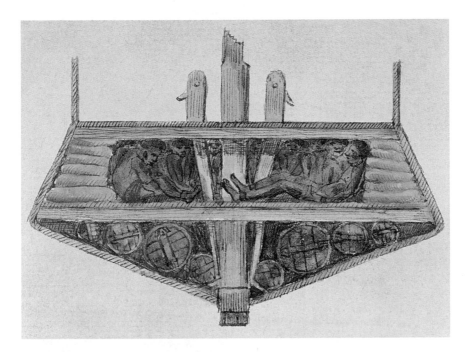

ABOVE LEFT

22 *John Wesley* (1789) after George Romney.
Methodism was started by a group of men
including John Wesley and his younger brother
Charles as a movement within the Church of
England, focused on a 'methodical approach'
to Bible study. (See page 164.)

ABOVE RIGHT

23 *Thomas Jefferson* (1805/21) by Gilbert Stuart.
Jefferson's Deism and rejection of traditional
Protestantism were clear: 'If by religion we
[mean] sectarian dogmas ... then ... this would
be the best of all possible worlds, if there were
no religion in it.' (See page 156.)

RIGHT

24 *William Wilberforce* (1833) by George Richmond. Since Quakers could not become members of parliament, Wilberforce was persuaded to become the leader of the parliamentary campaign against the slave trade. (See page 193.)

BELOW

25 *View of the Manchester and Liverpool Railway, taken at Newton, 1825*, by Charles Calvert. Allowing loans with interest began as a restricted innovation in Calvin's Geneva but had the unintended consequence of allowing the development of ideas about interest, liability, risk, profit, and dividend, which paved the way for the Industrial Revolution (epitomized by the advent of the railways). Through no fault of Calvin, modern capitalism was born. (See page 75.)

TOP

26 *Virginia Stock* (1836) engraved by Ingrey. Slavery began to be seen as a practice that offended Biblical and Enlightenment ideals or, as W. L. Garrison said: 'Convince me that liberty is not the inalienable birthright of every human being … and I will give [the Declaration of Independence] to the consuming fire. I do not know how to espouse freedom and slavery together.' (See page 191.)

ABOVE

27 A girl 'hurrier' in a Halifax coalmine in the 1840s, as pictured in the *Illustrated London News*. The caption reads: 'Naked to their waist; An iron chain fastened to a belt of leather runs between their legs'. Child labour, especially in dangerous industries, was the focus of intensive Protestant social action after the abolition of slavery. (See page 206.)

TOP

28 *Total Abstainers' Meeting in Sadler's Wells Theatre*
by George Cruikshank. Temperance and even
abstinence from all alcohol was part of a
'package' of social reforms pioneered by
Protestant social activists. (See page 163.)

ABOVE

29 *Pilgrims Going to Church* (1867) by George
Henry Boughton. Alexis de Tocqueville suggested
that the Pilgrims' Puritanism was the very thing
that provided a firm foundation for American
democracy. (See page 129.)

RIGHT

30 The abuse of alcohol (and other drugs) was seen as a religious evil and social ill that needed control. However, attempts at legal prohibition were wholly unsuccessful. (See page 251.)

BELOW LEFT

31 Suffragette Emmeline Pankhurst being arrested by Superintendent Rolfe while trying to present a petition to the king at Buckingham Palace in May 1914. (See page 244.)

BELOW RIGHT

32 *Dr Martin Luther King Jr* by Anthony Gruerio. King, who was a Protestant minister and a social activist, used both the Bible and the ideals of American democracy to fight bigotry and discrimination. (See page 228.)

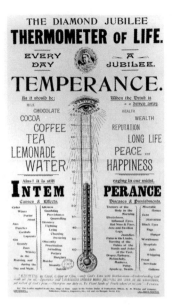

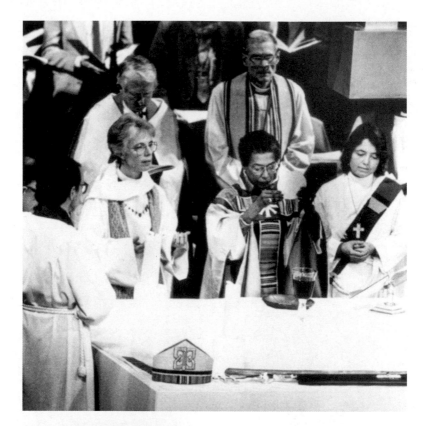

ABOVE
33 The election of 'gay' Bishop Gene Robinson has sparked as much debate as the election, in the 1980s, of black, female Bishop Barbara Harris, shown here celebrating Mass. (See page 238.)

LEFT
34 Bishop Gene Robinson. Archbishop Desmond Tutu, commenting on negative responses to the election of openly gay Robinson as bishop of Vermont by the parishioners in his diocese said: '[Anglicans] used to be known for embodying the attribute of comprehensiveness, of inclusiveness … God must look on and God must weep.' (See page 237.)

This was, in effect, a direct assault on the individualistic and experiential form of Protestant Christianity that had developed in America during the two Great Awakenings. Nothing could have been more distant or distinct from the evangelical preaching of the camp meetings and revivals. However, this articulated much of the thought lying behind Abolitionism. Moreover, this concept of Protestantism as a movement that was more about the community and the communal than the individual found as many echoes in the conflict resolution of Calvinist consistories as it did in the communal property of Anabaptists. Indeed, as noted earlier, individualism and experientialism were largely alien to much of Protestantism before the early nineteenth century, despite some superficial similarities to various forms of mysticism.

Rauschenbusch was condemned by the evolving fundamentalist movement as a modernizer, while members of the larger, wealthy denominations attacked his socialism. Both tended to argue that his ideas had no biblical basis. Rauschenbusch responded directly and uncompromisingly in *Christianity and the Social Crisis* (1907):

> No man shares his life with God whose religion does not flow out,
> naturally and without effort, into all relations of his life and
> reconstructs everything that it touches. Whoever uncouples the
> religious and the social life has not understood Jesus. Whoever sets
> any bounds for the reconstructive power of the religious life over the
> social relations and institutions of men, to that extent denies the
> faith of the Master.

Likewise, in his *Theology for the Social Gospel* (1917), he wrote that for John the Baptist, baptism was 'not a ritual act of individual salvation but an act of dedication to a religious and social movement'. However, critics of Rauschenbusch (then and now) argued that he neglected the needs of the individual as a moral and spiritual being in his fervour to reform society. In other words, he failed to teach that love for one's neighbour flowed directly from, and was required by, one's own love for God – a person must first be saved before he or she can do anything else.

The question, though, was much more complex. What was a saved person to do after being saved? Was the primary impulse to preach or to act? That is, was a saved person, while struggling to control his own individual sinfulness, meant to work to convince others of the need for the same individual experience of salvation? As a result of this activity, in time, would society be changed through the cumulative effect of saving individuals and the alteration of the sinful behaviour of those individuals? Or was it incumbent upon the believer to see that some evils in society were more than simply the cumulative result of the sins of individuals? That is, how many people needed to be converted before child labour would disappear or sweatshops become safe places to work or racial discrimination in hiring no longer happen? The Social Gospellers took the view that some evils in society needed to be confronted directly and that this was as important an act of 'Christian witness' to sinners as a camp-meeting sermon. Moreover, the eradication of these evils was in itself a godly, Christian act.

In this, the debate harkens back to those that have plagued or invigorated Protestantism since the days of the magisterial and radical reformers. Was Christianity a faith to be practised in this world or separated from it? Was it mostly about the believer and eternal destiny, or the believer's personal life and behaviour in this life? The Social Gospellers took the view that Christianity laid upon its adherents an obligation to fight battles in this world against evil, and that it was possible to win those battles (whether the war could be won by human agency was another matter). These battles did indeed involve personal struggle against individual ills (alcoholism, for example). However, the eradication of these individual sins would not overcome society's ills or sins. This required concerted group effort, not just person piety. Or to pose the issue in present-day circumstances: has a salvation experience and a personal relationship with Christ enjoyed by any given American made life healthier for workers slaving in remote sweatshops for a few pennies an hour to produce clothes for those same 'born-again'

Christians? Should it? If it should, but had not, Rauschenbusch and the Social Gospellers would ask, why not?

LIBERALISM

In a very real sense, the Social Gospellers were asking many of the same questions, with religious rhetoric and from a religious perspective, that secular adherents to the liberal values of the Enlightenment were asking at much the same time. As already noted, in America the language of 'values' and 'justice' is both religious (like the Social Gospellers or abolitionists using the Bible), and liberal (based on the rhetoric of the Declaration of Independence along with the Constitution and its first ten amendments, the Bill of Rights).

More generally, though, as an ideology, liberalism can trace its roots back to the humanism that subjected the medieval Western Church and its traditional truths to questioning. It also found articulation among the Whigs of the Glorious Revolution (1688) in Great Britain, whose assertion of their right to choose their king can be seen as a precursor to claims of popular sovereignty, as can the concessions extracted from Charles I by the Scottish Parliament in 1640. However, movements generally labelled as 'liberal' date from the Enlightenment, particularly the Whig party (Britain), the *philosophes* (France), and the movement towards self-government in colonial America. These movements politically opposed absolute monarchy, mercantilism (such as monopolies), and various kinds of religious orthodoxy and clericalism. They were also the first to formulate the concepts of individual rights under the rule of law, as well as the importance of self-government through elected representatives.

The definitive break with the past is normally understood as the point at which it was argued that free individuals could form the foundations of a stable society. Most would see John Locke and his *Two Treatises on Government* (1690) as key influences in the development of modern liberalism. He established two fundamental liberal ideas: economic liberty (the right to own and freely use property), and intellectual liberty (including freedom of conscience, which he noticeably did not extend to Catholics). This latter idea he further developed in *A Letter Concerning Toleration* (1689). Locke also stressed the earlier idea of natural rights, which he summed up as 'life, liberty and property' – not, interestingly, the 'life, liberty and pursuit of happiness' wording used in the Declaration of Independence. His 'natural-rights theory' would eventually develop into modern ideas about human rights. However, Locke believed that property was more important than the right to participate in government and public decision-making. In particular, he did not endorse democracy, since he feared that a 'mob' majority (in other words, the people) would be very likely to vote to take property away from the minority who had it (hence property requirements for voting in both Britain and America through much of the eighteenth and nineteenth centuries). Despite these caveats about the dangers of the majority, the idea of natural rights played a key role in providing the ideological justification for the American and French revolutions.

It is perhaps most interesting to note that many of the ideas of liberalism arose in two extremely different places – Catholic, absolutist France and Presbyterian Scotland. It is also worth noting that some key French thinkers actually found it advisable to argue from the safety of Calvinist Geneva. The late French Enlightenment saw two figures who would have tremendous influence on later liberal thought. Voltaire (pen-name of François-Marie Arouet, who spent periods of exile in England and Geneva) argued that the French should adopt constitutional monarchy, which he had seen in Britain, and disestablish the Second Estate (the nobility). The Genevan-born philosopher Jean-Jacques Rousseau argued for a natural freedom for mankind. Both argued, in different ways, for changes in political and social arrangements based around the idea that society can restrain a natural human liberty, but not obliterate its nature. For Voltaire, the concept was largely intellectual; for Rousseau, it was related to intrinsic natural rights, perhaps related to the philosophical ideas of Denis Diderot.

Rousseau, in particular, articulated many of the ideas that would find expression in the American and French revolutions, and, therefore, in the rhetoric (combined with the Bible) of many debates in America and else-where about social justice, racism and human rights. In America especially these ideas were regularly coupled with religion and the Bible, though it has to be said that the Founding Fathers rarely saw a need for this combination (see Deism, pages 155–7). Rousseau stressed the idea of a contract between government and people, which we have already met in Huguenot France and Civil War Britain (see pages 84, 132 and 134). He asserted that each person knows his own interest best. He argued that man was born free and that education was sufficient to restrain him within society, echoing some of the naivety about education seen in humanism. In his view the unity of a state came from the concerted action of consent, or the 'national will'. This unity of action would allow states to exist without being chained to pre-existing social orders, such as aristocracy. In time, these ideas became inter-twined with ideas coming from Scotland and from Enlightenment Germany. In particular, the writings of Scotsmen such as David Hume and Adam Smith, and the German philosopher Immanuel Kant, were crucial.

David Hume's contributions were many and varied, but the most important was his assertion that fundamental rules of human behaviour would overwhelm attempts to restrict or regulate them (*A Treatise of Human Nature*, 1739–40). Adam Smith argued that individuals could structure both moral (note the overlap with religion – this is an argument against State coercion in religion) and economic life without direction from the State, and that nations would be strongest when their citizens were free to follow their own initiative (individual choices and preferences). Indeed, he saw a very limited role for the State. Its primary task was to oversee those areas that could not be entrusted to the profit motive, such as preventing individuals from using force or fraud to disrupt competition, trade or production. This limited role was also apparent in his theory of taxation. Governments should levy taxes only in ways that did not harm the econ-omy and that 'The subjects of every state ought to contribute towards the support of the government, as nearly as possible, in proportion to their respective abilities [progressive taxation]; that is, in proportion [means-tested] to the revenue which they respectively enjoy under the protection of the state.'

It has to be said that an emphasis upon progressive rather than regressive tax (in other words, related to an ability to pay, such as graduated income tax, rather than the same amount levied on everyone, as with sales tax or VAT) is not an idea one might immediately associate with Smith, who is more often seen as the advocate of 'unfettered' market forces.

While Hume and Smith gave liberalism much of its economic and political thought, and Rousseau and Voltaire many of its key concepts, it was Kant who gave it much of its solid philosophical base. He stressed that a liberal, enlightened person thought autonomously, free of the dictates of external authority. He placed the active, rational human subject at the centre of the cognitive and moral worlds. With regard to knowledge, Kant argued that the rational order of the world as known by science could never be accounted for merely by the fortuitous accumulation of sense perceptions (that is, seeing a tree is not the same as interpreting it as a tree or categorizing it as an elm tree rather than an oak tree). Rather, the apparently objective order of nature and the causal necessity that operates within it are dependent upon the mind. With regard to morality, Kant argued that the source of the 'good' lies not in anything outside the person, either in nature (natural law) or given by God (revealed truth), rather only the good will itself. A good will is one that acts from duty in accordance with the universal moral law that the autonomous human being freely gives himself.

This did not mean that Kant rejected the idea of God, any more than the Deists did. However, his idea of God was radically different from that of traditional Christianity. Kant stated the practical necessity for a belief in God ('practical' being the key word) in his *Critique of Pure Reason* (1781). The idea of God is directly related to moral happiness as an expression of 'the supreme good'. The result is an intelligible moral world that 'is necessary from the practical point of view'. God, therefore, served a useful and practical purpose in man's rational and moral world. As we have seen, ideas like this underpinned the Deism of many of America's Founding Fathers, and must make one question their every use of the term 'God'. If Kant (or, indeed, Washington or Jefferson or Adams) had quoted the inscription on a modern American coin, 'In God we trust', he would have meant something very different from Calvin before him or even Rauschenbusch or Garrison or Martin Luther King Jr or Jerry Falwell after him.

Kant was also, like Smith, very distrustful of democracy, if by that one meant direct democracy. He believed that majority rule (the will of opinion polls) posed a threat to individual liberty, and stated, '[direct] democracy is, properly speaking, necessarily a despotism, because it establishes an executive power in which "all" [that is, the majority, even if only a majority of one] decide for or even against one who does not agree; that is, "all", who are not quite all, decide, and this is a contradiction of the general will with itself and with freedom.'

This fear of the dictatorship of the majority resulted in the system of checks and balances within the American Constitution. The goal was to ensure liberty by preventing the concentration of power in the hands of any one man – or any majority of men. Or, to put it another way, Kant and Smith remind us that direct democracy – the rule of the majority, be it 'moral' or not – would almost certainly have kept segregation in America well past the 1960s, and would certainly have kept most Catholics and Jews from entering America in the nineteenth century.

Liberalism was not in itself an explicitly religious or Protestant movement. However, as is obvious, it derived many of its views from ideas that came to the fore during the religious conflicts of the sixteenth and seventeenth centuries. Having seen the aftermath of attempts to coerce men's hearts and minds, as well as their behaviour, many concluded that support for freedom of the individual was the only logical position to hold. This was a crucial idea in the thinking of Abolitionism, which coupled these liberal and Enlightenment ideas with biblical calls to justice, equality and charity (particularly strong in the prophets of the Old Testament and Jesus's teachings in the Gospels). The Holiness Movement took this stress on the individual and experience (a perspective Kant would have understood – but probably deplored) and made it central to religion, in the process demolishing the idea that religion was 'enforceable'. The Social Gospel movement reacted against a perceived retreat into the individual and individualism by stressing Enlightenment ideas of equity and fairness (over the freedom of the 'marketplace') coupled with an expansion of the religious rhetoric of Abolitionism. As a group, these ideas and movements performed a complicated and interrelated dance that would lead to a dramatic expansion in the ideas of liberty and personal freedom in the mid- to late twentieth century and into the twenty-first century.

7

PROTESTANT LIBERALISM V. FUNDAMENTALISM

Jesus [was] an extremist for love: 'Love your enemies' ... Luther [was] an extremist: 'Here I stand; I can do none other' ... Lincoln [was] an extremist: 'This nation cannot survive half slave and half free' ... Jefferson [was] an extremist: 'All men are created equal'. So the question is not whether we will be [an] extremist but what kind of extremist will we be ... extremists for hate or ... for love ... [E]xtremists for the preservation of injustice ... or ... for the cause of justice?

Dr Martin Luther King Jr
In a letter from Birmingham Jail (1963)

PROTESTANTISM CAME INTO THE TWENTIETH century, the modern age, under grave threat. In the face of liberalism and secularization, it was retreating into a personal, individual experience. Its verities were challenged by a new form of biblical analysis that treated the Bible solely as an historical text, not a document of divine revelation. By the first few decades of the century, this Higher Criticism (see page 207) had suggested that most of the books of the Bible were significantly 'younger' than previously thought, and certainly not the work of the authors traditionally linked to them (for example, Moses as author of the first five books of the Old Testament, or St Paul as the author of many epistles in the New Testament). Subsequent analysis and discoveries have pushed these dates much further back and allowed the traditional ascriptions to be possible again. However, this lay well in the future at the beginning of the century. For Protestants of the time, it appeared that higher learning was directly assaulting the faith.

Also, the increasing pluralization and secularization of society, as well as the substantial splintering of Protestantism and the creation of new, non-orthodox denominations, such as Christian Science and the Latter-Day Saints, weakened the social and cultural 'consensus' of traditionally Protestant nations. However, just as Protestantism was able to mount a successful defence against the Enlightenment, the challenges of liberalism and secularization were not insuperable. Moreover, Protestantism responded with a pan-Protestant movement: evangelical fundamentalism. In the eighteenth and nineteenth centuries, similar pan-Protestant movements, such as Arianism, revivalism and the Social Gospel, gave life to many established denominations and, inevitably, produced new ones. Protestantism's propensity to 're-formation' was in some ways a great weakness, especially in the face of a well-organized Tridentine Catholicism, but it was also an exceptional strength. It has, for five centuries, allowed Protestantism to respond relatively quickly and effectively to changing cultural circumstances by reinventing itself for each new age.

However, it would be a mistake to think that the story of Protestantism in the twentieth century is solely about theology or biblical interpretation. This would be to suggest that the more radical tendency to stress a distinctly Protestant society and culture within the wider 'unsaved' society was less of an emphasis than in previous centuries, or that there was less interest in personal piety and devotion. Rather, Protestantism and Protestants were very actively involved in – indeed, led – movements that sought radically to alter Western culture. Just as importantly, co-religionists opposed these moves. The type of dispute that characterized the split between Luther and his desire (and that of most other magisterial reformers) to maintain the social status quo and men like Müntzer, who wanted to alter social structures as much as liturgy and theology, was still evident in the twentieth century.

RACIAL SUPERIORITY AND THE BIBLE

The best example of the debate about the status quo is race. And two of the best places to consider this issue and its relationship with Protestantism are the United States and South Africa, both of which spent the majority of the twentieth century upholding a system of segregation or apartheid. In both cases, some Protestant ministers were in the forefront of attempts to bring about racial equality, and other Protestant ministers were just as committed to ensuring that the separation and hierarchy of races was maintained.

During the nineteenth century arguments about race were largely subsumed in the wider debate about slavery. This has perhaps led to the tendency to confuse the two and to think that abolitionists were exponents of racial equality and integration. Very few believed in equality and even fewer (indeed, almost none) believed in integration. To the extent that this was a religious debate (and it was), the main debate revolved around the story of Noah and his three sons, and only much later about Simon the Cyrene, who carried Christ's cross part of the way to Golgotha (Mark 15:21; Luke 23:26). In the story of the flood, Noah and his wife were saved along with their three sons and their sons' wives. To celebrate their deliverance, the men in the family had a party at which Noah became drunk and passed out. One of the sons, Ham, then went to his father and looked at his private parts (the Bible gives no reason for this rather odd behaviour). Noah's other two sons covered their father's shame by walking in backwards with a coverlet between them. The story ends with Ham being 'cursed' to perpetual servitude to the others. The three sons are then said to have gone in different directions and founded new 'peoples' to repopulate the Earth. Ham went to Cush, more or less the southern part of Egypt and northern Sudan. This story was later used to support the idea that there were three 'races', although some might argue that being descended from Adam and Eve means that there is only one race – the 'human' race. Of course, there is no intrinsic reason to divide humanity into three races – European, African and Oriental – rather than four, if you include Native American, as was often done in nineteenth-century America, or more or even fewer.

Nevertheless, this story was seen as mandating that God eternally planned for there to be three distinct races and thus no mingling. In much the same way, some might argue that two biological genders means that God planned for there to be two sexes, and that one (female) is eternally subservient, though not necessarily inferior, to the other (male). Of course, there is no reason to make an intrinsic link between biological sex (the presence of a specific set of genitalia) and gender (adherence to a set of social norms about behaviour, such as wearing a dress or trousers). Others might use a similar line of reasoning to argue that Adam and Eve, rather than Adam and Steve, meant that God planned for all human sexual relationships to be between one man and one woman. (In fact, the Bible could be taken to support the idea that one man and as many women as he could afford to maintain or as were needed to produce a male heir was the 'normal' relationship.)

So Noah's story supported the idea of three races of which one was eternally subservient. Since Ham went off to found the nation of Cush in Africa, he represented the 'black' race (it is worth noting, though, that in the medieval period Ham, as founder of Canaan, was seen as Semitic, and thus used as an argument for the subservience of Jews to Gentiles). Blacks, therefore, were doomed by God to eternal servitude because of Ham's sin, in much the same way that all humans are touched by original sin because of Adam's fall. Much later, as Protestants struggled to find a theological or biblical basis for rejecting this argument, the story of Simon the Cyrene came to the fore. He was from Cyrenia, a Roman province in North Africa, and had carried Christ's cross, which had weighted on it all the sins of mankind. This was seen as 'paying' the debt incurred by Ham. Some have chosen to treat Simon, a man from North Africa, as an 'African', but there is no reason to think that someone from Roman North Africa was necessarily sub-Saharan. However, as a black man, it was possible for him to bear the burdens of all men and the curse was lifted. If nothing else, this brief digression into biblical analysis and the use of texts highlights the extreme emphasis placed on the Bible as the ultimate source of authority. One might have thought that Christ's injunction to treat others as one would want to be treated, and Paul's assertion that in Christ there was 'no Jew, no Gentile', might have been enough. However, the Noah story, and its traditional interpretation, had to be finessed by an equally 'clear' biblical 'answer'. Simon of Cyrene was perfect.

Obviously, a simple exchange of 'proof texts' (sections of the Bible used to 'prove' a specific viewpoint, often without any clear context) was not enough to eliminate racial inequality. Moreover, although Simon the Cyrene paid Ham's debt, this was not an argument for racial integration. As we shall see, though, the men (many of whom were Protestant ministers) who argued for both equality and integration, used the Bible, but with less of an emphasis upon specific texts and more upon the Bible's ethos, especially as seen in the New Testament and, in particular, in the teachings of Jesus in the Gospels.

RACE IN THE UNITED STATES

Although racial equality and integration were key issues in the latter part of the twentieth century, the main thrust of the American civil-rights movement through much of the late nineteenth and twentieth century was an attempt to limit the impact of (legal) segregation and moves (largely in the former Confederate states of the South) to erode or eliminate access to levers of political and social power. Thus, the main thrust of the movement was to gain access to high-quality education, secure employment and, wherever possible, the ballot box.

After the Civil War (1861–5), the United States extended civil rights to African-Americans. The Thirteen Amendment to the Constitution (1865) outlawed slavery, but did not provide citizenship. Bizarrely, citizenship based simply on being born on American soil was not extended retroactively to those previously denied citizenship; the same 'anomaly' meant that Native Americans born on 'reservations' (used as models for the South African 'homeland' system) had to be given citizenship. In 1868 the Fourteenth Amendment was ratified by the states granting African-Americans citizenship. In theory, this gave black persons born in the United States equal protection under the law, while the Fifteenth Amendment (1870) provided the right to vote to all citizens regardless of race. During Reconstruction (1865–77), northern (federal) troops occupied the South and enforced these new constitutional amendments. This, along with the temporary disenfranchisement of most southern white men for service in the Confederate army, allowed many blacks to take prominent positions in society, including elective office.

None of these moves, of course, involved women: female enfranchisement would have to await another amendment in 1920. Since many debates in American society and culture revolve around the 'correct' interpretation of key secular texts (the Constitution and the Declaration of Independence) and sacred texts (the Protestant Bible), it is worth pausing to consider the implications of these amendments. They make clear that without them it was not possible to 'read into' the Constitution protection against discrimination based on sex or race. Indeed, the need to amend the Constitution suggests that, as a text, it was understood at the time (well into the late twentieth century) that ideas about protection, equality and citizenship inherent in the text referred specifically to white males.

Reconstruction ended following the Compromise of 1877 between northern and southern whites. The compromise ended the federal military occupation of the South, giving southern whites a free hand to reinstitute discriminatory practices. In exchange, southerners aquiesced in the contentious election of Rutherford B. Hayes, a Republican largely supported by northerners, over his opponent, Samuel J. Tilden, a Democrat. Subsequently, the judiciary undermined the scope of the amendments designed by radical Republicans, who spearheaded Reconstruction, to eliminate both governmental and private discrimination by legislation. A string of Supreme Court decisions made it clear that the new amendments did not require 'equality'. *Plessy* v. *Ferguson* (1896) built on an earlier decision (1883) that had allowed individual and businesses to discriminate by accepting the constitutionality of 'separate but equal'. States were now free to introduce legal apartheid. While the Supreme Court had previously overturned state statutes that excluded African-Americans from juries or systematically disenfranchised them (and continued to do so in the years after *Plessy*), it endorsed segregation in nearly every other sphere of public and private life. As Justice John M. Harlan, the only member of the court to dissent from the decision, predicted:

> If a state can prescribe, as a rule of civil conduct, that whites and
> blacks shall not travel as passengers in the same railroad coach, why
> may it not so regulate the use of the streets of its cities and towns as

to compel white citizens to keep on one side of a street, and black citizens to keep on the other? Why may it not, upon like grounds, punish whites and blacks who ride together in street cars or in open vehicles on a public road or street?

Harlan's predictions were, in fact, accurate, as the court soon extended *Plessy* to legalize segregated schools, while in *Berea College* v. *Kentucky* (1908), the court upheld a Kentucky statute that had forced Berea College, a private institution, to stop teaching blacks and whites in an integrated setting. Thus, in 1883 the court said that private individuals and businesses could not be stopped from discriminating, but in 1908 it ruled that they could be *forced* to discriminate – an interesting example of conservative judicial activism supported by an argument based on the 'original' intent of the Constitution's writers, which was most definitely *not* racial equality or integration.

Many states, particularly in the South, saw *Plessy* and *Berea* as blanket approval for restrictive laws, generally known as Jim Crow laws. African-Americans were not allowed to share a taxi with whites or enter a building through the same entrance. They had to drink from separate water fountains, use separate rest-rooms, attend separate schools, be buried in separate cemeteries and even swear on separate Bibles. Blacks were excluded from restaurants and public libraries. Many parks barred them with signs that read 'Negroes and dogs not allowed'. One municipal zoo went so far as to list separate visiting hours. The etiquette of racial segregation was even harsher, particularly in the South. African-Americans were expected to step aside to let a white person pass, and black men dared not look any white woman in the eye. Black men and women were addressed by their first names, without the dignity of Mr, Mrs or Miss. Whites referred to a black man of any age as 'boy' and a black woman as 'girl'. Although the Supreme Court had declared overt forms of disenfranchisement to be unconstitutional, southern officials disenfranchised nearly all eligible African-American voters through 'white primaries', poll taxes, literacy tests, gerrymandering, economic reprisals and selective use of (often state-supported) terrorism to discourage blacks from registering to vote.

In some states, particularly Alabama, the state used the criminal justice system to re-establish a form of slavery or serfdom, sentencing black males to years of working without pay for private employers, such as the Tennessee Coal, Iron and Railroad Company (a subsidiary of US Steel), which paid the state for their labour. Extrajudicial punishment (that is, violent intimidation) was even more brutal. During the last decade of the nineteenth century and the first decades of the twentieth century, thousands of black males were lynched by white vigilantes (terrorists), sometimes with the overt assistance of state officials. In some cases, such as Elaine County, Arkansas (1919), and Tulsa, Oklahoma (1921), lynching escalated into mass murder, as rampaging whites killed large numbers of blacks. No whites were charged with crimes in any of those massacres; in fact, so confident were whites of their immunity from prosecution for lynching that they not only took photographs of their victims, but made postcards out of them. (These were often sent to blacks in the community with brief messages, such as 'See what we do …'.) It is worth remembering that black Americans knew the dangers of state-sponsored terrorism in America long before 9/11.

In addition to excluding blacks from equal participation in many areas of public life, white society also kept blacks in a position of economic subservience or marginality. Black farmers in the South often found themselves held in economic bondage as sharecroppers or tenant farmers, while employers and labour unions generally restricted African-Americans to the worst-paid and least desirable jobs. Relatively undistinguished jobs, such as working as a Pullman porter or a hotel doorman, became prestigious positions in black communities, where steady, well-paid employment was hard to find. The Jim Crow system that excluded African-Americans from many areas of economic life led to the creation of a vigorous, but stunted economic life within the segregated sphere: black newspapers sprang up throughout the North, while black-owned insurance and funeral establishments acquired disproportionate influence in both economic and political spheres.

The black, mostly Protestant churches filled the void created by the lack of any meaningful political role for blacks. The leadership role of black churches in the civil-rights movement was a natural extension of their structure and function. They offered their members opportunities to exercise roles denied them in society as a whole. Throughout their history, the black churches have served not only as places of worship, but also as sources of communal information, credit unions and 'people's courts' to solve disputes. However, many black churches were apolitical, serving more as a means of organizing relief for their parishioners than mounting a challenge to the economic, political or social structures that kept African-Americans in subjugation. New religious movements, such as the Holiness Movement (see pages 186–91), that expanded rapidly in the first decades of the twentieth century as the originally integrated Pentecostal movement segregated itself, reinforced the apolitical and quietist (Pietist) approach of many black churchgoers.

At the turn of the century the educator Booker T. Washington was regarded, particularly by the white community, as the foremost spokesman for African-Americans in the United States. Washington, who was the principal of Tuskegee Institute (founded in 1881 to educate male and female black teachers), preached a message of self-reliance, in which he urged blacks to concentrate on improving their economic position rather than demanding social equality until they had proved that they 'deserved' it. Publicly, he accepted the continuation of Jim Crow laws and segregation in the short term, but privately helped to fund court cases challenging the laws. The prominent African-American academic and activist W. E. B. Du Bois and others in the black community rejected Washington's 'apology' for segregation. In 1905 Du Bois and William Monroe Trotter convened a meeting of black activists on the Canadian side of the river at Niagara Falls, and issued a manifesto calling for universal manhood suffrage, elimination of all forms of racial segregation, and extension of education (academic, not just vocational, as Washington emphasized) on a non-discriminatory basis.

Black activism was able to make some inroads into the system of segregation through cases heard by the Supreme Court. In its early years, the National Association for the Advancement of Colored People (NAACP, founded 1909) concentrated on attacking Jim Crow laws, successfully challenging the Louisville, Kentucky, ordinance that required residential segregation (*Buchanan v. Warley*, 1917), and Oklahoma's 'grandfather law', which exempted most white voters from a law that disenfranchised African-American citizens (*Guinn v. United States*, 1913). The NAACP also lobbied for the commissioning of African-Americans as officers in the First World War, and against the introduction of racial segregation into federal civil-service employment (1913), which President Thomas Woodrow Wilson had introduced, saying 'segregation is not a humiliation but a benefit'. It is important to recall that Wilson, largely remembered for his calls for ethnic and national self-determination after the First World War, was a Virginia segregationist.

On 17 May 1954 the Supreme Court ruled on *Brown v. Board of Education of Topeka (Kansas)* on the constitutionality of separate education: 'The segregation of white and colored children in public schools has a detrimental effect upon the colored children. The impact is greater when it has the sanction of the law; for the policy of separating the races is usually interpreted as denoting the inferiority of the Negro group.' In its unanimous ruling, the court declared that *Plessy v. Ferguson*, which established the 'separate but equal' practice of segregation, was itself unconstitutional, and ordered that segregation be 'phased out over time'. This approach, however, was clearly unable to deliver consistent, comprehensive or immediate success.

By 1955, therefore, many blacks (and white supporters of equality) had become frustrated by attempts to implement desegregation by federal and state governments, especially in the face of massive resistance by proponents of racial segregation. In defiance, they adopted a combined strategy of direct action with non-violent resistance. The ensuing acts of civil disobedience produced crisis situations that often forced state governments to respond immediately. Some of the different forms of civil disobedience employed included boycotts (successfully used in the Montgomery, Alabama Bus Boycott, 1955–6), sit-ins (such as the influential Greensboro, North Carolina sit-in, 1960), and marches (such as the Selma to Montgomery marches in Alabama, 1965).

In response to these actions, local authorities attempted to outlaw and harass the mainstream civil-rights organizations throughout the Deep South. Alabama effectively barred the NAACP from operating in 1956 by requiring it to give the state a list of its members, then banning it as an illegal organization when it failed to do so (no similar attempt was made to identify and/or ban the Ku-Klux-Klan). While the Supreme Court ultimately reversed the order, for a few years in the mid-1950s the NAACP was unable to operate. In its place the Rev. Fred Shuttlesworth began the Alabama Christian Movement for Human Rights (ACMHR) in June 1956. Thus, churches in particular and local grassroots organizations stepped in to fill the gap, and brought with them a much more energetic and broader base in the local population than the more 'judicial' approach of groups such as the NAACP.

The most important step forward came in Montgomery, Alabama, where long-time NAACP activists Rosa Parks and Edgar Nixon prevailed on the Rev. Dr Martin Luther King Jr to lead the Montgomery Bus Boycott of 1955–6. Activists and church leaders in other communities, such as Baton Rouge, Louisiana, had used the boycott in recent years, although those efforts often withered away after a few days. In Montgomery, on the other hand, the Montgomery Improvement Association (created to lead the boycott) managed to keep it going for over a year until the federal government forced Montgomery to desegregate its buses. The success in Montgomery made King a nationally known figure and triggered other bus boycotts, such as the highly successful Tallahassee, Florida, boycott the following year.

In 1957 the leaders of the Montgomery Improvement Association, Dr King and Rev. John Duffy, joined with other church leaders (such as Rev. C. K. Steele of Tallahassee, Rev. T. J. Jemison of Baton Rouge, and Rev. Fred

Shuttlesworth of Montgomery) who had led similar boycott efforts to form the Southern Christian Leadership Conference (SCLC). Headquartered in Atlanta, Georgia, the SCLC did not attempt to create a network of chapters the way the NAACP had, but rather offered training and other assistance for local efforts to fight segregation, while raising funds, mostly from northern sources, to support these campaigns. It made non-violence both its central tenet and its primary method of confronting racism.

Non-violence, however, was not the response these activists met. Rather, the extremely religious, conservative and Protestant white South responded with violence both from vigilantes and the legal organs of the state. Students, who had led a series of successful, high-profile sit-ins at lunch counters, on park benches and in library reading rooms formed into another group in 1960 – the Student Nonviolent Coordinating Committee. (The plethora of groups involved in the civil-rights movements reminds us that it is not just Protestantism that can have a penchant for creating multiple groups theoretically engaged in the same activity.) The first campaign of the student-led group was conducting 'freedom rides', in which activists travelled by bus through the Deep South to desegregate companies' bus terminals, as required by federal law.

This was enormously dangerous non-violent activity. In Alabama alone, one bus was firebombed at Anniston, riders were severely beaten in Birmingham, and in Montgomery a mob charged another bus, knocking one rider unconscious with a crate and beating a photographer from *Life* magazine in the face with his own camera. A dozen men surrounded a white student from Fisk University and beat him with a suitcase, knocking out his teeth. The freedom riders did not fare much better in jail, where they were crammed into tiny, filthy cells and sporadically beaten. In Jackson, Mississippi, some male prisoners were forced to do hard labour in extremely high temperatures. Others were transferred to the Mississippi State Penitentiary at Parchman, where their food was deliberately over-salted and their mattresses were removed. Sometimes the men were suspended from the walls by 'wrist breakers'. Typically, the windows of their cells were shut tight on hot days, making it hard for them to breathe.

Similar violence met attempts to desegregate education. When the University of Mississippi was forced to allow a black student to enrol, the response that night was extreme. White students and other whites began rioting, throwing rocks at the US marshals guarding the black student. This soon turned to firing on the marshals. Two people, including a French journalist, were killed, twenty-eight marshals suffered gunshot wounds, and 160 others were injured. After the Mississippi Highway Patrol withdrew its troopers from the campus, President John F. Kennedy sent the army to the campus to quell the uprising.

It is interesting to note that although black Christian (that is, Protestant) organizations were active in the civil rights movement, they were often criticized for not being radical enough. For some, non-violence by the ministers meant non-action. This changed in 1963 when the SCLC moved to integrate downtown businesses in Birmingham, Alabama. This effort was, ironically, aided by the tactics of local authorities, in particular Eugene 'Bull' Connor, the Commissioner of Public Safety, who had lost a recent election for mayor to a less rabidly segregationist candidate, but refused to accept the new mayor's authority. The campaign used a variety of non-violent methods of confrontation, including sit-ins, kneel-ins at local churches, and a march to the county building to mark the beginning of a drive to register voters. The city, however, obtained an injunction barring all such protests. Convinced that the order was unconstitutional, the campaign defied it and prepared for the mass arrest of its supporters. Dr Martin Luther King Jr elected to be among those arrested on 12 April 1963.

The campaign, however, began to falter as fewer and fewer volunteers came forward willing to risk arrest. SCLC organizers came up with a bold and controversial alternative, calling on high-school students to take part. When more than a thousand of them left school on 2 May to join the demonstrations in what would come to be called the Children's Crusade, more than six hundred were arrested. Initially, the police acted with restraint. However, on the next day another thousand students gathered at a church, and Bull Connor unleashed police dogs on them, then turned on the city's fire hoses (set at a pressure capable of peeling bark off a tree or separating bricks from mortar). Via television, the nation watched horror-struck as fire hoses knocked down schoolchildren and police dogs attacked unarmed demonstrators.

National outrage forced President Kennedy to intervene and organize a compromise between the activists and local businessmen to end segregation in public facilities, to eliminate discriminatory hiring practices, to arrange for the release of jailed protesters, and to establish regular means of communication between black and white leaders. Not everyone in the black community approved of the agreement. The Rev. Fred Shuttlesworth was particularly critical, lacking any faith in the willingness of the official white community to keep its side of the arrangement. The reaction from parts of the white community was even more violent. The Gaston Motel, which had served as the SCLC's unofficial headquarters, was bombed, as was the home of King's brother, the Rev. A. D. King. Four months later, on 15 September, Ku-Klux-Klan members bombed the Sixteenth Street Baptist Church in Birmingham, killing four young girls.

Of course, much of this debate was conducted within the context of American society and culture. Thus, much of the rhetoric and argument focused on ideas found not in the Bible, but the 'canonical' texts of America's secular 'religion' – the Constitution and the Declaration of Independence. However, the leading role of Protestant ministers in the movement speaks to the importance of Christian ideals in the civil-rights movement. Indeed, one cannot hear King's 'I have a dream speech' without noticing this twin emphasis upon the Bible and the Constitution. It was as much a Protestant sermon as a very American speech.

> Five score years ago, a great American, in whose symbolic shadow we
> stand today, signed the Emancipation Proclamation. This momentous
> decree came as a great beacon light of hope to millions of Negro
> slaves who had been seared in the flames of withering injustice.

It came as a joyous daybreak to end the long night of their captivity. But one hundred years later, the Negro still is not free. One hundred years later, the life of the Negro is still sadly crippled by the manacles of segregation and the chains of discrimination. One hundred years later, the Negro lives on a lonely island of poverty in the midst of a vast ocean of material prosperity. One hundred years later, the Negro is still languishing in the corners of American society and finds himself an exile in his own land.

So we have come here today to dramatize a shameful condition. In a sense we have come to our nation's capital to cash a check. When the architects of our republic wrote the magnificent words of the Constitution and the Declaration of Independence, they were signing a promissory note to which every American was to fall heir. This note was a promise that all men, yes, black men as well as white men, would be guaranteed the unalienable rights of life, liberty, and the pursuit of happiness ... Now is the time to make real the promises of democracy. Now is the time to rise from the dark and desolate valley of segregation to the sunlit path of racial justice. Now is the time to lift our nation from the quicksands of racial injustice to the solid rock of brotherhood. Now is the time to make justice a reality for all of God's children ...

I have a dream that one day this nation will rise up and live out the true meaning of its creed: 'We hold these truths to be self-evident: that all men are created equal.' I have a dream that one day on the red hills of Georgia the sons of former slaves and the sons of former slave owners will be able to sit down together at the table of brotherhood ... I have a dream that one day every valley shall be exalted, every hill and mountain shall be made low, the rough places will be made plain, and the crooked places will be made straight, and the glory of the Lord shall be revealed, and all flesh shall see it together ...

This will be the day when all of God's children will be able to sing with a new meaning, 'My country, 'tis of thee, sweet land of liberty, of thee I sing. Land where my fathers died, land of the pilgrim's pride, from every mountainside, let freedom ring' ... And when this happens, when we allow freedom to ring, when we let it ring from every village and every hamlet, from every state and every city, we will be able to speed up that day when all of God's children, black men and white men, Jews and Gentiles, Protestants and Catholics, will be able to join hands and sing in the words of the old Negro spiritual, 'Free at last! Free at last! Thank God Almighty, we are free at last!'

King and other civil-rights leaders were striking notes meant to resonate in a largely Protestant cultural milieu. They knew their audience. Appeals to specifically American documents were vital, but so was a wider appeal to the power of the Gospel message to change a society, a culture and the individuals within it.

The religious leaders of the civil-rights movement did not question the 'American-ness' or 'Christian-ness' of the whites who supported segregation. Rather, they used the language of America and Protestantism to call those same whites (fellow citizens and fellow Protestants) to live up to their own values. Both civil-rights workers and segregationists lived in an environment that accepted the power of the ideas of the Constitution *and* the Bible radically to alter not only individuals, but also whole societies. The shared American value of citizenship and the Christian concept of brotherhood were powerful ideas in the arsenal of those wishing to destroy racial discrimination. Nevertheless, these shared ideas did not stop many leading whites from arguing, even from pulpits, that neither the Constitution nor the Bible aimed at racial integration or the end to 'white supremacy'. Luther's call to destroy the peasants found its echo in pulpits across the South (and also the North), declaring racial integration to be the end of 'Protestant America'.

Just as importantly, it has to be remembered that civil rights were not just a Protestant affair. The parish structure of Catholicism meant that segregation had had only a limited impact, though segregation by 'neighbourhood' could, and did, lead to effective segregation of the parishes. Moreover, Jews were strongly involved in the fight against racial discrimination – many because they had been the victim of Hitler's 'race' laws. For example, the Jewish philanthropist Julius Rosenwald funded dozens of primary schools, secondary schools and colleges for black youths. He gave, and led the Jewish community in giving, to some two thousand schools for black Americans, including Howard, Dillard and Fisk universities. At one time, some 40 per cent of southern blacks were learning at these schools. In addition, about half the civil-rights lawyers who worked in the South were Jewish. Leaders of the Jewish Reform Movement were arrested with King in St Augustine, Florida, in 1964 after a challenge to racial segregation in public accommodations.

RACE IN SOUTH AFRICA

Just as importantly, the fight against racial discrimination was not just an American event. Nor was it something largely related to Protestant groups, such as Methodists and, especially, Baptists, who tended to supply many of the ministers involved in the American movement. The other great example of the fight against racial discrimination that had a significant input from Protestants was in South Africa during the fight against apartheid (the Afrikaans word for 'segregation'). Although the creation of apartheid is usually attributed to Afrikaner-dominated governments, it is a legacy of British colonialism, which introduced a system of 'pass laws' in the Cape Colony during the nineteenth century. This was designed to regulate the movement of blacks from 'tribal regions', supposedly independently governed under British administration, to areas occupied by whites and coloureds (those of mixed race) under direct British rule. Pass laws not only restricted the movement of blacks, but also prohibited movement from one district to another without a signed pass.

It is also important to recall that Protestantism was and is just as capable of fighting the fight for conservatism, as with Luther in the sixteenth century and segregationist white ministers in twentieth-century America. Thus, attempts by the ruling United Party in South Africa during the Second World War to relax segregation were ended after the 1948 general election, when the National Party formed a coalition with the Afrikaner Party under the Protestant cleric Daniel François Malan. It immediately began implementing strict apartheid. Legislation was passed prohibiting mixed marriages. Miscegenation (interracial sexual activity) was outlawed, individuals were classified by race, and a classification board was created to rule in questionable cases. The Group Areas Act, 1950 became the heart of the apartheid system, designed to separate the racial groups geographically into 'reservations' called 'homelands'.

During the 1950s and 1960s, when segregation was collapsing in the United States, it was being given even greater strength in law in South Africa. The Separate Amenities Act, 1953 created, among other things, separate beaches, buses, hospitals, schools and universities. The pass laws were further strengthened: blacks and coloureds were compelled to carry identity documents, which became passports by which migration to white South Africa could be limited and controlled.

In the United States efforts by civil-rights activists to overturn segregationist legislation largely relied on judicial activism. The same approach was attempted in South Africa with disastrous consequences. J. G. Strijdom, the prime minister after Malan, moved to strip coloureds and blacks of what few voting rights they had. The previous government first introduced the Separate Representation of Voters Bill in 1951, but the validity of the ensuing Act was challenged. The Cape Supreme Court upheld the Act, but the Appeal Court upheld the appeal and found the Act to be invalid on the grounds that such substantive changes to constitutional structures required a two-thirds majority in a joint sitting of both houses of Parliament. The government then introduced the High Court of Parliament Bill, which gave Parliament the power to overrule decisions of the court. This too was declared invalid by both the Cape Supreme Court and the Appeal Court. In

1955 the government increased the number of judges in the Appeal Court from five to eleven, and filled the resulting vacancies with pro-Nationalist judges. In the same year they introduced the Senate Act, which increased the Senate from 49 seats to 89, which eventually left the National Party in control of 77 seats. With these changes, a joint sitting of Parliament was able to pass the Separate Representation of Voters Act, 1956, which removed coloureds from the common voters' roll in the Cape and established a separate roll for them.

Just as in America, one of the leading voices fighting discrimination was a Protestant minister – actually an Anglican bishop. Arising from the heart of a normally conservative denomination, Desmond Tutu was able to use his 'bully pulpit' to attack apartheid. When family finances forced him to abandon his ambition of becoming a doctor, he became a teacher, but left in 1957 in protest against the Bantu (Black) Education Act, which institutionalized segregated teaching and brought black education under governmental control (ending 'mission' schooling). He turned to theology, was ordained an Anglican priest in 1960 and became chaplain at the University of Fort Hare, a hotbed of dissent and one of the few quality universities for black students in the southern part of Africa.

In 1962 Tutu left his post as chaplain and travelled to King's College, London, where he received his BA and MA in theology. Returning to South Africa in 1967, he used his sermons to highlight racial discrimination. In 1972 he returned to Britain, where he was appointed vice-director of the Theological Education Fund of the World Council of Churches. He returned to South Africa in 1975 and was appointed Anglican Dean of Johannesburg, the first black person to hold that position. He took a leading role in the fight against apartheid in 1976 after the Soweto Riots (which began as a protest against the compulsory use of Afrikaans as a language of instruction in all schools sparking a nationwide uprising against apartheid). As Bishop of Lesotho (1976–8) and Secretary-General of the South African Council of Churches, he led a campaign against apartheid, which had the support of almost all the churches in South Africa. Most importantly, he supported boycotts (especially the economic one) against South Africa, even though these often had a very detrimental impact on blacks. In 1984 he was awarded the Nobel Peace Prize, and in 1986 he became primate (leader) of the Anglican Church of South Africa.

Repeatedly, Tutu has called not only for the end to discrimination as a Christian necessity, but also spoken of the need for reconciliation and forgiveness between the races, between the oppressors and the oppressed. However, in recent years he has made clear that his opposition to discrimination was not based solely on race. Rather, he has been a leading voice in calls for an end to discrimination against homosexuals. (His US counterpart in this campaign was Coretta Scott King, widow of Dr Martin Luther King Jr.) In 2005 he articulated his response to discrimination in the context of his Protestant reading of the Bible:

> I am deeply saddened at a time when we've got such huge problems ...
> that we should invest so much time and energy in this issue ... I think
> God is weeping ... Jesus did not say, 'If I be lifted up I will draw some'.
> Jesus said, 'If I be lifted up I will draw all, all, all, all, all. Black, white,
> yellow, rich, poor, clever, not so clever, beautiful, not so beautiful. It's
> one of the most radical things. All, all, all, all, all, all, all, all. All belong.
> Gay, lesbian, so-called straight. All, all are meant to be held in this
> incredible embrace that will not let us go. All ... Isn't it sad, that in
> a time when we face so many devastating problems – poverty,
> HIV/AIDS, war and conflict – that in our [Protestant Anglican]
> Communion we should be investing so much time and energy on
> disagreement about sexual orientation? [Anglicans] used to be known
> for embodying the attribute of comprehensiveness, of inclusiveness,
> where we were meant to accommodate all and diverse views, saying
> we may differ in our theology but we belong together as sisters and
> brothers [the Anglican Communion] now seems hell-bent on excom-
> municating one another. God must look on and God must weep.

The rhetoric is very much the same as that found in King's 'I have a dream speech'. This is both speech and sermon. It is defying attempts by some to read the Bible as a document of discrimination and hate. It highlights the question of authority in a Protestantism in which each believer is a priest and the Bible is there to be read and understood and interpreted by each.

Indeed, the issue of homosexuality, which has come to prominence at the beginning of the twenty-first century, highlights this question of authority and the role of religion as a tool for social control or social change. Thus, the recent election of 'gay' bishop Gene Robinson has sparked as much debate as the election in the 1980s of the black, female bishop Barbara Harris – both elected (unlike English Anglican bishops) within the American Episcopal (Anglican) Church. In America it has also combined and complicated the interplay of religion (the Bible) and Americanism (the Constitution and Declaration of Independence). Thus, in 2002 the president (Sandy Rios) of Concerned Women for America could say:

> To compare rich, privileged homosexual lobby groups allied with transsexuals and sadomasochists to brave civil rights crusaders – who risked their lives to advance freedom – insults every black American who overcame real injustice and poverty … It's time for the homosexual lobby to stop co-opting the black civil rights struggle. The [National Gay and Lesbian] Task Force's agenda of promoting perversion – including public homosexual sex, sadomasochism and bisexuality – would offend the vast majority of African-Americans who understand the difference between God-designed racial distinctions and changeable, immoral behavior.

In 1994 Coretta Scott King had just as strongly argued:

> For too long, our nation has tolerated the insidious form of discrimination against this group of Americans, who have worked as hard as any other group, paid their taxes like everyone else, and yet

have been denied equal protection under the law ... I believe that
freedom and justice cannot be parceled out in pieces to suit political
convenience. My husband, Martin Luther King, Jr. said, 'Injustice
anywhere is a threat to justice everywhere'. On another occasion he
said, 'I have worked too long and hard against segregated public
accommodations to end up segregating my moral concern. Justice is
indivisible.' Like Martin, I don't believe you can stand for freedom
for one group of people and deny it to others. The great promise of
American democracy is that no group of people will be forced to
suffer discrimination and injustice.

And again, in 1998, she argued:

I still hear people say that I should not be talking about the rights of
lesbian and gay people and I should stick to the issue of racial justice.
But I hasten to remind them that Martin Luther King Jr. said,
'Injustice anywhere is a threat to justice everywhere'. I appeal to
everyone who believes in Martin Luther King Jr.'s dream to make
room at the table of brother and sisterhood for lesbian and gay people.

Both women believe in the Bible. Both are speaking from a Protestant background. Both refer to American values. But who has the authority to decide
which is right? This remains the dilemma for Protestants.

However, in America, unlike most other places, calls for civil rights
involved a combination of specific secular Enlightenment ideals (derived
from the Constitution and the Declaration of Independence) and biblical
ideas of justice and brotherhood. Thus, Tutu's approach is much more
explicitly biblical and Protestant, with some references to more general
ideas of human rights. Dr King, on the other hand, weaves quotations from
Jesus with those of Thomas Jefferson, with little evidence that one is being
treated as more authoritative than the other. This approach says much
about the melding together in American Protestantism of ideas about the

singular authority of the Bible with an extreme reverence (whereby they become almost 'holy') for the key documents of America's foundational, secular ideology (or, better, 'faith'). Indeed, it might well not be an over-statement to suggest that American Protestantism has added Jefferson, James Madison, George Washington, Benjamin Franklin and John Quincy Adams to Matthew, Mark, Luke, John, and Paul. Arguments over the 'orig-inal intent' of the Founding Fathers are very similar to debates about bibli-cal interpretation fought out by 'liberals' and 'fundamentalists', to which we must now give some attention.

SCIENCE AND THE BIBLE

As we have seen time and again, Protestantism was not just a movement about lifestyles or social injustice. It has always been that, but it has also been about theology, beliefs and worship. In the course of the twentieth century, while some Protestants have focused on the same sort of issues that fired the Social Gospellers, others have been engaged in a war more reminiscent of the struggles between Calvinists and Arminians in the early seventeenth century. Indeed, this struggle (between modernists/liberals and fundamentalists/evangelicals) has come to dominate much of the Protestant world.

Modernism is a term that covers a variety of political, cultural and artis-tic movements rooted in the changes in Western society at the end of the nineteenth century and beginning of the twentieth century. Broadly speak-ing, modernism describes a series of progressive cultural movements in art and architecture, music, literature and the applied arts that emerged in the decades before 1914. Central to the modernist synthesis were common assumptions and ideas, including the religious norms found in Christianity (especially Protestantism), scientific norms found in classical physics, and doctrines that asserted that the depiction of external reality from an objective standpoint was in fact possible. From the 1870s onwards the ideas that history and civilization were inherently progressive and that progress was always good came under increasing attack. Coupled with this was a re-examination of accepted cultural norms, values and ideas. In particular, this had a profound impact on religion and views about the structure of society.

Thus, two of the most disruptive thinkers of the period were Charles Darwin in biology, and Karl Marx in political science. Darwin's theory of evolution by natural selection undermined the religious certainties of the general public, and the sense of human uniqueness. The notion that human beings were driven by the same impulses as 'lower animals' proved to be difficult to reconcile with the idea of an ennobling spirituality. Karl Marx seemed to present a political version of the same proposition: problems with the economic order were not temporary (the result of 'evil' robber barons or momentary glitches in the market system), but were fundamentally contradictions within the 'capitalist' system. Both suggested that the prevailing systems governing not only the body (the market) but also the soul (Protestantism and its emphasis upon the unique authority of a literal reading of the Bible) were fundamentally flawed. In the 1890s this led to a strand of thinking that asserted it was necessary to reject previous norms entirely, instead of merely revising past knowledge in the light of current discoveries.

Indeed, in today's world this has led to a general perception that science is somehow opposed to Protestantism, or rather, to revealed religion. Historically, this has not been the case. Protestantism was largely ambivalent or neutral on matters scientific. Primarily, as noted repeatedly, this was because, yet again, there was a lack of a central, overarching institution or mechanism for unified action. This left Protestants speaking to and about science with many voices. Two examples will suffice to illuminate Protestantism's complex relationship with science. Both also relate, importantly, to interpretations of Scripture. One, the response to the views of Charles Darwin, continues to reverberate today. The second, based on the views of the early astronomers Galileo and Copernicus, were controversial in their time, but are largely ignored today.

When the Catholic Church condemned Galileo and his Copernican ideas that the Earth rotated on its axis and revolved around the sun, the Church was simply upholding a literal reading of the Bible. Numerous passages made clear that the Earth did not and could not move (Psalms 93:1, 96:10). Straightforward historical accounts (Joshua 10:12–13, 2 Kings 20:9–11) taught that the sun moved (how else could it stand still or go into reverse?) around the Earth. While some Protestant theologians and ministers were equally alive to the threat to biblical infallibility posed by this heliocentrism, others were simply convinced of its obvious rightness. Their solution was to reinterpret the troublesome passages. God was simply speaking in a manner intelligible to readers. That God must have known they would draw a conclusion that was factually wrong and that the Bible nowhere corrected this 'misconception' was of little concern. The science and mathematics of heliocentrism were obvious and irrefutable, so the biblical meaning had to be adjusted since the Bible could not teach an obvious scientific error. The Catholic response was unified and institutional: while it accepted that Copernican astronomy and mathematics were useful, it denounced their 'reality' and upheld the 'clear and obvious' meaning of Scripture.

Most Protestants, on the other hand, seemed to take scientific and philosophical changes in their stride. Well into the late nineteenth century, most Protestants simply took the view that any apparent conflict between revealed truth and science (whether geological, archaeological or astronomical) was simply man using his God-given abilities more fully to understand God's creation. Thus, science enabled a greater, fuller, more correct understanding of the Bible. Darwinian ideas, especially as these came to impinge not only on the age of the Earth but also the means of man's creation, began to place this relationship under stress. While many Protestants seemed to have had little trouble accepting a less than literal reading of the creation timeline, any suggestion that man was anything less than a unique creation was resisted.

Interestingly, Catholicism has largely been able to accept a non-literal reading of Genesis, as well as adopting heliocentrism in the nineteenth century. It still tends to reject those aspects of evolution that suggest a mechanism without divine control. Protestantism, on the other hand, has either accepted both evolutionary theory and a non-literal reading of Genesis, or, as in most conservative, evangelical denominations, has used a defence of the literal interpretation of Genesis to rebut both evolution and geology. Attempts to reconcile science and the Bible, through 'planned' or 'designed' creationism, have proven problematic for both scientists and most conservative Protestants.

What lies at the root of the problematic relationship between Protestantism and science? Primarily, it is the understanding of what scientific inquiry is doing. To many Protestants in the seventeenth, eighteenth and even the nineteenth centuries science was revealing more and more of God's wondrous creation, and thereby God's will and mind. New understandings arising from this investigation added to and clarified, but did not contradict or repudiate, truth revealed in the Bible. In more recent times many Protestants have come to view scientific inquiry as a methodology almost intentionally designed at undermining revealed truth. Where science had previously been a godly, Christian investigation into God's handiwork to discover yet greater detail of His marvellous works, science has now become a tool for destroying faith – especially in the truthfulness of the Bible, or, more accurately, the truthfulness of some interpretations of the Bible. The crux of the problem seems to be that science, previously conducted by 'believers', is now largely the preserve of 'non-believers' (or so it appears to many Protestants).

However, the key point remains that Protestantism is thoroughly divided on its relationship with science. Catholicism is not – at least not as an institution. Not only does Catholicism have a means to evaluate scientific discoveries, but this same mechanism allows Catholicism, over time, to evolve its views *vis-à-vis* any given scientific idea. Protestantism, on the other hand, cannot. Individual Protestants and individual Protestant denominations are left to interpret science rather as they are left to interpret the Bible. Where, for example, science seems to support conservative Protestant ideas, such as recent discoveries making apostolic authorship of the New Testament books more plausible, these same Protestants will seize upon science, its methods and its conclusions. Where science seems to contradict entrenched beliefs and biblical interpretations, Protestants either alter their views or, as is more likely nowadays, attack science as an opponent of belief.

This increasingly negative reaction to science arose from the modernist drive to question all things and, in particular, to suggest that man was not a unique creation. It united with liberal ideas about society and culture and increasingly called into question accepted norms. As we have seen, this allowed for a trenchant and, in the end, devastating critique of racial discrimination based on ideas of white supremacy buttressed with specific interpretations of key biblical passages. This also led to a less effective critique of the role of women and their relationship with men, and, more recently, the question of rights for homosexuals. In all cases, both advocates and exponents have used a mixture of ideas based on nature (reality), revealed truth (the Bible) and normality (tradition). However, unlike the case of civil rights based on race, the debates on women's rights and gay rights have involved women and gay people on both sides of the argument. For example, women led the fight during the 1970s and 1980s against the American Equal Rights Amendment, and many gays strongly oppose the entire concept of 'gay marriage'. Thus, conservative Protestant women often make strong arguments for the subservience of women to men, and homosexuals will argue against attempts to turn their relationships into 'imitations' of heterosexual relationships. One cannot imagine a significant number of blacks in the 1950s, for example, advocating their own inferiority towards whites, or being in favour of laws refusing to recognize interracial marriages!

LIBERAL AND MODERNIST INFLUENCES

This mixing of liberalism's emphasis upon 'inherent rights' and modernism's undermining of accepted values and norms continues to have a profound impact, not least in the reaction it has sparked among conservative religious and secular political opponents. The ideas of individual liberties, personal dignity, free expression, religious tolerance, private property, universal human rights, transparency of government, limitations on government power, popular sovereignty, national self-determination, privacy, enlightened and rational policy, the rule of law, fundamental equality, a free-market economy and free trade were all radical notions in the eighteenth century. Today all are accepted as policy goals in most nations.

However, 'liberalism' means different things in different places, and in particular has a very different connotation in the USA than in Europe. In America liberalism is usually understood to refer to modern liberalism, as contrasted with conservatism, and is often used as a term of abuse. American liberals endorse regulation for business, a (limited) social-welfare state, and support broad racial, ethnic and religious tolerance. In Europe, on the other hand, liberalism is not only contrasted with conservatism and Christian Democracy, but also with socialism and social democracy. In some countries, European liberals share common positions with (conservative) Christian Democrats. Thus, liberals in Europe are generally hostile to any attempts by the State to enforce equality in employment by legal action against employers, whereas in the USA many liberals favour such affirmative action. Liberals in general support equal opportunity, but not necessarily equal outcome. Most European liberal parties do not favour employment quotas for women and ethnic minorities as the best way to end gender and racial inequality. However, all agree that arbitrary discrimination on the basis of race or gender is morally wrong.

Liberalism continues to have an impact in four key areas: politics, culture, economy and society. In politics liberalism supports the idea that individuals are the basis of law and society, and that society and its institutions exist to further the ends of individuals. Political liberalism stresses the social contract (so strongly advocated and developed during the French Wars of Religion, and later the Enlightenment), under which citizens make the laws and agree to abide by those laws. It is based on the belief that individuals, not their priests or ministers, know what is best for them. When dealing with cultural issues, liberalism focuses on the rights of individuals pertaining to conscience and lifestyle, including such issues as sexual freedom, religious freedom and protection from government intrusion into private life. It would take as its basic tenet the view expressed by the philosopher, political economist and advocate of utilitarianism John Stuart Mill: 'The sole end for which mankind are warranted, individually or collectively, in interfering with the liberty of action of any of their number, is self-protection. That the only purpose for which power can be rightfully exercised over any member of a civilised community, against his will, is to prevent harm to others. His own good, either physical or moral, is not a sufficient warrant.' Thus, basing laws on revealed truth (the Bible) and a standard of morality that focuses on entirely private or consensual activities would be rejected.

Economic liberalism stresses individual rights of property and freedom of contract. It advocates laissez-faire capitalism, meaning the removal of legal barriers to trade and cessation of government-bestowed privilege, such as subsidy and monopoly. Economic liberals want little or no government regulation of the market. Interestingly, therefore, this type of liberalism would be directly opposed to the communalism of the 'radical' Reformation. Indeed, it is well worth remembering that a Protestant critique of liberal ideas can come from not only the fundamentalist right, but also the radical left. Economic liberalism may well find itself rejected not only by some types of 'communal' Protestantism, but also by social liberals who wish to protect individuals from the juggernaut of uncontrolled market forces. According to the tenets of this form of liberalism, since individuals are the basis of society, all individuals should have access to basic necessities of fulfilment, such as education, economic opportunity and protection from harmful macro-events beyond their control. To social liberals, these benefits are considered rights. To the social liberal, ensuring positive rights is a goal that is continuous with the general project of protecting liberties. Social liberalism advocates some restrictions on economic competition, such as anti-trust laws and price controls on wages (minimum wage laws). It also expects governments to provide a basic level of welfare, supported by taxation. In the nineteenth century, as we have seen, this mixed message of liberalism could pit 'conservative' proponents of market liberalism, such as holders of monopolies, against Social Gospellers arguing for a 'decent' wage and good working conditions. Both groups contained leading Protestant ministers, and both groups used the Bible to argue their positions.

The Bible may be somewhat scathing of the greed of the rich, but it does not question their right to get rich, be rich or stay rich. At the same time it is also extremely disparaging of the ill treatment of widows and orphans. The question is how to make these ideas a reality in society. Conservatives could quite legitimately argue that Paul told slaves to be content with their lot and obey their masters – surely a strong argument against radical or revolutionary change in favour of hierarchy and traditional socio-cultural structures. At the same time, Jesus's one great display of violent, angry emotion was the overturning of the money-changers' tables in the Temple in Jerusalem (Matthew 21:12, Mark 11:15). Again, we return to the question not only of authority (who decides which of these is the 'main' message of the Bible), but also of interpretation (is Jesus's action simply against a specific behaviour unique to first-century Jerusalem, or a more general point about greedy businessmen?).

During the course of the twentieth century, liberal, modernist Protestantism came to suggest that the Bible was more a document providing general guidance for the modern age rather than a detailed, specific blueprint for society and individuals. They also rejected the idea that it was able to provide any 'revealed' information on science – in particular, geology. Thus, there was little problem in rejecting not only the Bible's geocentrism, but also the specifics of the creation story (or stories) in Genesis. These simply taught the general idea that God had created the universe, not the specifics of the timescale of that creation, which was couched in terms understandable to readers of the time. Fundamentalists rejected this new interpretative approach, which, they argued, allowed any and all verses of the Bible to be ignored or excised. Secular conservatives rejected the radicalism inherent in this more liberal approach to traditional Protestantism, and its traditionally conservative views about society and culture.

FUNDAMENTALISM

Just as modernism and liberalism were not specifically Protestant, or even religious, phenomena, opposition to these movements has not been necessarily Protestant or religious. In comparative religion, fundamentalism has come to refer to several different understandings of religious thought and practice through literal interpretation of religious texts, such as the Bible or the Koran, and sometimes also to anti-modernist movements in various religions. Fundamentalism is characterized by a sense of embattled alienation in the midst of the surrounding culture, even where the culture may be nominally, or even greatly, influenced by the adherents' religion. The term can also refer specifically to the belief that one's religious texts are infallible and historically accurate, despite apparent contradictions with 'science'.

Fundamentalism, as the term is used at the start of the twenty-first century, is a fairly recent phenomenon closely linked with the events in 1920s' American Protestantism (for example, the fundamentalist–modernist controversy in the Presbyterian Church). Since then the term has been exported and applied to a wide variety of religions, including Buddhism, Judaism and Islam. Fundamentalism is not the same thing as the Revivalist movements of the eighteenth- and nineteenth-century awakenings (see pages 160–4), although it does derive many practical approaches to religion, such as style of worship and emphasis upon a personal, emotional 'experience', from these sources.

Fundamentalism describes a return to what are considered the defining or founding principles of a religion on the basis that the fundamental principles upon which the larger religious group was supposedly founded have become corrupt. The 'fundamentals' of the religion have been jettisoned by neglect or lost through compromise. Fundamentalist movements are therefore founded upon the same religious principles as the larger group, but the fundamentalists more self-consciously attempt to build an entire approach to the modern world based on strict fidelity to those principles, to preserve a distinctiveness both of doctrine and of life.

The term itself is borrowed from the title of a four-volume set of books called *The Fundamentals*, published in 1909 by the Bible Institute of Los Angeles (BIOLA, now Biola University) and edited by R. A. Torrey, a minister affiliated with the Moody Bible Institute in Chicago. Initially, the project was funded by Lyman Stewart, president and co-founder of the Union Oil Company of California. The books were a republication of a series of essays that were sent by mail to every minister in America. They appealed to all Christians to affirm specific fundamental doctrines, such as the Virgin Birth and bodily resurrection of Jesus. These essays came to be representative of the fundamentalist–modernist controversy that started in the late nineteenth century within American Protestantism, and continued through the 1920s.

Fundamentalism is, therefore, a movement through which its adherents attempt to rescue religious identity from absorption in modern Western culture. This 'minority' believes that modernism had made irreversible progress in the wider religious community, and it is now necessary to assert a separate identity based upon the fundamental or founding principles of the religion. Fundamentalists believe their cause to have grave, even cosmic importance. They see themselves as protecting not only a distinctive doctrine, but also a vital principle, and a way of life and of salvation. Community, comprehensively centred upon a clearly defined religious way of life in all of its aspects, is the promise of fundamentalist movements.

In Christianity, fundamentalists are 'born-again' and 'Bible-believing' Protestants, as opposed to 'mainline', 'liberal', 'modernist' Protestants, who represent 'Churchianity' rather than 'true' Christianity. In Islam they are *Jama'at* (religious enclaves with connotations of close fellowship) self-consciously engaged in *jihad* (struggle) against Western culture that suppresses authentic Islam (submission) and the God-given (*Shari'ah*) way of life. In Judaism, they are *Haredi* (Torah-true) Jews. These groups insist on a sharp boundary between themselves and the faithful adherents of other religions, and between a 'sacred' view of life and the 'secular' world.

However, Protestant fundamentalists, who describe themselves thus, strongly dislike any wider application of the term, or any implication that

Protestant fundamentalism (which is 'truth') is in any way similar to fundamentalism in any other (false) religions. Obviously, this does not stop these groups from actively cooperating in society and politics in the face of the 'common foe' – secular modernism. In addition, many Muslims object to the use of the term 'fundamentalist' because all Muslims believe in the absolute inerrancy of the Koran, and Western writers use the term only to refer to extremist groups. Furthermore, many strongly dislike being placed in the same category as Christian fundamentalists, whom they see as being religiously incorrect. Moreover, unlike Christian fundamentalist groups, Islamist groups do not use the term 'fundamentalist' to refer to themselves. Thus, the term is most accurately used to refer to Protestant groups that happily call themselves fundamentalist.

For these Protestants, the key issue is the view one has about the Bible. This does not, however, suggest an authoritative interpretative model, but it does limit the range of interpretations available. The Bible is considered the authentic and literal word of God. Fundamentalist beliefs depend on the twin doctrines that God articulated his will precisely to prophets, and that followers also have a reliable and perfect record of that revelation. Fundamentalists believe that no person has a right to change it or disagree with it, though, again, this highlights the issue of authority and interpretation. Self-described Protestant fundamentalists see their Scripture, a combination of the Hebrew Bible and the New Testament, as both infallible and historically accurate. The New Testament represents a new covenant between God and human beings, which is held to fulfil the Old Testament in regard to God's redemptive plan. On the basis of this confidence in Scripture, many fundamentalist Christians accept the account of Scripture as being literally true.

Of course, this belief in the inerrancy of the 'literal' Bible has some inherent problems. Who decides which parts are literal and which metaphorical or symbolic? Most would argue that common sense is the guide, which brings us back to the idea that the Bible is clear, plain and simple in its meaning. This inevitably raises the same issue that divided

Luther and Zwingli in Marburg – what does 'is' mean? Or, as William Jennings Bryan put it when arguing against Clarence Darrow during the Scopes (Monkey) Trial (1925) about evolution and creationism: 'I believe that everything in the Bible should be accepted as it is given there; some of the Bible is given illustratively. For instance: "Ye are the salt of the earth". I would not insist that man was actually salt, or that he had flesh of salt, but it is used in the sense of salt as saving God's people.'

But why can it not be taken literally that men are made of salt? Why must the word 'day' in Genesis be literally a twenty-four hour period? This question of authority and interpretation has haunted Protestantism since Marburg, and fundamentalism has not yet solved it. Nevertheless, it is an attempt to react against an interpretative model (liberal modernism) that suggested the Bible was not itself necessarily the sole or unique source of authority.

This has also led to the construction of a set of values and morals based on interpretations of Bible passages in a way that relates them to events, trends, issues and ideas never specifically addressed in the Bible. Examples of things that fundamentalists might believe important to avoid are modern translations of the Bible, alcoholic drinks or recreational drugs, tobacco, modern popular music (including Christian contemporary music), 'folk' instruments, such as guitars and drums, in worship, dancing, mixed bathing (an increase in lust is directly related to a decrease in clothing) and gender-neutral or trans-gender clothing and hairstyles.

Not surprisingly, many of the claims and goals of modern, predominantly American, fundamentalist Protestantism echo those of the reformers of the sixteenth century. Fundamentalists claim both that they practise their religion as the first Church adherents did and that this is how religion should be practised. In other words, a Christian ought to believe and practise as those who knew and followed Jesus during his time on Earth. The communal-property aspects of the apostolic church in Jerusalem are noticeable by their absence. Thus, modern American Protestant fundamentalists would be appalled by the 'heresy' of sixteenth-century radical reformers who rejected private property, and consider them advocates of the atheistic evil of communism, which, until its implosion, was a greater threat than even secular modernism.

Many criticisms of the fundamentalist position have been offered. Some of the most common are that the theological claims made by fundamentalist groups cannot be proven, are irrational, or are demonstrably false and contrary to scientific evidence — as understood by opponents of fundamentalism. Another criticism is that the rhetoric of these groups offers an appearance of uniformity and simplicity, yet within each faith community, one actually finds different texts of religious law that are accepted; each text has varying interpretations. Consequently, each fundamentalist faith is observed to splinter into many mutually antagonistic groups. They are often as hostile to each other as they are to other religions, though they are at least upholding the traditional tendency of Protestantism continually to subdivide.

The most significant critique, though, relates to the process by which the 'inerrant, infallible' Word of God becomes known to individual believers. As a text on the shelf, these critics argue, the Bible could well be both infallible and inerrant. However, the minute a person reads the text and attempts to understand or explain it, human fallibility and interpretation become an inextricable part of the process. God's Word can be infallible and inerrant, but man's interpretation and understanding of it cannot. It is fair to say that, for the most part, this issue is simply ignored by fundamentalists, or the suggestion is made that in some manner the Holy Spirit intervenes to ensure the correct interpretation. Obviously, as we have seen time and time again, the claim of guidance by the Holy Spirit is also likely to produce multiple and contradictory interpretations.

A general criticism of fundamentalism is the claim that fundamentalists are selective in what they believe and practise. For instance, the book of Deuteronomy (25:5–6) dictates that if a man's brother dies without a son, he must marry his widowed sister-in-law. Yet fundamentalist Christians do not adhere to this doctrine, despite the fact that it is not contradicted in the New Testament (even though Jesus is asked a specific question about the practice and does not suggest that it should cease – for example, Matthew 22:24–8). However, defenders of fundamentalism argue that according to New Testament theology, large parts, if not all, of the Mosaic Law (which includes not only the Ten Commandments, but also dietary rules and a host of other regulations for almost every aspect of life) are not normative for modern Christians, though there is no explicit New Testament guide for deciding which bits are normative and which are not. Other fundamentalists argue that only certain parts of the Mosaic Law, parts that rely on universal moral principles (again, how does one decide which are universal and which not?), are normative for today. Therefore, in their view, there is no contradiction between such passages in the Old Testament and their belief in biblical infallibility.

The key debate as it has developed in American Protestantism appears on the surface to relate to specific passages of the Bible, such as the Genesis creation account, or explicit Old Testament injunctions against homosexuality. However, this belies the deeper issue of authority and interpretation. When considered in this light, this debate is as old as Protestantism itself. Protestants of every variety accept the authority of the Bible: some wish to limit the understanding of this authoritative position by the use of words such as 'literal', 'inerrant' and 'infallible'. They would all accept that the Bible is God's Word – as did Luther, Calvin and Zwingli. The problem, though, arises in interpretation. Protestantism continues to lack any structure for settling disputes about biblical interpretation. To mix metaphors, once Luther had opened Pandora's box and let out the genie of the priesthood of all believers, it became impossible to control the results. In that sense, the comment made by Cardinal Walter Kaspar on the fortieth anniversary of the publication of Second Vatican Councils decree on ecumenism, *Unitatis Redintegratio*, in 2004 is quite true: 'Protestant Christians do not wish to be a church in the same way as the Catholic Church understands itself as a church; they represent a different type of church and for this reason they are not a church in the Catholic meaning of the word.'

No better example of this problem can be advanced than the reaction of Protestants and Catholics to Mormonism. In modern America conservative Catholics, Protestants, Jews and Mormons (and, more recently, even conservative Muslims) have united to oppose secularism and modernism. And yet most conservative Christians would reject the very idea that Mormonism is a form of Christianity. For example, the Southern Baptist Convention has said:

> Christian theologians, however, know that Mormonism is essentially different in its basic theological structure from that of historic Christianity. Mormons believe, for example, that God, called Heavenly Father, is a physical man of flesh and bone who once lived on a world like our own. Through righteous living, obedience to his Heavenly Father, and Celestial Marriage, he progressed to become the god of our universe ... Mormons are undeniably polytheistic. Jesus Christ, according to [Mormon] doctrine, is also one of Heavenly Father's spirit children who has attained godhood. Heavenly Father, Jesus Christ, and the Holy Ghost are three of many gods of other worlds.

Or, more recently, in Tal Davis's *A Closer Look at the Book of Mormon* (2001):

> The Church of Jesus Christ of Latter Day Saints (Mormons) used to teach with some vehemence that 'Christians' were doomed to hell. More recently, though, they have tried to insist that they, too, are Christians. Given their numbers, they claim that they are one of the 'mainline' Christian denominations. But Mormon theology distorts Christian doctrine on most major issues; they have become rather reticent in their new stance towards Christianity about their teaching that 'men [*sic*] can become gods'.

Catholicism is just as vehement in its views on Mormonism. Indeed, as early as Pope Leo XIII's encyclical on marriage (1880) the Church said: 'Again, in the very beginning of the Christian Church [such heresies] were repulsed and defeated, with the like unremitting determination, the efforts of many who aimed at the destruction of Christian marriage, such as the Gnostics, Manichaeans, and Montanists; and in our own time Mormons ... and communists.'

Catholicism has an inherent structure based on tradition and the Bible interpreted, maintained and explained through the magisterial function of the Church, embodied in the papacy, for deciding what is and is not heresy. Protestantism does not. A Protestant may say what he or she thinks is the meaning of a particular verse, but there is no mechanism by which Protestantism can do that. Indeed, this very lack of a system for limiting the priesthood of all believers, or for agreeing on the clear, plain, and simple message of the Bible, continues to plague Protestantism, as it has done since its inception.

CONCLUSIONS

Obviously, this volume is not intended to be a comprehensive history of Protestantism. Indeed, in some senses it it not a history at all. Rather it is a consideration of those features that seem to be unique to Protestantism through the centuries and that, perhaps, explain the societies and cultures that have been largely, if not predominantly, influenced by Protestantism. Clearly, this is not meant to explain everything. Nor is it even a thesis on the grand scale of Max Weber's, though it will perhaps be worth while to take a few brief moments to consider Weber's thesis as it has had an enduring impact on ideas about Protestantism.

This volume has, however, made an attempt to see Protestantism as more than just 'magisterial' churches and their successors, or even as traditionally 'orthodox'. There is a tendency (and danger) in accepting the idea that Protestantism is basically the denominations deriving from Lutheranism, Calvinism and Anglicanism. This would suggest that the radical reforming groups, such as the Hutterites and Mennonites, were not Protestant. Moreover, it would overlook the important strand among groups arising out of the Reformation, which called into question the entire Christian understanding of God and Jesus (for example Socinians, anti-Trinitarians, Unitarians), as well as those that have added sacred texts to the Protestant Bible, but would still consider themselves to be, broadly speaking, both Protestant and Christian (Jehovah's Witnesses, Christian Scientists, Mormons). Instead, by allowing these strands of the Protestant story to appear and reappear, this volume has tried to stress the diversity and religious 'creativity' of the accidental revolution began by Luther. Only when one considers Protestantism in this wider meaning can one really begin to discuss its impact and 'genius' in shaping the modern world. It was this very question that absorbed Weber.

Maximilian Weber was a German political economist and sociologist who is considered one of the founders of modern sociology (the scientific study of human society). His major works deal with the rationalization in sociology of religion and government, but he also wrote much in the field of economics. In his writings Weber argued that religion was one (stressing only one) of the reasons for the different ways the cultures of the West and the East had developed.

Weber's three main themes were the effect of religious ideas on economic activities, the relation between social stratification and religious ideas, and the specific characteristics of Western civilization. His goal was to find reasons for the different developmental paths of the cultures of the West and the East. In analysing his findings, Weber maintained that Calvinist and, more widely, Christian religious ideas had had a major impact on the development of the economic systems of Europe and the United States, but noted that they were not the only factors in this development. Other notable influences, Weber maintained, included the rationalism of scientific pursuit, merging observation with mathematics, the science of scholarship and jurisprudence, rational systematization of governmental administration, and economic enterprise. In the end, the study of the sociology of religion, according to Weber, merely explored one phase of 'freeing [man] from magic', that 'disenchantment of the world' that he regarded as an important characteristic of Western culture.

In his book *The Protestant Ethic and the Spirit of Capitalism* (1904–5), Weber argued that he was not presenting a detailed study of Protestantism (nor does this volume); it was to be an introduction to his later works, especially his studies of interaction between various religious ideas and economic behaviour. In that book Weber put forward the thesis that the 'Puritan' (that is, Calvinist) ethic and ideas influenced the development of capitalism. Traditionally, deep religious devotion had been accompanied by a rejection of mundane or worldly affairs, including economic pursuit, but this, Weber argued, was not the case in Calvinism.

He defined 'the spirit of capitalism' as the ideas and habits that favoured the rational pursuit of economic gain. Weber pointed out that such a spirit was not limited to Western culture, when considered as the attitude of individuals, but that such individuals – 'heroic entrepreneurs', as he called them – could not by themselves establish a new economic order (capitalism). Among the tendencies identified by Weber were the greed for profit with minimum effort, the idea that work was a curse and a burden to be avoided, especially when it exceeded what was enough for modest life. He said that 'in order that a manner of life well adapted to the peculiarities of capitalism could come to dominate others, it had to originate somewhere, and not in isolated individuals alone, but as a way of life common to whole groups of man.'

After defining this spirit of capitalism, Weber argued that there were many reasons to look for its origins in the religious ideas of the Reformation. Indeed, he was not the first to notice or suggest an affinity between Protestantism and the development of the commercial spirit. Weber argued that certain types of Protestantism, notably Calvinism, favoured the rational (one might say organized) pursuit of economic gain, and that these worldly activities had been given positive spiritual and moral meaning: for example, success was equated with 'God's blessing'. It was not the goal of those religious ideas, but rather a by-product – the inherent and unintended logic of those doctrines.

Needless to say, there have been many critiques of Weber's ideas, and innumerable examples can be put forth showing that Calvinists were not enthusiastic capitalists. Likewise, capitalism was not unknown among Catholics – the conquest of the New World by the Spanish was a type of privatized imperialism that would have made the industrialists Andrew Carnegie and Henry Ford proud. However, what Weber tried to do was to consider those aspects of Protestantism that seemed unique compared with other religions and other Christian denominations, and then to consider their practical implications.

This volume, on a much less grand or comprehensive scale, follows the same approach. The predominant feature of Protestantism from its outset relates to ideas about authority and interpretation. In rejecting the structure of Western medieval Christianity, with its reliance on councils, creeds and the papacy, Protestantism set in motion a chain of events largely antithetical to the wishes of its earliest proponents. Luther, Zwingli and Calvin did not desire to establish separate denominations, let alone serve as catalysts for the formation of literally thousands of them. They would look on in horror at the modern Protestant stress on personal, emotional experience, with its lack of emphasis upon doctrine. They would be appalled by its individualism, and consider its Arminian-based theology of salvation to be heretical.

Nevertheless, Martin Luther did more than rupture Western medieval Christianity – he made it impossible to hold even its smallest fragments together. In itself, this would suggest that the history of Protestantism is simply a history of schism and woe. Many a Catholic onlooker would be inclined to agree. But this would be much too simplistic. Luther and the other early reformers did something much more dramatic, and that, in the long run, had considerably more positive consequences. They suggested that the relationship between man and truth (as revealed by God in the Bible) was not mediated; there was no one between the individual person and God's Word. This was revolutionary. Yes, it meant that there could eventually be as many denominations of Protestantism as there could be Protestants. It also meant that any Bible verse might be interpreted differently by every single reader. Traditionalists in the sixteenth century, and both Catholic and Protestant conservatives since, have seen this as extremely dangerous.

But it is also amazingly liberating. This suggests that the individual is personally and uniquely responsible for what he or she believes, for how he or she interprets God's Word, for how it is worked out in his or her own life and behaviour. Chaos results, but it is a creative and explosively inventive chaos. It is a chaos that can allow for radical new ideas to spring seemingly from nowhere in a matter of decades, if not days. No council or pope was needed to hold meetings and conclaves to decide that slavery was wrong: William Wilberforce and his colleagues simply searched their Bibles and their hearts, and went out to abolish it. Dr King and Archbishop Tutu did not need external authority or the *magisterium* of the Church to lead them to reject racial discrimination. The Social Gospellers fought against inhuman working conditions and hopeless homes filled with despair because that was the charge they found in their Bible. The Diggers, Quakers, Mennonites, Hutterites and hosts of others then and now held their world up to the measuring rod in their Bible and found their societies wanting. Then went about constructing new ones.

And yet each of these groups faced opposition from other Protestants – at times violent, vicious opposition. Segregationist ministers attacked King and Tutu. 'God-fearing, church-going' southerners fire-bombed black churches. The Anglican Church owned slaves and grew rich off their toil. Churches, bishops, elders, ministers and priests called on secular authorities to root out exponents of radical social and cultural change, especially when the radicalism touched private property. The freedom to read and interpret the Bible that could produce a Wilberforce railing in Parliament against slavery was the very same as the one that could produce a state governor like George Wallace standing at the entrance to the University of Alabama surrounded by armed guards and shouting, 'Segregation today, segregation tomorrow, segregation for ever!' Both believed that their ideas found support in, and were required by, the Bible.

So one cannot see Protestantism as some great driving force for modernity or progress. It has been, but it has also been a staunch opponent of both. Rather, its inherent tendency to schism, its lack of a mechanism of authority, its inability to put the genie of freedom back in the bottle has tended to favour change. It has the ability to hasten change and to allow individuals to be motivated quickly and enthusiastically. By placing a burden of responsibility on each person for his or her beliefs or actions, Protestantism introduced into society an incentive for individual, immediate action. This did not free the individual; rather, in a very real sense, it bound the individual even more tightly. No one could sit back and leave the faith to others, to mediation, to priests, bishops, councils or popes. This new faith required, even demanded, individual attention and personal action. That action has led to innumerable schisms, but it has also provided one of the dynamic forces driving many Western cultures and societies not only to close introspection, but also to swift and dramatic change.

The lack of a mechanism for authority means that Protestantism cannot be a Church in the sense that Roman Catholicism is a Church. It also means that no one had to wait to approve Dr King's arguments – they were thrown into the marketplace of ideas and won on their merit. They were persuasive and effective precisely because they challenged a predominately Protestant America to turn to its Bible and its secular documents and dare to find a justification for hate and discrimination. The individuals who heard King's challenge understood their responsibility to read and decide for themselves. Luther never intended to introduce individualism into his world, but he did so. However, that individualism, in the Protestant context, is not a freedom to do whatever you want: rather, it is the weighty, terrifying burden to be responsible for what one does and believes. The challenge of Protestantism to its adherents is to read the Bible and then to stand, alone, as a priest before God. Protestantism replaced a mechanism of authority with a recipe for chaos. In the process, it inadvertently forced individuals to become active, participating citizens in a new type of Christendom.

GLOSSARY
OF NAMES

Names are arranged alphabetically by first name for monarchs and their wives, by last word for those with titles (e.g. Duke of Alva appears under 'A'), and by surname for all others. Those marked with an asterisk (*) have their own entries.

JOHN QUINCY ADAMS (1735–1826) was a politician and founding father of the United States, who served both as the first vice president (1789–97), and as its second president (1797–1801). He was defeated for re-election in the 'Revolution of 1800' by Thomas Jefferson*. Adams was a sponsor of the American Revolution in Massachusetts, and a diplomat in the 1770s. He was a driving force for independence in 1776 – in fact, Jefferson called him the 'Colossus of Independence'. As a statesman and author, Adams helped define a set of republican ideals that became the core of America's system of political values: the rejection of hereditary monarchy in favour of rule by the people, hatred of corruption, and devotion to civic duty.

JANE ADDAMS (1860–1935) was an American social worker, sociologist, philosopher and reformer. She was also the first American woman to win the Nobel Peace Prize, and a founder of the US Settlement House Movement, which provided housing for poor women.

SYDNEY E. AHLSTROM (1919–84) was a professor of history at Yale University. His most significant publication was *A Religious History of the American People* (1972).

THOMAS AIKENHEAD (c.1678–97) was a Scottish student from Edinburgh, who was prosecuted and executed on a charge of blasphemy for anti-Trinitarianism. He further predicted that Christianity would be 'utterly extirpated' by 1800. Although he pleaded for mercy during the hearing, and attempted to recant his views, he was sentenced to death by hanging. On the gallows he stated his belief that moral laws were devised by humans rather than a divine being. He was the last person hanged for blasphemy in Britain.

ALBRECHT OF HOHENZOLLERN (1490–1545), appointed cardinal in 1518, was Elector and Archbishop of Mainz (1514–45), and Archbishop of Magdeburg (1513–45). He borrowed 21,000 ducats from the Fugger banking family to buy his appointment to Mainz, and obtained permission from Pope Leo X* to sell indulgences to repay this loan as long as half the money collected was sent to Rome (to help pay for the building of St Peter's basilica). Johann Tetzel* was hired to sell these indulgences, and it was as a disgusted response to Tetzel's activities that Martin Luther* wrote his famous 'Ninety-five Theses'.

ALEXANDER II (1818–81) was the Tsar of Russia from 1855 until his assassination. He was also the Grand Duke of Finland. In 1861 he emancipated the serfs.

3RD DUKE OF ALVA (1507–82), born Fernando Álvarez de Toledo y Pimentel, was a Spanish general and governor of the Spanish Netherlands (1567–73). He was nicknamed the 'Iron Duke' by Protestants because of his harsh rule and cruelty. Tales of atrocities committed during his military operations in Flanders became part of Dutch and English folklore, forming a new and central component of the anti-Spanish 'Black Legend', in which English-speaking (especially North American) Protestants portrayed the Spanish (and Catholicism) as particularly brutal and backwards.

DUKE OF ANJOU AND ALENÇON (1555–84), born Hercule François, was the youngest son of Henry II* and Catherine de' Medici*. Deformed by childhood smallpox, he was called 'my little frog' by Elizabeth I* and 'my little ape' by his own brother, Henry III*. In 1574, following the death of his brother Charles IX* and the accession of Henry III*, he became heir to the throne. In 1579 he was invited by William I of Orange-Nassau* to become hereditary sovereign to the United Provinces. In 1580 the Dutch Estates General granted him the title 'Protector of the Liberty of the Netherlands', and he became the sovereign. In 1583, after leading a disastrous campaign against Antwerp, he abdicated and fled to France.

JACOBUS ARMINIUS (1560–1609) was a Dutch theologian and (from 1603) professor of theology at the University of Leiden. He was a harsh critic of the variety of Calvinism common in the Dutch Reformed Church.

ARCHDUKE OF AUSTRIA (1559–1621), born Albert Ernst, was the son of Maximilian II* and the Infanta Maria, daughter of Charles V* and Isabella of Portugal. He held numerous titles, including Duke of Luxemburg and Archbishop of Toledo. He was appointed Governor of the Low Countries in 1595, and in 1599 was released from his religious commitments by Pope Clement VIII in order to marry Isabella*, daughter of Philip II* of Spain. Together they became joint sovereigns of the Seventeen Provinces of the Low Countries.

2ND BARON BALTIMORE (1605–75), born Caecilius (Cecil) Calvert, inherited the new colony of Maryland on the death of his father in 1632. (His father had been granted it by Charles I*.) He thus became Maryland's first proprietary governor, though he never visited the colony. As a Catholic, he ensured that Maryland was open to Catholic immigration and that Catholicism was practised there.

ROBERT BARCLAY (c.1648–90) was a Scotsman and one of the Quakers' most eminent writers. He wrote Truth Cleared of Calumnies (1670) and a Catechism and Confession of Faith (1673).

JAN VAN BATENBURG (c.1495–1538) was the illegitimate son of a Dutch nobleman and rose to prominence himself as a town mayor. During the early 1530s, he converted to Anabaptism. His sympathies originally lay with the Anabaptists of Münster, but in 1535 the Anabaptists from Groningen (later called the Batenburgers) urged him to declare himself as 'a new David'. Before long, he had established a new and completely

independent sect, which quickly became the most extreme of all the early Anabaptist movements. In their theology, everything on earth was theirs to do with as they pleased. There was nothing wrong in making a living by robbing 'infidels', by which they meant anyone who was not a member of their sect; indeed, killing infidels was pleasing to their God. They shared the views of the Münsterites on polygamy and property: all women and all goods were held in common.

STEPHEN (ISTVÁN) BÁTHORY (1533–86) was Prince of Transylvania (1571–86), then King of Poland and Grand Duke of Lithuania (1575–86). When he became ruler of the Polish-Lithuanian Commonwealth, he left Transylvania for Poland, appointing his elder brother, Christopher, as viceroy. Although a Catholic and enthusiastic supporter of the Jesuits, he largely respected the multi-denominational settlements in his kingdoms.

DAVID BEATON (c.1494–1546) was Archbishop of St Andrews and the last Scottish cardinal prior to the Reformation. He was assassinated by a band of pro-Protestant conspirators avenging the execution of George Wishart*.

ROBERT BELLARMINE (1542–1621), a Roman Catholic cardinal, was a Jesuit theologian and academic. He is a saint (canonized 1930) and is one of only thirty-three Doctors of the Church (declared 1931) who were those ecclesiastical writers so honoured on account of the great advantage the whole Church has derived from their doctrine.

LOUIS DE BERQUIN (1485–1529) was a leading French humanist and evangelical. He was repeatedly arrested for his supposed Lutheran views, but was protected by Francis I*. When he was finally condemned as a heretic in 1529, Francis did not intervene in the hasty judicial process, and Berquin was burnt at the stake.

MARY MCLEOD BETHUNE (1875–1955) worked for the election of Franklin D. Roosevelt to the US presidency in 1932, and tried to get his support for a proposed law (the Costigan–Wagner Bill) against lynching. Although the bill was not passed, it did raise more public awareness of the lynching issue. She was also a member of Roosevelt's 'black cabinet'.

THEODORE BEZA (1519–1605) was a French Protestant theologian and scholar who played an important role in the early Reformation. He was a disciple of John Calvin* and lived most of his life in Switzerland. Although a key figure in the Reformation in Lausanne, he was forced out by the city's overlords in Berne. Settling in Geneva, he succeeded Calvin as the city's chief pastor in 1564.

JOHN BIDDLE (1616–62) is often referred to as the 'Father of English Unitarianism'. In 1644 he was questioned by the local authorities at Gloucester to answer charges brought against him for anti-Trinitarian views. He wrote a manuscript entitled *Twelve Arguments Drawn out of the Scriptures* (1644), for which he was again arrested. In 1652 he established a small Socinian congregation in London. Although repeatedly arrested under the Commonwealth, the protection of Oliver Cromwell* kept him safe. Following the Restoration, he was against arrested and fined under common law (not any religious statute) for his beliefs. Unable to pay the fine, he was jailed and died while incarcerated.

TONY BLAIR (b. 1953) is the Prime Minister of the United Kingdom, First Lord of the Treasury, minister for the Civil Service, leader of the UK Labour Party, and Member of Parliament for Sedgefield in County Durham. As a member of the Cabinet, he is also a Privy Counsellor.

GIORGIO BLANDRATA (c.1515–88) was an Italian physician and polemicist. He spent a year at the Italian (Protestant) church in Geneva, where he spread anti-Trinitarian ideas. He then went to Poland, where he became court physician to the Milanese dowager queen Bona Sforza. Although she had been instrumental in the

burning of one of Poland's first anti-Trinitarian 'martyrs' Melchior Weygel in 1539, the writings of Bernardino Ochino* had altered her views, converting her to Protestantism. He later spread his ideas in Transylvania, but returned to Italy and Catholicism (as with many on the fringe of the Reformation his denominational loyalties were very fluid) with a fortune amassed from his work as a medical doctor to the 'rich and famous'.

WILLIAM BOARDMAN (1810–86), an American pastor and teacher, was the author of *A Higher Christian Life* (1858), which was a major international success and helped ignite the Higher Life movement. His work attracted international attention, especially in England.

JAN BOCKELSON (c.1509–36), also known as John of Leiden, was an Anabaptist leader. He was the illegitimate son of a Dutch mayor, and a tailor's apprentice by trade. In 1534 he became King of Münster. He set up a theocracy, led a communalistic and polygamous state, and may have taken as many as sixteen wives. When Münster fell to the combined Catholic and Lutheran army besieging the city in 1535, he was captured.

ANNE BOLEYN (c.1504–36) was the second wife and queen-consort of King Henry VIII*, and the mother of Elizabeth I*. She was beheaded when Henry tired of her inability to produce a male heir.

DIETRICH BONHOEFFER (1906–45) was a German Lutheran pastor, theologian and participant in the German resistance movement against Nazism. He was involved in plots planned by members of the *Abwehr* (the German Military Intelligence Office) to assassinate Adolf Hitler. He was arrested in 1943 and eventually hanged.

WILLIAM BRADFORD (1590–1657) was a leader of the Pilgrim settlers of the Plymouth Colony in Massachusetts, and became its governor. He was the second signer and primary architect of the Mayflower Compact. As Governor of Plymouth, he is also credited as being the first to proclaim what popular American culture views as the first Thanksgiving.

GUILLAUME BRIÇONNET (1472–1534) was the Bishop of Meaux from 1516. Here he began to implement a programme of ecclesiastical reform, working to improve monastic discipline and the training of his clergy. The evangelical humanists he invited to help implement his reform programme became known as the Circle of Meaux.

GORDON BROWN (b. 1951) is the Chancellor of the Exchequer of the United Kingdom and a Labour Party politician. Formerly the Member of Parliament for Dunfermline East (1983–2005), he is now MP for Kirkcaldy and Cowdenbeath following a reorganization of parliamentary constituencies in Scotland. He is widely expected to succeed Tony Blair* as leader of the Labour Party and prime minister.

WILLIAM JENNINGS BRYAN (1860–1925) was an American lawyer, statesman and politician, and a three-time Democratic Party nominee for President of the United States. One of the most popular speakers in American history, he was noted for his deep, commanding voice. Bryan was a devout Presbyterian, a strong proponent of popular democracy, an outspoken critic of banks and railroads, a dominant figure in the Democratic Party, a peace advocate, a prohibitionist, an opponent of Darwinism, and one of the most prominent leaders of the Progressive Movement. He was called the 'Great Commoner' because of his total faith in the goodness and rightness of the common people.

MARTIN BUCER (1491–1551) was a German Protestant reformer. In 1522 he was pastor at Landstuhl in the Palatinate, and travelled extensively propagating Protestantism. After his excommunication in 1523, he made his headquarters at Strasburg. In 1549 he moved to England and was appointed Regius Professor of

Divinity at Cambridge University. Edward VI* and Edward Seymour, Duke of Somerset*, showed him much favour, and he was consulted on the revision of the Book of Common Prayer. In 1557, six years after his death, he was branded a heretic by commissioners of Mary I*, so his body was exhumed and burnt, and his tomb demolished; it was subsequently restored by order of Elizabeth I*.

GEORGE BUCHANAN (1506–82) was a Scottish historian and humanist scholar, and tutor of James VI*. So great was his reputation for learning and his flair for administration that in 1567, although a layman, he was made Moderator of the General Assembly of the Church of Scotland. He was the last lay person to be elected to the post until Alison Elliot, the first female moderator, was appointed in 2004.

GUILLAUME BUDÉ (1467–1540) was a great French humanist. He persuaded Francis I* to establish the Collegium Trilingue (later the Collège de France), in Paris, and the library at Fontainebleau. The latter subsequently moved to Paris, where it became the present-day Bibliothèque nationale.

JOHN BUNYAN (1628–88) was a Christian writer and preacher. He wrote *The Pilgrim's Progress* (1678), arguably the most famous Christian allegory.

JACOB BURCKHARDT (1818–97) was a Swiss historian of art and culture. His work *The Civilization of the Renaissance in Italy* (1860) was the most influential interpretation of the Italian Renaissance in the nineteenth century, and is still widely read.

CAECILIUS CALVERT (*see* 2nd Baron Baltimore)

JOHN CALVIN (1509–64) was a French Protestant theologian during the Reformation, and was a central developer of the system of Christian theology called Calvinism or reformed theology. In Geneva he rejected papal authority, established a new scheme of civic and ecclesiastical governance, and created a safe haven from which reformed theology was propagated. He is renowned for his teachings and writings, especially *Institution of the Christian Religion* (1536).

JIMMY (JAMES EARL JR) CARTER (b. 1924) was the thirty-ninth President of the United States (1977–81) and the 2002 Nobel Peace laureate. Previously, he was the Governor of Georgia (1971–5).

THOMAS CARTWRIGHT (1535–1603) was one of the key early leaders of what would become English Puritanism. He criticized the hierarchy and constitution of the Church of England, which he compared unfavourably with the primitive Christian Church's structures.

CATHERINE OF ARAGON (1485–1536), as the first wife of Henry VIII*, was Queen-consort of England. Henry tried to have their twenty-four year marriage annulled because she failed to provide him with a male heir. Only one of their six children, Princess Mary (later Mary I*), survived. She refused to acknowledge the divorce and took the issue to the law, but she lost and was forced to leave the royal court. She was separated from her daughter, who was declared illegitimate, and was sent to live in remote castles in humble conditions in the hope that she would surrender to the inevitable; she never accepted the divorce and signed her last letter 'Catherine the Queen'. Henry did not attend her funeral, nor did he allow Princess Mary to do so.

CATHERINE DE' MEDICI (1519–89), as the wife of King Henry II*, was Queen of France and mother to the last three kings of the Valois dynasty.

WILLIAM CECIL (1520–98) was an English politician, the chief adviser of Elizabeth I*, and lord high treasurer from 1572.

JOHN 'JOHNNY APPLESEED' CHAPMAN (1774–1845) was an American pioneer nurseryman and missionary for the Church of the New Jerusalem, founded by Emanuel Swedenborg. He introduced the apple to large parts of Ohio, Indiana and Illinois by planting small nurseries (hence his nickname). He became an American legend while still alive, portrayed in works of art and literature, largely because of his kind and generous ways, and his leadership in conservation.

CHARLES I (1600–49) was King of England, King of Ireland and King of Scots. He engaged in a struggle for power with the parliaments and peoples of his three kingdoms. He was a staunch advocate of the divine right of kings, which led many of his subjects to fear that he was attempting to gain absolute power.

CHARLES II (1630–85) was the King of England, King of Scots, and King of Ireland from 1649. His reign was racked by political factions and intrigue, and it was at this time that the Whig and Tory political parties first developed. He converted to Roman Catholicism on his deathbed.

CHARLES V (1500–58) was ruler of the Burgundian territories, King of Spain, King of Naples and Sicily, Archduke of Austria, King of the Romans or German King and Holy Roman Emperor, but formally abdicated from these last two posts. The vast extent of his territories led to him being described as ruling an empire 'on which the sun does not set'.

CHARLES IX (1550–74) became King of France following the death of his elder brother Francis II*, and was crowned in 1560. In 1572 he oversaw the massacre of thousands of Huguenots (Protestants) in and around Paris in what became known as the St Bartholomew's Day Massacre.

CHARLES CHAUNCY (1592–1672) was an Anglo-American clergyman and educator. He was president of Harvard College (now University) from 1654 to 1672.

PETR CHELČICKÝ (1390–1460) was a Christian and political leader and author in Bohemia. He was influenced by the ideas of John Wyclif* and Jan Hus*, and was a communist in the original Christian sense of wanting complete equality in the Christian community. There could be no rich or poor, as the Christian relinquished all property and status. Christians could expel evil persons from their community, but could not compel them to be good. He believed in equality, but also that the State should not force it upon society.

CHRISTIAN IV (1577–1648) was the King of Denmark and Norway from 1588. Active in the Protestant cause during the opening phases of the Thirty Years War, he was, despite being defeated, able to leave the conflict without losing any territory. His most important contribution to the struggle was bringing Sweden into the war on the Protestant side.

CLEMENT VI (1291–1352), born Pierre Roger, was the fourth of the Avignon popes (elected May 1342). He issued the bull *Unigenitus* (1343), which justified papal supremacy and the sale of indulgences, and was used in response to the attack on indulgences by Martin Luther* in his 'Ninety-five Theses'.

CLEMENT VII (1342–94), born Robert of Geneva, was the first antipope of the Western Schism (see Urban VI*). He was elected to the papacy in 1378 by the French cardinals who opposed Urban VI, and was based in Avignon.

CLEMENT VII (1478–1534), born Giulio di Giuliano de' Medici, was a cardinal (1513–23) and pope from 1523. He refused to grant Henry VIII* a divorce from Catherine of Aragon*. Days before his death he commissioned Michelangelo* to paint the *Last Judgement* in the Sistine Chapel.

LINDA COLLEY (b. 1949) is a British historian widely known for her book *Britons: Forging the Nation, 1707–1837* (1992), which explored the development of a British national identity following the 1707 Acts of Union. She is currently Shelby M. C. Davis Professor of History at Princeton University in the USA.

FRANCIS COLLINS (b. 1950) is a physician–geneticist noted for his landmark discoveries of disease genes and his leadership of the Human Genome Project. He is director of the National Human Genome Research Institute in Bethesda, Maryland.

EUGENE 'BULL' CONNOR (1897–1973) was a police official in the state of Alabama at the height of the American civil-rights movement, a member of the Ku-Klux-Klan, and a staunch advocate of racial segregation. He called Lee Harvey Oswald (the assassinator of John F. Kennedy*) 'a southern hero like John Wilkes Booth' (the assassinator of Abraham Lincoln*).

GASPARO CONTARINI (1483–1542) was an Italian diplomat whom Pope Paul III unexpectedly made a cardinal (in 1535) in order to bind an able man of evangelical disposition to Rome. He and his friends, who formed the Catholic evangelical movement of the *Spirituali*, believed that reform of abuses was sufficient not only to correct the Catholic Church, but also to heal the breach with the Protestants.

NICOLAUS COPERNICUS (1473–1543) was the Polish astronomer who formulated the first modern heliocentric theory of the solar system. His key text, *De revolutionibus orbium coelestium* (1543), is considered the starting point of modern astronomy. Among the great polymaths of the Scientific Revolution, Copernicus was a mathematician, astronomer, jurist, physician, classical scholar, Catholic cleric, governor, administrator, diplomat, economist and soldier. Amid these extensive responsibilities, astronomy served as no more than a hobby. Nonetheless, his conception of the sun (rather than the Earth) at the centre of the solar system is considered among the most important scientific landmarks.

THOMAS CRANMER (1489–1556) was the Archbishop of Canterbury during the reigns of

Henry VIII* and Edward VI*. He is credited with writing and compiling the first two Books of Common Prayer, which established the basic structure of Anglican liturgy for centuries, and stand as examples of the English language at its finest. He was one of the first Anglican martyrs, being burnt in 1556 for heresy by Mary I*.

OLIVER CROMWELL (1599–1658) was an English military and political leader best known for making Great Britain a republic. A religious-conversion experience made religion the central fact of his life and actions. A brilliant soldier, he rose from the ranks to command the army. Politically, he took control of England, Scotland and Ireland as lord protector from 1653 until his death.

THOMAS CROMWELL (c.1485–1540) was an English statesman and chief minister to King Henry VIII*. While Cromwell was in office, Henry's government was far more open to religious reform than subsequently.

CHARLES DARWIN (1809–82) was an eminent English naturalist who achieved lasting fame by convincing the scientific community that species develop over time from a common origin. His theories explaining this phenomenon through natural and sexual selection are central to the modern understanding of evolution as the unifying theory of the life sciences, essential in biology, and important in other disciplines, such as anthropology, psychology and philosophy.

FERENC DÁVID (1510–79) was the founder of the Unitarian Church in Transylvania.

DANIEL DEFOE (1660–1731) was an English writer, journalist and spy, who gained enduring fame for his novel Robinson Crusoe (1719). He helped popularize the genre in Britain, and is sometimes referred to as the founder of the English novel. A prolific and versatile writer, he wrote over five hundred books, pamphlets and journals on various topics, including politics, crime, religion, marriage, psychology and the

supernatural. He was also a pioneer of economic journalism.

CHARLES DICKENS (1812–70) was an English novelist who achieved worldwide popularity during his career, winning acclaim for his rich storytelling and memorable characters. Considered one of the English language's greatest writers, he was the foremost novelist of the Victorian era, as well as a vigorous social campaigner.

JAMES DOBSON (b. 1936) is a conservative evangelical Christian and psychologist who presents a daily radio programme called Focus on the Family, broadcast on over 6000 stations worldwide in more than a dozen languages. He is also founder (1977) and chairman of the board of a non-profit organization of the same name based in Colorado Springs.

STEPHEN DOUGLAS (1813–61), known as 'the Little Giant', was an American politician from the frontier state of Illinois, and was a Democratic Party nominee for president in 1860. He lost to Abraham Lincoln*, also from Illinois. As one of the most important leaders in Congress in the 1850s, he helped shape the Third Party System; he also wrote the highly controversial Kansas–Nebraska Act, 1854, which reopened the slavery question.

TOMMY (THOMAS CLEMENT) DOUGLAS (1904–86) was a Scottish-born Baptist minister who became a prominent Canadian social-democratic politician. As leader of the Saskatchewan Co-operative Commonwealth Federation (CCF) from 1942, and the seventh premier of Saskatchewan (1944–61), he led the first socialist government in North America, and introduced universal public 'medicare' to Canada. When the CCF united with the Canadian Labour Congress to form the New Democratic Party, he was elected as its first federal leader (1961–71).

FREDERICK DOUGLASS (1818–95) was an American abolitionist, editor, orator, author, statesman and reformer. Called 'the Sage' or 'the Lion of Anacostia', he was one of the most prominent figures of African-American history during his time and one of the most influential lecturers and authors in American history.

W. E. B. Du Bois (1868–1963) was an African-American civil-rights activist, sociologist, educator, historian, writer, editor, poet, scholar and socialist. He became a naturalized citizen of Ghana in 1963.

Johann Eck (1486–1543) was a theologian and defender of Catholicism during the Protestant Reformation. He argued effectively and convincingly that the beliefs of Martin Luther* and Jan Hus* were similar.

Edward VI (1537–53) became King of England, Ireland and France (in this last case he ruled only the town and surrounding district of Calais) in 1547 at nine years of age. As the son of Henry VIII* and Jane Seymour*, Edward was the third monarch of the Tudor dynasty, and England's first ruler to be Protestant at the time of ascending to the throne. His entire rule was directed through a council of regency as he never reached maturity. It was during this time that Thomas Cranmer* implemented the Book of Common Prayer. Edward's reign was marked by increasingly harsh Protestant reforms and an economic downturn.

Jonathan Edwards (1703–58) was a colonial American Congregational preacher, theologian and missionary to Native Americans. He is known as one of the greatest and most profound American evangelical theologians. His work is very broad in scope, but he is often associated with his defence of Calvinist theology and the Puritan heritage.

George Eliot (1819–80) is the pen name of Mary Anne Evans, a leading English writer of the Victorian era. Her novels, set largely in provincial England, are admired for their realism and psychological insight.

Elizabeth I (1533–1603) was Queen of England, the sixth and final monarch of the Tudor dynasty. She was also Queen of France (in name only) and Queen of Ireland from 17 November 1558. Sometimes referred to as the 'Virgin Queen' because she never married, or 'Gloriana' or 'Good Queen Bess', she was immortalized by Edmund Spenser (c.1552–99) in his poem The Faerie Queene. Elizabeth restored England and Ireland (at least officially) to Protestantism after her predecessor, Mary I*, had briefly returned them to obedience to Rome.

Thomas Emlyn (1663–1741) was an English nonconformist divine. He was dismissed from his preaching post for publishing An Humble Inquiry into the Scripture Account of Jesus Christ (1702). He is said to have been the first English preacher definitely to describe himself as 'Unitarian'.

Desiderius Erasmus (c.1469–1536) was a Dutch humanist and theologian. Although he remained a Catholic, he was a famous and severe critic of the apparent abuses perpetrated by the Roman Catholic Church. He produced new Latin and Greek editions of the New Testament, and wrote the Manual of a Christian Knight (1502) and In Praise of Folly (1509).

Jerry Falwell (b. 1933) is an American evangelical pastor and televangelist. He is the founding pastor of the Thomas Road Baptist Church in Virginia. He also founded the Moral Majority movement (1979) and Liberty University (1971). He has associated himself with 'Bible-believing, independent, local-church oriented, Baptist fundamentalism'. He changed affiliations from the more traditional Baptist Bible Fellowship International to the mainly conservative Southern Baptist Convention, and ended his self-identification with fundamentalism in favour of evangelicalism.

Guillaume Farel (1489–1565) was a French evangelist and a founder of the Reformed Church in Neuchâtel, Berne, Geneva and the Pays de Vaud. He is most often remembered for having persuaded John Calvin* to remain in Geneva in 1536, and for persuading him to return there in 1541, after their joint expulsion in 1538. Together with Calvin, Farel worked to train missionary preachers who spread the Protestant cause to other countries, especially France.

ALEXANDER FARNESE (1545–92), the nephew of Philip II* of Spain and of Don John of Austria, was Duke of Parma and Piacenza and Governor of the Spanish Netherlands. He led a significant military and diplomatic career in the service of Spain, and fought in the Battle of Lepanto (1571).

MARGARET FELL (1614–1702), the 'Mother of Quakerism', was one of the founding members of the Religious Society of Friends. She is counted among the 'Valiant Sixty', a group of early Quaker preachers and missionaries.

FERDINAND I (1503–64) was Holy Roman Emperor from 1556. When his brother, Charles V*, concluded that the enormous Habsburg 'Empire' was too large to be manageable, he placed Ferdinand in charge of the Austro-German half. Ruling first on his father's behalf and later in his own right, he pursued a pro-Catholic yet conciliatory policy towards the Protestants in his possessions.

FERDINAND II (1578–1637), of the House of Habsburg, was the Archduke of Styria, King of Hungary and Holy Roman Emperor. He was also a devout Catholic. His recognition as King of Bohemia and his suppression of Protestantism precipitated the early events of the Thirty Years War.

CHARLES GRANDISON FINNEY (1792–1875) has often been called 'America's foremost revivalist'. He was a major leader of the Second Great Awakening.

GEORGE FOX (1624–91) was an English Dissenter and a major early figure – often considered the founder – of the Religious Society of Friends, commonly known as the Quakers.

JOHN FOXE (1516–87) was the author of the famous *Book of Martyrs* (1563). Converted to Protestantism under Henry VIII (whose 'reform' he rejected as 'too Catholic'), he was active in the Edwardian church but forced into exile in Strasburg, then Frankfurt, and, finally, Basle. He returned to England after Mary I's* death serving as a priest in Norwich for a while before settling in London and devoting himself to his literary works. He fell foul of Elizabeth I's* moderate reform in his rejection of vestments (clerical robes) and complicated her relations with France by his ardent support for French Protestants.

FRANCIS I (1494–1547) was crowned King of France in 1515. Renowned for his interest in humanism, he appointed the great French humanist Guillaume Budé* as chief librarian, and began to expand the royal collection. Francis employed agents in Italy to look for rare books, manuscripts and artworks. While he dramatically expanded the library, there is also good evidence that he actually read the books he bought. He set an important precedent by opening his library to scholars from around the world in order to facilitate the diffusion of knowledge. In 1537 Francis signed the Ordonnance de Montpellier, decreeing that his library be given a copy of every book sold in France. His collection thus became the basis of the present-day Bibliothèque nationale in Paris.

FRANCIS II (1544–60) was the King of France and husband to Mary Queen of Scots*. He was crowned, aged fifteen, upon the death of his father, Henry II*, but died the next year from an ear infection that led to a fatal brain abscess.

BENJAMIN FRANKLIN (1706–90) was a founding father of the United States – probably one of the best known. He was a leading author, politician, printer, scientist, philosopher, publisher, inventor, civic activist and diplomat. As a scientist, he made major contributions to physics through his discoveries and theories regarding electricity. As a political writer and activist, he, more than anyone, invented the idea of an American nation, and, as a diplomat during the American Revolution, he secured the French alliance that made independence possible.

FREDERICK III (1463–1525), also known as 'Frederick the Wise', was Elector of Saxony (from the House of Wettin) from 1486. He was among the princes who pressed the need for reform upon Maximilian I, Holy Roman Emperor, and in 1500 he became president of the newly formed *Reichsregiment* (council of regency). Initially, Frederick was Pope Leo X's* candidate for Holy Roman Emperor in 1519, but the pope eventually helped secure the election of Charles V* whose powerful position in Italian politics was a greater concern to the pope. Frederick ensured Martin Luther* would be heard at the Diet of Worms (1521), and subsequently took him into protective custody at Wartburg Castle. In 1523 he agreed to end the veneration of relics

GALILEO GALILEI (1564–1642) was an Italian physicist, astronomer and philosopher who is closely associated with the Scientific Revolution. His achievements include improvements to the telescope, a variety of astronomical observations, and effective support for the ideas of Copernicus*. He has been variously referred to as the 'Father of Modern Astronomy', the 'Father of Modern Physics' and the 'Father of Science'.

MOHANDAS KARAMCHAND GANDHI (1869–1948) was a major political and spiritual leader of the Indian independence movement. He was the pioneer of *Satyagraha*, resistance through mass civil disobedience, strongly founded upon *ahimsa* (non-violence), which became one of the strongest philosophies for freedom struggles worldwide. He was assassinated by a Hindu fanatic.

STEPHEN GARDINER (c.1497–1555) was Bishop of Winchester (1531) under Henry VIII*, was jailed in the Tower of London under Edward VI*, and was lord chancellor during the reign of Mary I*.

WILLIAM LLOYD GARRISON (1805–79) was a prominent US abolitionist, journalist and social reformer. He is best known as the editor of the radical abolitionist newspaper the *Liberator*, and as one of the founders of the American Anti–Slavery Society.

WILLIAM GLADSTONE (1809–98) was a British Liberal Party statesman and prime minister (1868–74, 1880–5, 1886 and 1892–4). He was a notable political reformer, known for his populist speeches.

PETER GONESIUS (Piotr z Goniàdza, c.1525–73) was a Polish political and religious writer, a thinker and one of the spiritual leaders of the Polish brethren. He, along with Gregory Pauli, offered anti-Trinitarian opposition to traditional Calvinist ideas at the second synod of the Polish Reformed Church (1556).

BILLY GRAHAM (b. 1918) is an American Protestant evangelist who has been a spiritual adviser to many US presidents. He is one of the most prominent members of the Southern Baptist Convention.

CONRAD GREBEL (c.1498–1526), son of a prominent Swiss merchant and councilman, was a co-founder of the Swiss Brethren movement and is often called the 'Father of Anabaptism'. Along with Felix Mann, he disputed with Ulrich Zwingli* in Zurich.

GRAHAM GREENE (1904–91) was a prolific English writer of novels, plays, short stories, travel books and criticism whose works explore the ambivalent moral and political issues of the modern world. Although he objected strongly to being described as a 'Catholic novelist' rather than as a 'novelist who happened to be Catholic', Catholic religious themes are at the root of many of his novels, including *Brighton Rock* (1938) and *The Power and the Glory* (1940). Works such as *The Quiet American* (1955) also showed his keen interest in the workings of international politics.

HUGO GROTIUS (1583–1645) worked as a jurist in the Dutch Republic and laid the foundations for international law, based on natural law. He was also a philosopher, Christian apologist, playwright and poet.

2ND DUKE OF GUISE (1519–63), named François, was a French soldier and politician, the uncle of Mary Queen of Scots*. His younger brothers included Charles, Cardinal of Lorraine, and Louis, Cardinal of Guise. Among his numerous military successes was the capturing of Calais from the English in 1558. He was killed by a Huguenot at the siege of Orléans.

GUSTAVUS II ADOLPHUS (1594–1632), referred to by Protestants as the 'Lion of the North', was King of Sweden from 1611. He is the only Swedish king to be styled 'the Great'. His intervention on the Protestant side during the Thirty Years War turned the tide of battle against the Catholic imperial forces and led to a stalemate that secured Protestantism's position in the Holy Roman Empire. He died in battle at Lützen in Germany.

HENRY II (1519–59), a member of the Valois dynasty, became King of France in 1547 upon the death of his brother, Francis I*. In 1559, during celebrations to mark the Treaty of Cateau-Cambrésis with his long-time enemies, the Habsburgs, and the marriage of his daughter Elizabeth to Philip II of Spain*, he was mortally wounded while participating in a joust. A sliver from a shattered lance pierced his left eye, penetrated his brain and came out via his ear. Despite the efforts of a royal surgeon, he died.

HENRY III (1551–89) was king from 1574 (upon the death of his brother, Charles IX*). He was also briefly King of the Polish-Lithuanian Commonwealth (1574) – a post he abdicated. In 1588, at his sanction, the 3rd Duke of Guise and his brother the Cardinal of Guise were murdered by guardsmen at the Palace of Blois. This act led to a Catholic revolt against Henry and forced him into supporting the claims to

be the heir to the throne of his cousin, Henry Bourbon (later Henry IV*). He was assassinated by a Dominican friar.

HENRY IV (1553–1610) was the first monarch of the Bourbon dynasty in France. As a Huguenot, he was involved in the Wars of Religion, and converted to Catholicism (for the second time in his life) before ascending to the throne in 1598. One of the most popular French kings (he was nicknamed 'Henry the Great' and 'Good King Henry'), he showed great care for the welfare of his subjects and displayed an unusual religious tolerance for the time. He promulgated the Edict of Nantes, which guaranteed religious liberties to Protestants and thereby effectively ended the civil wars. He was assassinated by a fanatical Catholic.

HENRY VIII (1491–1547), the second monarch of the Tudor dynasty, was King of England and Lord of Ireland (later King of Ireland) from 1509. He is famous for having been married six times in his efforts to have a son. He 'divorced' two wives by execution, having already broken with Rome when the pope would not grant his first annulment. This led him to introduce Protestantism to his kingdoms. He wielded perhaps the most extensive powers of any English monarch, and brought about the dissolution of the monasteries, and the union of England and Wales.

MELCHIOR HOFFMAN (c.1495–1543) was an Anabaptist prophet and a visionary leader in northern Germany and the Netherlands. His views on salvation were a type of Gnosticism (technically, Valentinianism), a mystical approach in Christianity's first centuries that placed an emphasis on 'hidden' knowledge and (in this case) rejected the traditional and orthodox understanding of God (the Trinity) and Christ (as both fully God and fully human in one person). Hoffman believed that while all are elected to salvation, only the regenerate may receive baptism, and those who sin after regeneration sin against the Holy Spirit and cannot be saved. His followers were known as Hoffmanites or Melchiorites.

SEBASTIAN HOFMEISTER (1476–1533), known in writing as Oeconomus or Oikonomos (literally 'housekeeper', but in this context 'manager' – the Greek version of his German name), was a Swiss Franciscan monk and religious reformer who was prominent in the early debates of the Reformation. He was the central reformer in Schaffhausen, and continued his reforming work in Zurich, St Gallen and Basle.

RICHARD HOOKER (1554–1600) was an influential Anglican theologian. He is arguably the co-founder (with Thomas Cranmer* and Matthew Parker*) of Anglican theological thought.

THOMAS HOWARD (see 3rd Duke of Norfolk)

BALTHASAR HÜBMAIER (c.1480–1528) was an influential German/Moravian Anabaptist leader. He was one of the most well-known and respected Anabaptist theologians of the Reformation.

JAN HUS (1369–1415) was a Czech religious thinker, philosopher and reformer, and master at Charles University in Prague. His followers were known as Hussites. The Catholic Church condemned his teachings as heresy. He was excommunicated in 1411, condemned by the Council of Constance, and burnt at the stake.

ISABELLA CLARA EUGENIA (1566–1633) was Infanta of Spain and Portugal, and subsequently became Archduchess of Austria and the joint sovereign of the Seventeen Provinces of the Low Countries. Shortly before he died, her father Philip II* renounced his rights to the Netherlands in favour of Isabella and her husband, the Archduke of Austria*.

JAMES VI / JAMES I (1566–1625) was the first monarch to style himself King of Great Britain.

He ruled in Scotland as James VI from 1567. Then, from the 'Union of the Crowns' in 1603, he reigned in England and Ireland as James I. He was the first Stuart monarch of England, succeeding the last Tudor monarch, Elizabeth I*.

THOMAS JEFFERSON (1743–1826) was the third President of the United States (1801–09), the principal author of the Declaration of Independence (1776), one of the most influential founding fathers, and a vigorous promoter of the ideals of republicanism in the United States, despite being a slave-owner.

T. J. JEMISON (b. 1914) is a pastor and was President of the National (Black) Baptist Convention (1982–94). He led a short and partially successful mass boycott of the bus service in Baton Rouge, Louisiana, in 1953, which was a precursor to the Montgomery Bus Boycott launched two years later. He was one of the founders of the Southern Christian Leadership Conference (1957).

JERRY B. JENKINS (b. 1949) is an American novelist and biographer. He is best known as co-author of the Left Behind series of books written with Tim LaHaye*. His works usually feature evangelical Christians as protagonists.

JOHN XXIII (1370–1419), born Baldassare Cossa, was pope during the Western Schism (see Urban VI*) and is officially regarded by the Catholic Church as an antipope. He was one of the seven cardinals who, in May 1408, convened the Council of Pisa, which elected Pope Alexander V in 1409. Cossa succeeded him a year later.

JOHN GEORGE I (1585–1656) was Prince-Elector of Saxony. Although a Lutheran, in 1618 he supported the claims of the Catholic Ferdinand II* to the throne of Hungary rather than those of the Calvinist Elector of the Palatinate, Frederick V, which hopelessly divided Protestant forces in the early phases of the Thirty Years War.

JOHN PAUL II (1920–2005), born Karol Józef Wojtyla, was pope from 1978 until his death more than twenty-six years later, making his the second-longest pontificate in modern times (Pius IX reigned thirty-one years). He was the first and only Polish pope, and the first non-Italian pope since the Dutch pontiff Adrian VI in the 1520s.

JOHN II SIGISMUND ZÁPOLYA (d. 1571), the son of John Zápolya, was the King of Hungary from 1540 until his abdication in 1570. He then became the first Prince of Transylvania. He passed the Edict of Torda (1568), the first decree of religious freedom in the modern history of Europe, and supported the establishment of the Unitarian Church in Transylvania.

SAMUEL JOHNSON (1709–84), often referred to simply as Dr Johnson, was one of England's greatest literary figures: a poet, essayist, biographer and lexicographer, and often considered the finest critic of English literature. He was also a great wit and prose stylist.

ANDREAS KARLSTADT (1486–1541) was a Christian theologian during the Protestant Reformation. He had a turbulent relationship with Martin Luther*. In 1524 Karlstadt was exiled from Saxony for his more radical reforming ideas. When the Peasants' Revolt broke out, Karlstadt was threatened as he was seen as a supporter of the peasants and their more radical approach to reform, and wrote to Luther asking for help. Luther agreed and Karlstadt lived secretly in Luther's house for eight weeks. However, he had to sign a retraction (*Apology ... Regarding the False Charge of Insurrection ... Made against Him*) and was not allowed to preach. Karlstadt lived as a peasant in various towns in Saxony until 1529, when he retracted his retraction.

THOMAS À KEMPIS (1380–1471) was a German Renaissance Catholic monk and author of *Imitation of Christ*, one of the best-known books on Christian devotion.

CHARLES KENNEDY (b. 1959) is a Scottish politician who was the leader of the Liberal Democrats, the third-largest political party in the United Kingdom, from 1999 to 2006.

JOHN F. KENNEDY (1917–63) was the thirty-fifth President of the United States until his assassination. He was the first and (so far) only Catholic president. He took a keen interest in the US civil-rights movement and demonstrated a sure touch in foreign affairs, particularly the Cuban Missile Crisis and the building of the Berlin Wall.

CORETTA SCOTT KING (1927–2006) was the wife of the assassinated civil-rights activist Martin Luther King Jr*, and a noted community leader in her own right.

MARTIN LUTHER KING JR (1929–68) was the most famous leader of the American civil-rights movement, a political activist and a Baptist minister. In 1964 he became the youngest man to be awarded the Nobel Peace Prize (for his work in promoting non-violence and equal treatment for different races).

JOSEPH KNIGHT (n. d.) was a slave born in Africa and sold in Jamaica to a Scottish owner. Taken to Scotland in 1769, a ruling in England three years later cast doubt on the legality of slavery under the common law, and the court pronounced slavery illegal in Scotland. However, it also held that Knight was an enforced apprentice, which remained lawful, so they bound him to return to the service of his master for 'perpetual servitude'.

JOHN KNOX (c.1514–72) was a Scottish religious reformer who took the lead in reforming the Church in Scotland along the principles outlined by John Calvin*. He is widely regarded as the father of the Protestant Reformation in Scotland and of the Church of Scotland. He and his views were disliked by Elizabeth I* largely as a result of the rabid sexism in his *First Blast against the Monstrous Regiment of Women* (1558).

TIM LAHAYE (b. 1926) is an American conservative fundamentalist Christian minister, author and speaker. He is best known for the Left Behind series of apocalyptic fiction that he co-wrote with Jerry B. Jenkins*.

RICHARD LAND (b. 1950) is president of the Ethics and Religious Liberty Commission, the public-policy entity of the Southern Baptist Convention, a post he has held since 1988. He was the primary author of the 'Land letter', an open letter sent to President George W. Bush by leaders of the religious right in October 2002, which outlined a 'just war' argument in support of the subsequent military invasion of Iraq. In 2001 President Bush appointed him to the US Commission on International Religious Freedom, a federal agency, where he continues to serve.

WILLIAM LAUD (1573–1645) was Archbishop of Canterbury and a fervent supporter of Charles I*, whom he encouraged to believe in divine right. His support for Charles, absolute monarchy, and his persecuting of opposing views led to his beheading in the midst of the English Civil War. He was a staunch supporter of episcopacy against Presbyterianism and Congregationalism. His support for rituals, vestments, kneeling and candles led to his being accused of popery (i.e. Catholicism) by his Puritan opponents.

JOHN OF LEIDEN (see Jan Bockelson)

LEO X (1475–1521), born Giovanni de' Medici, was pope from 1513 to his death. He is known primarily for his failure to stem the Protestant Reformation and for commissioning the present St Peter's basilica in Rome.

LEO XIII (1810–1903), born Vincenzo Gioacchino Raffaele Luigi Pecci, was elected as pontiff in 1878. Known as the 'Pope of the Working Man', he worked to encourage understanding between the Church and the modern world. He firmly reasserted the scholastic doctrine that science and religion coexist, and required the study of leading

medieval theologians such as Thomas Aquinas. He said that it 'is quite unlawful to demand, defend, or to grant unconditional freedom of thought, or speech, of writing or worship, as if these were so many rights given by nature to man'. He is most famous for his social teaching, in which he argued that both capitalism and communism are flawed. His bull Apostolicae Curae (1896) declared Anglican ordination invalid, while granting recognition to ordinations in Orthodox churches (although they were still considered illicit since they were not in communion with, or submission to, Rome). His apostolic letter Testem Benevolentiae (1899) condemned the heresy called Americanism – the acceptance of supposedly anti-Catholic principles embraced by the United States, such as absolute freedom of the press, liberalism, individualism, and complete separation of Church and State.

ABRAHAM LINCOLN (1809–65) was an American politician who was elected as the sixteenth President of the United States in 1861, the first president from the Republican Party. Today he is best known for ending slavery and preserving the Union during the American Civil War. His influence was magnified by his powerful rhetoric; his Gettysburg Address rededicated the nation to freedom and democracy. He was assassinated by John Wilkes Booth, who supported the Confederacy and opposed the ending of slavery.

THEOPHILUS LINDSEY (1723–1808) was an English Unitarian theologian. His chief work is An Historical View of the State of the Unitarian Doctrine and Worship from the Reformation to Our Own Times (1783).

DAVID LLOYD GEORGE (1863–1945) was a British Liberal Party statesman who, as prime minister (1916–22), guided Britain, the British Empire and the Commonwealth through the First World War and the post-war settlement.

JOHN LOCKE (1632–1704) was an influential English philosopher. In epistemology (the theory of knowledge) he has, along with David Hume, often been classified as a British empiricist. He is equally important as a social-contract theorist, and argued that a government could be legitimate only if it received the consent of the governed through a social contract and protected the natural rights of life, liberty and estate. If such consent was not given, argued Locke, citizens had a right of rebellion. He was one of the few major philosophers who became a minister of government. His ideas had an enormous influence on the development of political philosophy, and he is widely regarded as one of the most influential Enlightenment thinkers and contributors to liberal theory. His writings, along with those of many Scottish Enlightenment thinkers, influenced the American revolutionaries, as reflected in the American Declaration of Independence.

LOUIS XIII (1601–43), called 'the Just', was King of France from 1610. During his minority, when he was under the guidance of his chief minister, Cardinal Richelieu*, Catholic France entered the Thirty Years War on the side of the Protestants.

LOUIS XIV (1638–1715) ruled as King of France and Navarre from 14 May 1643. He was known as the 'Sun King', 'Louis the Great' or the 'Great Monarch', and ruled France for seventy-two years, the longest reign of any French or other major European monarch. In 1685 he revoked the Edict of Nantes (proclaimed by Henry IV in 1598), which had given legal recognition and protection to France's Protestants (Huguenots). Belief in Protestantism was not outlawed, but any practice of it was. Over 200,000 Huguenots fled the kingdom.

IGNATIUS LOYOLA (1491–1556) was the principal founder and first superior-general of the Society of Jesus (Jesuits), a religious order of the Catholic Church professing direct service to the pope.

MARTIN LUTHER (1483–1546) was a German monk, priest, professor, theologian and church

reformer. His teachings inspired the Reformation and deeply influenced the doctrines and culture of (especially) the Lutheran and (more generally) Protestant traditions.

MARGARET S. MCWILLIAMS (1875–1952) was the first president of the Canadian Federation of University Women, wrote a number of books on history and politics, served as a city councillor during the Depression, and in 1943 chaired the subcommittee on Post-war Problems for Women for the Canadian government's committee on reconstruction. For more than thirty years she held regular 'current events' classes, providing education in politics for women.

DANIEL FRANÇOIS MALAN (1874–1959) was a cleric and Prime Minister of South Africa from 1948 to 1954. He is seen as the champion of Afrikaner nationalism, and his government introduced strict apartheid policies.

1ST EARL OF MANSFIELD (1705–93), born William Murray, was a British judge and politician who is recognized as the founder of English mercantile law. Through his famous judgment in the case of James Somerset* he played a key role in ending slavery in England.

MARGARET OF PARMA (1522–86) was the illegitimate daughter of Charles V*, Holy Roman Emperor. From 1559 to 1567 she was regent of the Netherlands.

MARGUERITE OF NAVARRE (1492–1549), also known as Marguerite of Angoulême, was the queen-consort of King Henry II of Navarre. As a patron of humanists and reformers, and as an author in her own right, she was an outstanding figure of the French Renaissance. Many modern historians and feminists would consider her to be the 'first modern woman'.

MARTIN V (c.1368–1431), born Oddone Colonna, was pope from 1417 to 1431. His election ended the Western Schism, which had seen two, and even three, popes vying for supremacy.

KARL MARX (1818–83) was an immensely influential German philosopher, political economist and revolutionary. He is most famous for his analysis of history, summed up in the opening line of the introduction to the *Communist Manifesto*: 'The history of all hitherto existing society is the history of class struggles.' He believed that the downfall of capitalism was inevitable and that it would be replaced by communism.

MARY I (1500–58), also known as Mary Tudor, was the daughter of Henry VIII* by his first wife Catherine of Aragon*, and was Queen of England and Ireland from July 1553 until her death. She is best known for briefly returning England to Roman Catholicism.

MARY QUEEN OF SCOTS (1542–87) reigned from 1542 until she abdicated in 1567, but thirteen of those years were spent in France with her family there. During that time abroad she married the dauphin, and on his accession (as Francis II*), became Queen-consort of France (1559–60). She returned to Scotland in 1561, but was forced to abdicate in favour of her son, James VI*, when she was unable to control her Protestant lords. Mary fled to England in 1568, where she was taken into custody and imprisoned at Carlisle Castle. After much prevarication, Elizabeth I* had her cousin tried for treason and executed.

COTTON MATHER (1663–1728) was a socially and politically influential Puritan minister, prolific author and pamphleteer. The son of the influential minister Increase Mather, he is often remembered for his persecution of witches.

MATTHIAS II (1557–1619), of the House of Habsburg, reigned as King of Hungary, King of Bohemia and Holy Roman Emperor. He was conciliatory towards his Protestant subjects.

JAN MATTHYS (*c.*1500–34) was a charismatic Anabaptist leader, regarded by his followers as a prophet. Originally an Amsterdam baker, he was converted to Anabaptism through the ministry of Melchior Hoffman* in the 1520s. He was one of the leaders of Anabaptist Münster, and was killed leading thirty followers against the armies besieging the city, believing that he would triumph just as Gideon had.

MAURICE OF NASSAU (1567–1625) was Prince of Orange from 1618 to 1625. He became *stadtholder* (governor-general or viceroy) of Holland and Zeeland in 1585, of Guelders, Overijssel and Utrecht in 1590, and of Groningen and Drenthe in 1620. Appointed captain-general of the Dutch army in 1587, he organized the rebellion against Spain into a coherent, successful revolt. Indeed, he proved himself to be among the best military strategists of his age.

MAXIMILIAN I (1459–1519), called 'the Great', was a Wittelsbach ruler of Bavaria and a prince-elector of the Holy Roman Empire. He played a leading part in founding the Catholic League. Through his general Johann Tserclaes von Tilly* he also took a leading role in the Thirty Years War.

MAXIMILIAN II (1527–76), a member of the Habsburg dynasty, was King of Bohemia from 1562, King of Hungary from 1563, and Emperor of the Holy Roman Empire from 1564.

THOMAS FRANCIS MEAGHER (1823–67) was an Irish revolutionary, who also served in the US Army as a brigadier-general during the American Civil War.

PHILIPP MELANCHTHON (1497–1560) was a German professor and theologian, a key leader of the Lutheran Reformation, and a friend and associate of Martin Luther*.

ANDREW MELVILLE (1545–1622) was a Scottish scholar, theologian and religious reformer. He was famous for his clashes with

James VI*, especially for saying: 'Sirrah, ye are God's silly vassal; there are two kings and two kingdoms in Scotland: there is king James, the head of the commonwealth; and there is Christ Jesus, the king of the Church, whose subject James VI is, and of whose kingdom he is not a king, not a lord, not a head, but a member.' He was deprived of all offices by James, and banished from Scotland. He ended his life as rector (1611–22) of the Huguenot University of Sedan in France.

MICHELANGELO BUONARROTI (1475–1564), born Michelangelo di Lodovico Buonarroti Simoni, was an Italian Renaissance painter, sculptor, architect and poet. Despite making few forays beyond the arts, his versatility in the disciplines he took up was of such a high order that he, along with his fellow Florentine Leonardo da Vinci, is often considered a contender for the title of the archetypal Renaissance man.

KARL VON MILTITZ (1490–1529) was a papal nuncio (ambassador) and a Mainz Cathedral canon. He met Martin Luther* in Altenburg (1519) and negotiated a tentative settlement over the sale of indulgences: Luther would remain silent on the matter, write the pope a conciliatory letter, and publish a tract supporting papal authority. Luther's silence was contingent on the silence of his opponents; Johann Tetzel* and Albrecht of Hohenzollern* would be disciplined. Luther was not to be forced to recant. Although these negotiations proved fruitless, Luther did publish a letter to the pope, along with a tract dedicated to him – On the Freedom of a Christian (1520).

THOMAS MORE (1478–1535) was an English lawyer, author and statesman. During his lifetime he earned a reputation as a leading humanist scholar, and occupied many public offices, including that of Lord Chancellor (1529–32). More coined the word 'Utopia', a name he gave to an ideal, imaginary island nation whose political system he described in a book of that name published in 1516. He is chiefly remembered for his principled refusal to accept the claim of

Henry VIII* to be the supreme head of the Church of England, a decision that ended his political career and led to his execution as a traitor. In 1935, four hundred years after his death, More was canonized by Pope Pius XI, and was later declared the patron saint of lawyers and statesmen. He shares his feast day, 22 June, with St John Fisher, the only bishop during the English Reformation under Henry VIII to maintain his allegiance to the pope.

THOMAS MÜNTZER (c. 1490–1525) was an early Reformation German pastor who was a rebel leader during the Peasants' Revolt. From 1517 to 1519 Müntzer stayed in Wittenberg and was influenced by Andreas Karlstadt* and Martin Luther*.

WILLIAM MURRAY (see 1st Earl of Mansfield)

3RD DUKE OF NORFOLK (1473–1554), born Thomas Howard, was a prominent Tudor politician. He was the uncle of Anne Boleyn* and Catherine Howard, both of whom married Henry VIII*. Following the accession of Edward VI*, Norfolk was imprisoned on suspicion of treason and forfeited his dukedom. Released by Mary I* in 1553, and his dukedom restored, he showed his gratitude by leading the forces sent to put down the rebellion of Sir Thomas Wyatt, who had protested against the queen's marriage to Philip II* and had planned to put Princess Elizabeth* on the throne in Mary's place. The result of Norfolk's suppression of the Wyatt Rebellion was Elizabeth's imprisonment in the Tower and the execution of Lady Jane Grey (the granddaughter of Henry VIII's sister).

BERNARDINO OCHINO (1487–1564) was an Italian reformer and an intimate friend of the famous Spanish mystic Juan de Valdes. In 1538 he was elected Vicar-General of the (Franciscan) Order of Friars Minor Capuchin. Embracing Protestantism, he fled to Geneva, where he was warmly received by John Calvin*. He served as a minister in Augsburg, but had to escape imperial Catholic troops there, so fled to England, where he served as a prebendary (canon) of Canterbury, receiving a pension from Edward VI*. He fled Mary I* for Zurich, which he also fled, for Poland, in 1563, when his writings implied an acceptance of polygamy and a rejection of the Trinity.

DANIEL O'CONNELL (1775–1847), known as 'the Liberator' or 'the Emancipator', was Ireland's predominant political leader in the first half of the nineteenth century, championing the cause of the downtrodden Catholic population. He campaigned for Catholic emancipation and repeal of the union between Ireland and Great Britain. He is remembered in Ireland as the founder of a non-violent form of Irish nationalism, and also for the mobilization of the Catholic community as a political force in order to achieve emancipation.

JOHANN OECOLAMPADIUS (1482–1531) was a German religious reformer. His original name was Hussgen or Heussgen, which he changed to Hausschein, and then into its Greek equivalent Oecolampadius (from oikos meaning 'house', and lâmpada, 'lamp'). He was one of the leading reformers in Basle.

JOEL OSTEEN (b. 1963) is the senior pastor at Lakewood Church in Houston, Texas, North America's largest and fastest-growing church congregation, averaging approximately 35,000 adult attendees every week in 2005. He is also the author of Your Best Life Now (2005).

PHOEBE PALMER (1807–74) was an evangelist and writer who promoted the doctrine of Christian Perfection. She is considered one of the founders of the Holiness Movement in the USA, and the Higher Life movement in the UK.

MATTHEW PARKER (1504–75) was Archbishop of Canterbury from 1559. He was one of the primary architects of the Thirty-nine Articles, the defining statements of Anglican doctrine.

ROSA PARKS (1913–2005) was an African-American seamstress and civil-rights activist, whom the US Congress dubbed the 'Mother of the Modern-day Civil Rights Movement'.

PAUL IV (1476–1559), born Giovanni Pietro Carafa, was an ambassador to England and then papal nuncio in Spain before becoming pope in 1555. Nationalism was the driving force of his papacy; the Habsburgs disliked him, so he allied with France. He also alienated the English and rejected the claim of Elizabeth I* of England to the crown. Staunchly anti-Semitic, he considered Jews to be undeserving of Christian love and that God had condemned them to slavery. His papal canon Cum nimis absurdum created a Jewish ghetto in Rome, where they were locked in at night. He also decreed that Jews should wear distinctive signs: yellow hats for men, and veils or shawls for women. The Roman ghetto was the last to be abolished in Western Europe during the pontificate of Pope Pius IX (1846–78).

WILLIAM PENN (1644–1718) was a leading Quaker who founded the Commonwealth of Pennsylvania, the British colony in America that became the US state. The democratic principles that he set forth in the Pennsylvania Frame of Government (1682) served as an inspiration for the US Constitution. He also published a plan for a United States of Europe: European Diet, Parliament or Estates (1693).

SAMUEL PEPYS (1633–1703) was an English naval administrator and Member of Parliament, famous chiefly for his diaries. Although he had no maritime experience, he rose by hard work and ability to be the chief secretary to the Admiralty under James II. The detailed private diary that he kept during 1660–9 was published after his death, and it provides a fascinating combination of personal revelation as well as eyewitness accounts of great events, such as the Great Plague of London (1665), the Second Dutch War (1665–7) and the Great Fire of London (1666).

PHILIP OF HESSE (1504–67), also known as 'Philip the Proud', was a leading champion of the Reformation and one of the most important

German rulers of the Renaissance. Contemporary accounts describe him as highly intelligent and gifted, but haughty and selfish.

PHILIP II OF SPAIN (1527–98) was the only legitimate son of Holy Roman Emperor Charles V*. He was the first official King of Spain, the King of Naples and Sicily, King of England (as king-consort of Mary I*), King of Portugal and the Algarve (as Philip I), and King of Chile. In 1557, owing to his predilection for military engagements, he was forced to declare Spain bankrupt. Although he lost the United Provinces to Protestantism he successfully (if not permanently) united Spain and Portugal and turned back the Ottoman threat in the western Mediterranean. The Armada he sent to bring England back into the Catholic fold was destroyed off the English coast – this loss, along with others inflicted by the Dutch broke the back of Spanish naval power for ever.

OBBE PHILIPS (1500–68) was one of the early founders of Dutch Anabaptism. The illegitimate son of a Catholic priest from Leeuwarden, Philips studied medicine and became a barber–surgeon. He ordained his brother, Dirk.

PIUS V (1504–72), born Antonio Ghislieri, was pope from 1566 and is a saint of the Roman Catholic Church. He standardized the Mass by promulgating the Roman missal (1570). This form of the Mass (commonly called the Tridentine Mass) remained essentially unchanged for 400 years, until the modern revision of the missal in 1970. He banished Jews from all ecclesiastical dominions, except Rome and Ancona, in 1569. He published the bull *Regnans in Excelsis* (1570), which declared Elizabeth I* a heretic and released her subjects from their allegiance to her. This changed the status of English Roman Catholics from religious dissidents to potential enemies of the state.

REGINALD POLE (1500–58) was an English prelate, Archbishop of Canterbury, and a cardinal of the Roman Catholic Church. He was the last

Catholic to hold that archbishopric, and died just a few hours after Mary I*, who had appointed him.

JOSEPH PRIESTLEY (1733–1804) was an English chemist, philosopher, Dissenting clergyman and teacher of anti-Trinitarian views. He is known for his investigations of carbon dioxide and the co-discovery (with Antoine Lavoisier) of oxygen.

WALTER RAUSCHENBUSCH (1861–1918) was a Christian theologian and minister. He was a key figure in the Social Gospel movement in the USA.

CHARLES LENOX REMOND (1810–82) was an African-American abolitionist and military organizer during the American Civil War. Born free in Salem, Massachusetts, he was an anti-slavery orator who spoke at public meetings in that state, as well as Rhode Island, Maine, New York and Pennsylvania. In 1838 the Massachusetts Anti-Slavery Society chose him as one of its agents, and in 1840 he went with William Lloyd Garrison* to the World Anti-Slavery Convention in London. Later he recruited black soldiers in Massachusetts for the Union Army during the Civil War, particularly for the famous 54th and 55th Massachusetts Infantry.

LUIS DE ZÚÑIGA Y REQUESENS (1528–76), Spanish governor of the Netherlands, had the misfortune to succeed the Duke of Alva* and to govern amid hopeless difficulties under the direction of Philip II* that saw troops under his control mutiny and Spain declare bankruptcy.

CARDINAL-DUC DE RICHELIEU (1585–1642), born Armand Jean du Plessis, was a French nobleman, clergyman and statesman. Consecrated as a bishop in 1607, he later entered politics, becoming a secretary of state in 1616. He rose rapidly in both the Church and the State, becoming a cardinal in 1622, and chief minister to Louis XIII* in 1624. He remained in office until his death.

NICHOLAS RIDLEY (c.1500–55) was an English clergyman. Bishop of Rochester (1549–50) and then Bishop of London (1550), he was deposed by Mary I* and died, along with fellow cleric Hugh Latimer (c.1485–1555), an Anglican Protestant martyr at the stake.

PAT ROBERTSON (b. 1930) is an American televangelist. He is the founder of numerous organizations and corporations, including the Christian Broadcasting Network, and is opposed to abortion and gay rights. He is an ordained minister in the Southern Baptist Church, but holds to a charismatic theology not commonly held among that denomination.

BERNHARD ROTHMANN (c.1495–c.1535) was a reformer and an Anabaptist leader in the city of Münster. Having been converted from Lutheranism by the Anabaptist disciples of Melchior Hoffman*, he began to preach against infant baptism. He was probably the most important theological voice in Anabaptist Münster, and seems to have died fighting when the city fell to a combined army of Catholics and Lutherans.

JEAN-JACQUES ROUSSEAU (1712–78) was a Genevan philosopher of the Enlightenment, whose political ideas influenced the French Revolution, the development of socialist theory, and the growth of nationalism. He also made important contributions to music both as a theorist and a composer. With his *Confessions* (1781–8) and other writings, he practically invented modern autobiography. His novel *Julie, ou la nouvelle Héloïse* (1761) was one of the best-selling fictional works of the eighteenth century, and was important to the development of Romanticism.

RUDOLF II (1552–1612) was an emperor of the Holy Roman Empire, King of Bohemia and King of Hungary. He was conciliatory towards his Protestant subjects.

JACOPO SADOLETO (1477–1547), a Roman Catholic cardinal, was an Italian humanist, jurist and poet. The great aim of his life was to win back the Protestants by peaceful persuasion rather than persecution.

JOSEPH SAUER (1872–1949) was a Catholic ecclesiastical and art historian whose great work, *History of Christian Art* (1908), closed with a masterful treatment of the Italian Renaissance. He was considered a liberal critic of the Catholic Church of the late nineteenth century.

MICHAEL SERVETUS (c.1511–53) was a Spanish theologian, physician and humanist whose interests ranged from astronomy and mathematics to jurisprudence and the Bible. He is renowned in the history of several of these fields, particularly medicine and theology. He developed an anti-Trinitarian theology and was condemned by Catholics and Protestants alike. Branded a heretic in Protestant Geneva, he was burnt at the stake there while already under sentence of death in Catholic Vienne (France).

EDWARD SEYMOUR (*see* 1st Duke of Somerset)

JANE SEYMOUR (c.1508–37) was the third wife of Henry VIII*. She died of post-natal complications following the birth of her only son, Edward VI*.

MENNO SIMONS (1496–1551) was an Anabaptist religious leader from Friesland in the Netherlands. His influence on Anabaptism in the Low Countries was so great that it has been suggested that their history be divided into three periods: 'before Menno, under Menno, and after Menno'. He was especially significant in coming to the Anabaptist movement in the north in its most troublesome days, and helping not only to sustain it, but also to establish it as a viable radical reformation movement. His followers became known as Mennonites.

ALBERT BENJAMIN SIMPSON (1843–1919) was a Canadian preacher, theologian, author and founder of the Christian and Missionary Alliance, an evangelical Protestant denomination emphasizing global evangelism.

ADAM SMITH (1720–90) was a Scottish political economist and moral philosopher. His *Inquiry into the Nature and Causes of the Wealth of Nations* (1776) was one of the earliest attempts to study the historical development of industry and commerce in Europe. That work helped to create the modern academic discipline of economics, and provided one of the best-known intellectual rationales for free trade, capitalism and libertarianism.

ROBERT PEARSALL SMITH (1827–99) was a lay leader in the Holiness Movement in the USA, and the Higher Life movement in Great Britain. His book *Holiness Through Faith* (1879) was one of the foundational works of the Holiness Movement.

FAUSTUS SOCINUS (1539–1604), also known as Fausto Sozzini, was a theologian and founder of the school of Christian thought known as 'Socinianism'. He was the nephew of Laelius Socinus* and, like him, questioned the traditional Trinitarian doctrine. He was influential among anti-Trinitarians in eastern Europe. Of his non-theological doctrines, the most important is his assertion of the unlawfulness not only of war, but of the taking of human life in any circumstances as well. Hence the comparative mildness of his proposals for dealing with religious and anti-religious offenders, though it cannot be said that he had grasped the complete theory of toleration. Hence too his contention, in common with Anabaptists, that magisterial office is unlawful for a Christian.

LAELIUS SOCINUS (1525–62) was an Italian humanist and reformer. Although he questioned aspects of the traditional understanding of the Trinity, he did not break with the other magisterial reformers on the issue.

1ST DUKE OF SOMERSET (c.1506–52), born Edward Seymour, was Lord Protector of England

between the death of Henry VIII* and his own indictment in 1549. He was the eldest brother of Jane Seymour*, who would become Henry's third wife. He was executed for treason.

JAMES SOMERSET (n. d.) was a young African slave who was purchased by Charles Stuart in Virginia in 1749. He was the subject of a landmark legal ruling in England (*see* 1st Earl of Mansfield).

FAUSTO SOZZINI (*see* Faustus Socinus)

PHILIPP JAKOB SPENER (1635–1705) was a German theologian known as the 'Father of Pietism'. Although he did not advocate the quietistic, legalistic and semi-separatist practices of Pietism, they were more or less involved in the positions he assumed or the practices he encouraged. The only three points on which he departed from the orthodox Lutheran faith of his day were the requirement of regeneration as the *sine qua non* of the true theologian, the expectation of the conversion of the Jews and the fall of the papacy as preludes to the triumph of the Church. He did not, like the later Pietists, insist on the necessity of a conscious crisis of conversion, nor did he encourage a complete breach between the Christian and the secular life.

JOHANN VON STAUPITZ (1460–1524) was a theologian and university preacher. He was vicar-general of the Augustinian order in Germany, and counsellor to Martin Luther* prior to Luther's break with Rome.

1ST EARL OF STRAFFORD (1593–1641), born Thomas Wentworth, was an English statesman, a major figure in the period leading up to the English Civil War. He was one of the more vocal supporters of the Petition of Right, which curbed the power of the king.

JOHANNES GERHARDUS STRIJDOM (1893–1958) was Prime Minister of South Africa from 1954 to 1958. His extreme policies resulted in the removal of Coloureds (people of mixed race) from the common voters' roll, and the extended 'treason trial' of 156 activists (including Nelson Mandela) involved in a 'Freedom Charter'.

ARTHUR TAPPAN (1786–1865) was an American abolitionist who, in 1833, co-founded the American Anti-Slavery Society with William Lloyd Garrison*. He served as its first president until 1840, when he resigned in protest at the society's support for women's suffrage and feminism.

LEWIS TAPPAN (1788–1883) was a New York abolitionist who, at the request of Connecticut abolitionists, was most responsible for making sure that captured Africans sailing on the *Amistad* had their freedom again. He and his brother Arthur Tappan* ensured they got able legal help, drummed up public support for their cause, and finally organized their return home to Africa. Among his revolutionary ideas, Lewis advocated intermarriage as the long-term solution to racial issues. He dreamt of a 'copper-skinned' America where race would not define any man, woman or child.

JOHANN TETZEL (1465–1519) was a German Dominican friar who is perhaps best known for selling indulgences during the sixteenth century; he even created a chart that listed a price for absolving each type of sin. It was partly in response to Tetzel's practice of selling indulgences that Martin Luther* wrote his 'Ninety-five Theses'.

MARGARET THATCHER (b. 1925) was Prime Minister of the United Kingdom from 1979 to 1990, the only woman to have served in that capacity. She had the longest continuous period in office since Lord Liverpool, who was prime minister from 1812 to 1827.

TOUSSAINT L'OUVERTURE (c.1743–1803), originally François Dominique Toussaint, was one of the leaders of the Haitian Revolution. Along with Jean-Jacques Dessalines, another leader of

the Revolution, he is considered one of the fathers of the Haitian nation.

JOHANN TSERCLAES VON TILLY (1559–1632) was a field marshal of the Holy Roman Empire. He had a string of important victories against the Bohemians, Germans and later the Danish, but was defeated by forces led by Gustavus II Adolphus*. Along with Albrecht von Wallenstein*, he was one the two chief commanders of the Holy Roman Empire's forces in the Thirty Years War. He commanded the forces that sacked Magdeburg in 1631 with the loss of more than 25,000 civilians. He was fatally wounded by a cannonball at the Battle of Rain.

ALEXIS-CHARLES-HENRI CLÉREL DE TOCQUEVILLE (1805–59) was a French political thinker and historian. The works for which he is most known are *Democracy in America* (1835 and 1840) and *The Old Regime and the Revolution* (1856). In both works he explored the effects of the rising equality of social conditions on both the individual and the State in Western societies.

DESMOND TUTU (b. 1931) is a South African cleric and activist, who rose to worldwide fame during the 1980s as an opponent of apartheid. He was elected and ordained the first black South African Anglican Archbishop of Cape Town, and primate of the Church of the Province of Southern Africa (now the Anglican Church of Southern Africa). He was awarded the Nobel Peace Prize in 1984. He is also a recipient of the Albert Schweitzer Prize for Humanitarianism.

URBAN VI (1318–89), born Bartolomeo Prignano, was elected pope in 1378. He took his first significant Church post when he became Archbishop of Acerenza in the Kingdom of Naples in 1364. He was consecrated Archbishop of Bari in 1377, and, on the death of Pope Gregory XI (r. 1370–8), was unanimously chosen as pontiff. He was the last pope not to be a member of the College of Cardinals. Five months after his election, the French cardinals met, claiming that their votes had been swayed by a fear of the Roman mob. They then elected Robert of Geneva, who took the title of Clement VII*. Thus began the Western Schism (1378–1417), which divided Christendom for nearly forty years.

PETER MARTYR VERMIGLI (1499–1562) was an Italian theologian and monk who became abbot of the Augustinian monastery in Spoleto. Having adopted Protestant ideas, he was repeatedly examined by Italian Catholic church authorities. In 1542 he fled to Pisa, and thence to another Italian reformer, Bernardino Ochino*, at Florence. From there he fled to Zurich, Basle and finally Strasburg, where, with support from Martin Bucer*, he was appointed professor of theology. He was invited to England by Archbishop Cranmer* in 1547. The following year he was appointed Regius Professor of Divinity at Oxford. Forced to flee England after the accession of Mary I*, he eventually settled in Zurich.

PIERRE VIRET (1511–71) was a Swiss Reformed theologian, the leading reformer in Geneva and Lausanne, which became a training ground for French-speaking Reformation preachers. He preached in both those places, and made missionary tours of France, preaching to crowds of thousands in Paris, Orléans, Avignon, Montauban and Montpellier. Riots and the destruction of religious art often followed his preaching, which was enthusiastically and emotionally iconoclastic.

VOLTAIRE (FRANÇOIS-MARIE AROUET) (1694–1778) was a French Enlightenment writer, essayist, Deist and philosopher. He was known for his sharp wit, philosophical writings and defence of civil liberties, including freedom of religion and the right to a fair trial. He was an outspoken supporter of social reform, despite strict censorship laws in France and harsh penalties for those who broke them. A satirical polemicist, he frequently made use of his works to criticize Church dogma and the French institutions of his day.

GEORGE WALLACE (1919–98) was an American politician who was elected four times as the Democratic Governor of Alabama and ran for US President five times (four as a Democrat and once as the American Independent Party candidate). He is best known for his pro-segregation attitude, which he later recanted.

ALBRECHT VON WALLENSTEIN (1583–1634) was a Bohemian soldier and politician who gave his services (including an army of up to 100,000 men) to Ferdinand II* during the Danish Period of the Thirty Years War. He asked for no payment except the right to plunder the territories that he conquered.

JIM WALLIS (b. 1948) is a Christian writer and left-wing political activist, best known as the founder and editor of *Sojourners* magazine and of the Washington-based Christian community of the same name. Wallis avoids political labels, but his advocacy tends to focus on issues of peace and social justice, earning him his primary support from the religious left. He is also known for his opposition to the religious right's fiscal and foreign policies. His books include *God's Politics: Why the Right Gets It Wrong and the Left Doesn't Get It* (2004).

RICK WARREN (b. 1954) is the founding and senior pastor of the moderate, 'mega-church' Saddleback Church in California. He is also the author of many Christian books, including *The Purpose-Driven Life* (2002), and is a major and controversial figure among American Southern Baptists. Many critics contend that he compromises on various doctrinal truths in his teachings, and that he espouses ecumenism, which, its opponents would argue, prioritizes Christian unity and cooperation over doctrinal 'purity'.

BOOKER T. WASHINGTON (1856–1915), born a slave in Virginia, became an American political leader, educator and author. In 1881 he founded the Tuskegee Institute, a training facility for teachers in Alabama. Under his direction, the students built their own buildings, produced their own food, and provided for most of their own basic necessities. The skills they acquired in the process were then shared with African-American communities throughout the South.

GEORGE WASHINGTON (1732–99) led America's Continental Army to victory over Britain in the American Revolutionary War (1775–83) and was later elected the first President of the United States. He served two four-year terms (1789–97), having been re-elected in 1792. Because of his central role in the founding of the United States, Washington is often referred to as the 'father of his country'. His devotion to republicanism and civic virtue made him an exemplary figure among early American politicians, though it did not lead him to emancipate his slaves.

EVELYN WAUGH (1903–66) was an English writer, best known for such satirical and darkly humorous novels as *Decline and Fall* (1928) and *Scoop* (1938), as well as for more serious works, such as *Brideshead Revisited* (1945), which were influenced by his own conservative Catholic outlook. Many of his novels depict the British aristocracy and high society, which he savagely satirized, but to which he was also strongly attracted.

MAXIMILIAN WEBER (1864–1920) was a German political economist and sociologist, and is considered one of the founders of the modern study of sociology and public administration.

THOMAS WENTWORTH (*see* 1st Earl of Strafford)

CHARLES WESLEY (1707–88) was the younger brother of John Wesley* and a leader of the Methodist movement. He is chiefly remembered for the many hymns he wrote.

JOHN WESLEY (1703–91) was an Anglican clergyman and theologian who was an early leader in the Methodist movement. Under his direction, Methodists became leaders in many social-justice issues of the day, including prison reform and Abolitionism. His greatest theological achievement was his promotion of what he termed 'Christian perfection', or holiness of heart and life. He always remained within the Church of England and insisted that his movement was well within the bounds of the Anglican Church.

GEORGE WHITEFIELD (1714–70) was a minister in the Church of England and one of the leaders of the Methodist movement, although he was Calvinist in his theology – as opposed to the Arminianism of John Wesley* and most other Methodists.

WILLIAM WILBERFORCE (1759–1833) was a British politician, philanthropist, abolitionist and leader of the parliamentary campaign against the slave trade.

WILLIAM I OF ORANGE-NASSAU (1533–84), also known as 'William the Silent', became Prince of Orange in 1544. He was the main leader of the Dutch revolt against the Spanish that set off the Eighty Years War (Dutch Revolt) and resulted in the formal independence of the United Provinces in 1648.

ROWAN WILLIAMS (b. 1950) became the Archbishop of Canterbury, Primate of All England and head of the worldwide Anglican Communion in 2003, the 104th person to hold the office. He is a distinguished theologian, and also a poet.

THOMAS WOODROW WILSON (1856–1924) was the twenty-eighth President of the United States. A devout Presbyterian and leading intellectual of the Progressive Era, he served as president of Princeton University, then became the reform governor of New Jersey in 1910. His administration imposed full racial segregation in Washington, and hounded from office considerable numbers of black federal employees. The segregation he introduced was kept in place by the succeeding Republican presidents, and was not finally rescinded until the Truman administration (1948–53).

GEORGE WISHART (c.1513–46) was a Scottish religious reformer and Protestant martyr. A proponent of the ideas of John Calvin* and Ulrich Zwingli*, he was arrested in 1545 at Ormiston in East Lothian on the orders of Cardinal Beaton*. He was handed over to Beaton, who had him burnt at the stake for heresy.

THOMAS WOLSEY (c.1473–1530) was a powerful English statesman and a cardinal of the Roman Catholic Church. He was slow in promoting attempts by Henry VIII* to annul his marriage to Catherine of Aragon*, so he was stripped of his offices.

FRANCES WRIGHT (1795–1852) was an American lecturer, writer, feminist, abolitionist and utopian. She advocated abolition, universal equality in education, and feminism. She also attacked organized religion, greed and capitalism.

JOHN WYCLIF (c.1320–84) was an English theologian and early proponent of reform in the Catholic Church. He prepared the first complete English edition of the Bible.

COUNT NICOLAUS LUDWIG VON ZINZENDORF (1700–60) was a German religious and social reformer and a bishop of the Moravian Church.

ULRICH (OR HULDRYCH) ZWINGLI (1484–1531) was the leader of the Protestant Reformation in Switzerland, and founder of the Swiss Reformed Churches. Independently of Luther*, who was a biblical academic, Zwingli arrived at similar conclusions to his by studying the Scriptures from the point of view of humanism.

FURTHER
READING

Abzug, R. H., *Cosmos Crumbling: American Reform and the Religious Imagination* (Oxford, 1994)

Ackerman, B., *The Future of Liberal Revolution* (New Haven, CT, 1992)

Allen, K., *Max Weber: A Critical Introduction* (London, 2004)

Armstrong, K., *The Battle for God: A History of Fundamentalism* (New York, 2001)

Bannister, R. C., *Social Darwinism: Science and Myth in Anglo-American Social Thought* (Philadelphia, 1989)

Barry, J., Hester, M., & Roberts, G. (eds), *Witchcraft in Early Modern Europe: Studies in Culture and Belief* (Cambridge, 1996)

Bireley, R., *The Refashioning of Catholicism, 1450–1700* (Basingstoke, 1999)

Branch, T., *At Canaan's Edge: America in the King Years, 1965–68* (New York, 2006)

Bratt, J. D., 'Religious Anti-revivalism in Antebellum America', *Journal of the Early Republic*, 24 (2004), pp. 65–106

Brown, C. L., *Moral Capital: Foundations of British Abolitionism* (Chapel Hill, NC, 2006)

Browne, E. J., *Charles Darwin: Voyaging* (Princeton, 1995)

— *The Power of Place* (Princeton, 2002)

Bumsted, J. M., and Van de Wetering, J. E., *'What Must I Do to Be Saved?': The Great Awakening in Colonial America* (New York, 1976)

Butler, J., *Awash in a Sea of Faith: Christianizing the American People* (Harvard, 1990)

Cameron, E., *The European Reformation* (Oxford, 1991)

Campbell, J. T., *Songs of Zion: The African Methodist Episcopal Church in the United States and South Africa* (Oxford, 1995)

Caponetto, S., *The Protestant Reformation in Sixteenth-century Italy*, SCES 43 (Kirksville, MO, 1998)

Conforti, J. A., *Jonathan Edwards, Religious Tradition and American Culture* (Chapel Hill, NC, 1995)

Cottret, B., *Calvin: A Biography* (Edinburgh, 2000)

Cowan, I. B., *The Scottish Reformation: Church and Society in 16th-century Scotland* (London, 1982)

Crowner, D., *The Spirituality of the German Awakening* (Mahwah, NJ, 2003)

Curtis, S., *A Consuming Faith: The Social Gospel and Modern American Culture* (Columbia, MO, 1991)

Davis, D. B., *Inhuman Bondage: The Rise and Fall of Slavery in the New World* (Oxford, 2006)

Dickens, P., *Social Darwinism: Linking Evolutionary Thought to Social Theory* (Philadelphia, 2000)

Dieter, M. E., *The Holiness Revival of the Nineteenth Century* (Metuchen, NJ, 1996)

Dorrien, G., *The Making of American Liberal Theology: Imagining Progressive Religion, 1805–1900*, vol. 1 (Louisville, KY, 2002)

Duffy, E., *The Stripping of the Altars: Traditional Religion in England, 1400–1580* (London, 1992)

Edwards, J., *The Jews in Christian Europe, 1400–1700* (London, 1991)

Eire, C. M. N., *War against the Idols: The Reformation of Worship from Erasmus to Calvin* (Cambridge, 1986)

Foner, E., and Brown, J., *Forever Free: The Story of Emancipation and Reconstruction* (New York, 2005)

Gamble, R. M., *The War for Righteousness: Progressive Christianity, the Great War, and the Rise of the Messianic Nation* (Wilmington, DE, 2003)

Gillespie, R., *Devoted People: Belief and Religion in Early Modern Ireland* (Dublin, 1997)

Gish, S. D., *Desmond Tutu: A Biography* (Orlando, FL, 2004)

Goertz, H-J., *The Anabaptists* (London, 1996)

Gould, P., *Barbaric Traffic: Commerce and Antislavery in the Eighteenth-century Atlantic World* (Harvard, 2003)

Greengrass, M. (ed.), *Conquest and Coalescence: The Shaping of the State in Early Modern Europe* (London, 1991)

Greengrass, M., *The French Reformation* (Oxford, 1987)

Gregory, B. S., *Salvation at Stake: Christian Martyrdom in Early Modern Europe* (Cambridge, MA, 1999)

Grell, O. P. (ed.), *The Scandinavian Reformation: From Evangelical Movement to Institutionalisation of Reform* (Cambridge, 1994)

Grell, O., and Scribner, B. (eds), *Tolerance and Intolerance in the European Reformation* (Cambridge, 1996)

Halper, Stefan, and Clarke, Jonathan, *America Alone: The Neo-Conservatives and the Global Order* (Cambridge, 2004)

Hempton, D., *Methodism and Politics in British Society, 1750–1850* (Stanford, 1984)

Henry, J., *The Scientific Revolution and the Origins of Modern Science* (Basingstoke, 2002)

Herman, A., *How the Scots Invented the Modern World: The True Story of How Western Europe's Poorest Nation Created Our World and Everything in It* (New York, 2001)

Hill, C., *The World Turned Upside Down* (London, 1985)

Hill, J., *Faith in the Age of Reason* (Downer's Grove, IL, 2004)

Himmelfarb, G., *The Roads to Modernity: The British, French, and American Enlightenments* (New York, 2004)

Huizinga, J., *Erasmus of Rotterdam* (London, 1952)

Hutchison, W. R., *The Modernist Impulse in American Protestantism* (Harvard, 1976)

Israel, J., *The Dutch Republic: Its Rise, Greatness and Fall, 1477–1806* (Oxford, 1995)

Kalberg, S., *Max Weber: The Confrontation with Modernity* (London, 2004)

Kamen, H., *European Society, 1500–1700* (London, 1984)

— *Inquisition and Society in Spain in the Sixteenth and Seventeenth Centuries* (London, 1985)

Kenyon, J., and Ohlmeyer, J. (eds), *The British and Irish Civil Wars: A Military History of Scotland, Ireland and England, 1638–1660* (Oxford, 1998)

Kirk, J. A., *Martin Luther King, Jr.* (London, 2005)

Kloczowski, J., *A History of Polish Christianity* (Cambridge, 2000)

Kors, A. C. (ed.), *Encyclopedia of the Enlightenment*, 4 vols (Oxford, 2003)

Kristol, I., *Neo-Conservatism: The Autobiography of an Idea* (London, 1995)

Lawrence, B. B., *Defenders of God: The Fundamentalist Revolt against the Modern Age* (San Francisco, 1989)

Lindberg, C. (ed.), *The European Reformations Sourcebook* (Oxford, 2000)

— *The Pietist Theologians: An Introduction to Theology in the Seventeenth and Eighteenth Centuries* (Oxford, 2006)

Lohse, B., *Martin Luther: An Introduction to his Life and Work* (Edinburgh, 1986)

Louw, P. E., *The Rise, Fall and Legacy of Apartheid* (Westport, CT, 2004)

Maag, E. (ed.), *The Reformation in Eastern and Central Europe* (Aldershot, 1997)

MacCulloch, D., *The Later Reformation in England, 1547–1603* (Basingstoke, 2000)

McLaughlin, K. E., *Caspar Schwenckfeld, Reluctant Radical: His Life to 1540* (New Haven, CT, 1986)

Marsden, G. M., *Fundamentalism and American Culture: The Shaping of Twentieth-century Evangelicalism, 1870–1925* (Oxford, 1980)

Moore, R. I., *The Formation of a Persecuting Society: Power and Deviance in Western Europe, 950–1250* (Oxford, 1987)

Muir, E., *Ritual in Early Modern Europe* (Cambridge, 1997)

Mullett, M. A., *The Catholic Reformation* (London, 1999)

Munck, T., *Enlightenment: A Comparative Social History, 1721–1794* (London, 2000)

Murdock, G., *Calvinism on the Frontier 1600–1660: International Calvinism and the Reformed Church in Hungary and Transylvania* (Oxford, 2000)

Naphy, W. G., *Sex Crimes from Renaissance to Enlightenment* (Stroud, 2002)

— *Born to be Gay: A History of Homosexuality* (Stroud, 2006)

Norman, E. R., *Church and Society in England, 1770–1970: A Historical Study* (Oxford, 1976)

Ó Siochrú, M. (ed.), *Kingdoms in Crisis: Ireland in the 1640s* (Dublin, 2000)

Pettegree, A. (ed.), *The Reformation World* (London, 2000)

Pettegree, A., Duke, A., and Lewis, G. (eds), *Calvinism in Europe, 1540–1620* (Cambridge, 1994)

Po-Chia Hsia, R., *The World of Catholic Renewal, 1540–1770* (Cambridge, 1998)

Potter, G. R., *Zwingli* (Cambridge, 1976)

Rawlyk, G. A., *The Canada Fire: Radical Evangelicalism in British North America, 1775–1812* (Kingston, ON, 1994)

Ryn, C. G., *America the Virtuous: The Crisis of Democracy and the Quest for Empire* (New Brunswick, NJ, 2003)

Scarre, G., *Witchcraft and Magic in 16th- and 17th-century Europe* (Basingstoke, 1987)

Scribner, R. W., *The German Reformation* (Basingstoke, 1986)

Stout, H. S., *The Divine Dramatist: George Whitefield and the Rise of Modern Evangelicalism* (Grand Rapids, MI, 1991)

Todd, M., *The Culture of Protestantism in Early Modern Scotland* (London, 2002)

Webb, A. K., *Beyond the Global Culture War* (London, 2006)

White, C. E., *The Beauty of Holiness: Phoebe Palmer as Theologian, Revivalist, Feminist, and Humanitarian* (Grand Rapids, MI, 1986)

White, J. F., *Protestant Worship and Church Architecture* (Oxford, 1964)

White, R. C., Jr. and Hopkins, C. H., *The Social Gospel: Religion and Reform in Changing America* (Philadelphia, 1975)

Wiesner-Hanks, M., *Christianity and Sexuality in the Early Modern World: Regulating Desire, Reforming Practice* (London, 2000)

Wigger, J. H., *Taking Heaven by Storm: Methodism and the Rise of Popular Christianity in America* (Oxford, 1998)

Williams, G. H., *The Radical Reformation* (Kirksville, MO, 1992)

INDEX

ACKNOWLEDGEMENTS

I would greatly like to thank Alan Clement of Wark Clements and Christopher Tinker of BBC Books for their unstinting support and advice in the production of this volume. Also, as ever, I am indebted to my closest family members (Arlene, Donald, Paul and Ruth) for their continual and constant encouragement.

PICTURE CREDITS